Christian Women
in INDONESIA

Angela —
I can see that you are
quite far along the road to
being a powerful and strong
leader. Thanks for being
all *there* in class!
Frances

Women and Religion
Amanda Porterfield *and* Mary Farrell Bednarowski
Series Editors

Other titles in Women and Religion

Building Sisterhood: A Feminist History of the Sisters, Servants of the Immaculate Heart of Mary
  Sisters, Servants of the Immaculate Heart of Mary, Monroe, MI

Emma Curtis Hopkins: Forgotten Founder of New Thought
  Gail M. Harley

Emma Newman: A Frontier Woman Minister
  Randi Jones Walker

Faith Cures, and Answers to Prayer
  Mrs. Edward Mix; Rosemary D. Gooden, ed.

Moon Sisters, Krishna Mothers, Rajneesh Lovers: Women's Roles in New Religions
  Susan J. Palmer

Moravian Women's Memoirs: Related Lives, 1750–1820
  Katherine M. Faull, trans. and ed.

O Sisters Ain't You Happy? Gender, Family, and Community Among the Harvard and Shirley Shakers, 1781–1918
  Suzanne R. Thurman

Rational Mothers and Infidel Gentlemen: Gender and American Atheism, 1865–1915
  Evelyn Kirkley

The Religious World of Antislavery Women: Spirituality in the Lives of Five Abolitionist Lecturers
  Anna M. Speicher

A Still Small Voice: Women, Ordination, and the Church
  Frederick W. Schmidt

Windows of Faith: Muslim Women Scholar-Activists of North America
  Gisela Webb, ed.

Christian Women *in* INDONESIA

A Narrative Study of Gender and Religion

Frances S. Adeney

 Syracuse University Press

Copyright © 2003 by Syracuse University Press
Syracuse, New York 13244–5160

All Rights Reserved

First Edition 2003
03 04 05 06 07 08   6 5 4 3 2 1

The paper used in this publication meets the minimum requirements
of American National Standard for Information Sciences—Permanence
of Paper for Printed Library Materials, ANSI Z39.48–1984.∞™

Library of Congress Cataloguing-in-Publication Data

Adeney, Frances S.
Christian women in Indonesia : a narrative study of gender and
religion / Frances S. Adeney.—1st ed.
    p. cm.—(Women and religion)
Includes bibliographical references (p.) and index.
ISBN 0-8156-2956-7
1. Christian women—Indonesia—History—20th century.
2. Women clergy—Indonesia—History—20th century. I. Title.
II. Series: Women and religion (Syracuse, N.Y.)
BR1220.A34 2002
305.43'204'09598—dc21
                                                          2002013514

Manufactured in the United States of America

For Jen Marion, Rina, and Peter
—resisters, creators, announcers

Frances S. Adeney is the William A. Benfield Associate Professor of Evangelism and Social Mission at the Louisville Presbyterian Theological Seminary in Louisville, Kentucky. She has held positions in religion and social ethics at the University of Southern California (1997–99), Satya Wacana University in Indonesia (1991–96), and New College, Berkeley (1988–91). Her publications include a chapter contributed to *Ethics and World Religions: Cross-Cultural Case Studies* (Maryknoll, NY: Orbis, 1999) and an interview of theologian John Cobb, which she coauthored in 1998 with Terry C. Muck in *Buddhist-Christian Studies*, vol. 18.

Contents

Acknowledgments   *ix*

PART ONE   **The Project**

1. Introduction to Part One
   Study Parameters and Findings   3

2. Indonesia
   Unity or Diversity?   16

3. Gender Ideologies
   Crisis or Opportunity?   32

4. The Challenge of University Life
   Inclusion or Exclusion?   53

5. Strategies of Resistance
   Independent Agents or Followers of God?   76

6. Strategies of Growth
   Everyday Practices or Feminist Innovations?   104

PART TWO Theory and Method

7. Introduction to Part Two
   Parameters and Use of Theory   129

8. Social Theory as Practice
   A North American Feminist in Indonesia   138

9. Using Theories Across Cultures
   Moral Development Theories as a Test Case   153

10. Feminist Theory versus Advocacy
    An Integrative Approach   172

Appendix
Dreyfus Skill Acquisition Model   193

Glossary   195

References   199

Index   213

Acknowledgments

I have been fascinated with other cultures and have desired to understand how religions interact with everyday life since my early twenties, when I headed off to Europe and Asia, returning four years later. This interest led me to experiment with teaching second graders about China, to research religious influences on Western psychologies, and to study the sociology of religion and social ethics at the Graduate Theological Union and the University of California at Berkeley. My interest in feminist approaches to religion and society was heightened when women students I met at Satya Wacana Christian University in Indonesia prodded me to analyze feminist concerns and their interaction with Christian institutions and gender ideologies in Indonesia.

Acknowledgment goes first to my Indonesian mentors, especially Marianne Katoppo in theology, whose ideas and practices are seminal to this work. *Ibu* Trimurti in matters of the revolution, Konta in economics, and Nunuk Prasetyo Murniati in psychology—each helped me to understand the uniqueness of the Indonesian milieu for exploring issues of women's emancipation, gender ideologies, and paths of resistance and social change. I owe thanks to colleagues in the Graduate Program in Religion and Society at Satya Wacana, especially Director John Titaley, who brought talented women into the program, and Sumartana, who demonstrated gender equality, a healthy pluralism, and an openness to new ideas.

I appreciate the opportunities I had to attend regional and national conferences of Protestant women in Java and Sulawesi, which supplemented my understanding of the goals of the women's movement in the Indonesian Church. Working as a consultant for the Women's Research Center at the university informed me regarding patterns of life in the villages as well as methods of research and organizational leadership styles exhibited by Indonesian women at the center. Finding retreat for my own spirit at a Trappist women's monastery near Salatiga put me in contact with Catholic women who had chosen a unique and dedicated path of difference. Working with undergraduate women as well as graduate students at the Jakarta Theological Seminary led me to a few exceptional undergraduate women and increased my conviction that something new was happening in Indonesia.

The opportunity to work intensively on this project presented itself during my sabbatical year, 1996–97. As a resident scholar at the Institute for Ecumenical and Cultural Research in Collegeville, Minnesota, I had the privilege of taking time to remember, to organize materials, to formulate my thesis, to find direction, and most of all to write.

I found invaluable encouragement from the faculty of the University of California's School of Religion and Center for Feminist Research during my time there as the Brooks Professor of Religion. From 1997 through 1999, the work was extended through graduate seminars and conversations with students and scholars. Presenting the Brooks Lecture in Religion in 1998 helped focus the analytical dimensions of the work.

In 1998 I was welcomed by the PERSETIA graduate studies program at Tomohon University in Sulawesi to teach feminist theology, to further the research, and to find out how economic reforms and political changes affected women in Indonesia.

This project could not have been completed without the help and support of friends and colleagues here in the United States and in Indonesia. My students and colleagues in Indonesia, both women and men, who told their stories and grappled with questions of theory, value, and method deserve a great deal of credit for this work. Students in my seminars and courses at the Graduate Theological Union and the University of Southern California contributed insights into the cross-cultural understanding that I sought. Friends and scholars at the Ecumenical Institute in Collegeville gave constructive critique and personal support.

I want to thank colleagues who offered insights on parts of the work or on the manuscript itself, especially Clare Fischer, Patrick Henry, Angela Dries, Don Miller, John M. Mulder, and Johanna Bos. Mary Bednarowski encouraged me to submit the book to the Women and Religion Series, and both she and Amanda Porterfield offered constructive suggestions for revision. The editorial work of Virginia Hearn amazed me, as did the patient optimism of Mary Selden Evans at Syracuse University Press. Cauleen Spatz and Lant Davis worked with a myriad of details in preparing the manuscript. Through all of these processes, my husband and best editor, Terry Muck, advised and encouraged me.

The analysis I present here has both local and global dimensions. Exploring religion as a locus for resistance to gender inequalities shows the complexity of the issues involved and the creativity of women addressing them. Applying models of moral development to women leaders in Indonesia highlights the variegated complexity of both gender construction and moral agency in a particular society while testing the usefulness of theories in a specific context. Offering a contextual theory and an interpretive methodology for developing theoretical tools for feminist scholars in conversation across cultures fosters comparisons and illumines limitations of feminist understandings in local contexts.

I hope, however, that what comes through most strongly in these pages are the stories of particular women in Indonesia—women who are seizing their moment of history to announce their equality to themselves and to the world.

PART ONE The Project

1

Introduction to Part One
Study Parameters and Findings

Women's voices are transforming religions and the way scholars and practitioners understand them. Some feminist scholars (such as Ruether, Carmody, and S. Young) are uncovering histories of women and their roles in religious institutions. Others (including Kanyoro and Oduyoye, Hassan and Gordon, and Williams) dare name the injustices perpetuated by those religious institutions. Feminist theologians in the world's religions (notably Fiorenza, Bos, Adler, Gross, and Chung) are critiquing dominant theologies and outlining new understandings of the divine, while feminist ethicists (such as Woolfe, Shiva, and Welch) are addressing pressing global problems from women's perspectives. Some feminist theorists (notably Falk and Gross, Fischer, Bednarowski, and Belenky, Clinchy, Goldberger, and Tarule) describe women's thought and practices, while others envision futures of equality and human flourishing (including Cooey, King, and Plaskow and Christ).

These contributions to the study of religion have stimulated renewed interest in the issue of religion and gender power. Amanda Porterfield argues that gender consciousness influenced a transformation in American religion that began in the late twentieth century (Porterfield 2001). The gender power embedded in women's critiques and constructive theologies in numerous religions contributes to what promises to be a third wave of the global women's movement that centers on spirituality (Adeney 1993).

The conversation between North American feminists and voices from Asia, Latin America, and Africa illuminates common theological themes among feminists in different religions and academic disciplines. That discourse highlights creative resistance strategies that may be applied in new contexts while showing up the limitations of feminist theory and advocacy in a particular locale. This conversation across cultures develops solidarity and fosters awareness of the global dimensions of the power of gender to effect change in both the theologies and the institutions of religions (Bednarowski 1999, 187).

Religion and Resistance in Indonesia

The idea of telling the stories of Christian women who used their religion as a form of gender resistance and moral agency arose in 1992 while I was teaching at Satya Wacana Christian University in central Java. The graduate program in religion and society was developing quickly, and we already had ten women students.

A women's group was taking shape, and that spring we gathered for a weekend retreat. The bonding that occurred during the extended time that we spent together inspired and grounded the subsequent work of the group. It marked the beginning of a process of empowerment that enabled individuals in that first group of graduate students to face the daunting tasks of doing master's degree work on gender issues at a Christian university in Indonesia.

I was awed by the energy produced during that simple retreat as we talked together, cooked and ate together, worshipped with candles, danced, performed homemade rituals, and slept overnight together, scattered about the big living room of the rustic cabin.

When I returned to campus on the following Monday, I found a petition posted on the graduate students' bulletin board. It featured a feminist hymn one of the students had taught us on the retreat—a hymn about a God who does not sit in heaven judging us but walks with us in our everyday struggles to find freedom and equality. It said at the bottom: "Who agrees with this? Please sign here." No one signed.

Invoking Christian theology to uphold the students' shared value of gender equality produced excitement at the retreat, an excitement not shared by other students and faculty on campus. Rather than welcoming feminist interpretations of an immanent God as co-worker and concerned friend to women in their struggle for equality, many ignored the women's call for affirmation.

In spite of discrimination, these women had come to the university to seek leadership in their religious institutions. Drawn from a variety of regions of Indonesia, they were influenced by differing indigenous views on gender. They recounted conflicting versions of Western Christian influences on the status and roles of women in Indonesia. Some argued that Western Christian influence led to liberality and expanded roles for women, others, that Christianity curtailed women's participation in public life. Regardless of different indigenous gender ideologies and varying assessments of Western religious influence on women's equal status in their regions, all of the women had chosen to study their religion more deeply. Feminist Christian theologies now challenged traditional Christian views.

The differences in gender ideologies and accounts of Western influence led to questions about the relationship among gender ideologies in Indonesia, colonial influences, and women's aspirations to leadership. Specifically, what religious, cultural, and social influences motivated Indonesian women to challenge patriarchal structures in church and society? How did they develop the moral agency needed to take a path that went against social conventions? What sustained them as they developed as Christian leaders? How did their actions affect the traditional social structures of family and church as the women used the power of their religion to foment social change?

Those questions concern feminist theorists and theologians in the West, making this study of particular interest to scholars in North America. Exploring a part of the women's movement in Indonesia uncovers an active stream of feminism that has been opaque to Western feminists. Examining the religion-identified resistance of Indonesian women opens up avenues for feminists in North America who seek gender justice within their religious institutions. Comparing the roles of moral agency and everyday practices in creating social change in the Indonesian setting can show strengths and shortcomings of advocacy efforts here. In addition, the contextual-relational theory and narrative method of this study charts a way for feminist theorists to integrate theory and advocacy in feminist scholarship.

Investigating the Issues

Ethnographic research to study the reasons for and results of this type of religion-identified resistance was carried out in Java and north Sulawesi between 1992 and 1998. The subjects were Christian women who chose religious leadership as a career: entering the pastorate, choosing a monastic life, or becoming educators.[1] For these women, religion was both a site of oppression and a resource for overcoming gender inequities.

Rather than leave their religious institutions, they used the intellectual discourse and beliefs of their religion to develop patterns of resistance to gender inequalities. Resisting pressures to conform to strong familial and social networks of control, these women claimed inclusion in their religious communities, deciding to break out of expected patterns of behavior for women. A sense of individual agency, combined with a religious calling and a conviction about the justice

---

1. This research study was done during a five-year residency in Indonesia as a professor. Bahasa Indonesia, the national language, was used for most interviews and information gathering. The research on women is based on work with twenty university graduate students over the course of five years. In addition, we worked with three seminary graduate students and forty undergraduate seminary students during one year; conducted twenty in-person interviews with women leaders, one with the abbess, and four written "interviews" with cloistered Trappist monks; and interacted with six women professors. Information was also gathered through working as a consultant with the Women's Research Center (one year), a regional church women's group (one year), and the Graduate Students' Women's Group (four years). Trips to Bali, Lombok, Sumba, Ceram, and Sulawesi, as well as conference attendance at women's functions in Java, Sulawesi, Ambon, and Sangir Terlau, augmented the research. Information was gathered from men who came from many different Indonesian islands during faculty and class interactions in central Java and Jakarta. Conversations with church leaders in Java and Ambon are also included. Further research was carried out in 1998 during a two-month stay at the University of Tomohon in north Sulawesi. During that time, information was gathered from twenty-four university and seminary students from nine institutions in Indonesia.

of women's equality, served to strengthen the women's resolve to choose a path that many saw as strange. After choosing the course of development as leaders within the intellectual and religious institutions of university and church, many women developed practices that sustained them and led them to success in their chosen vocations.

In this study, I have identified common practices used by these aspiring leaders, sometimes in new ways: practicing hospitality, creating beauty, and honoring relationships. Some women used those practices to support their resistance to social conventions and to pursue leadership in their religious communities. Other women using the same practices were deterred by those practices from reaching their goal of attaining leadership. I have used theories of gender ideology and moral agency to analyze the factors that enhanced individual agency and strengthened the women's resolve to follow a different path than their peers. I have gathered new interpretations of meaning and spirituality that took shape as women reflected on those daily practices. In addition, I have noted changes in their communities and society resulting from their work on women's issues and their lifestyles as church leaders.

In this study, I have assembled narratives of the experiences of women students and colleagues based on interviews, conference notes, and participant observation during my five years of living and teaching university graduate students in Indonesia.[2] Those students comprised the first generation of Christian women to do graduate-level work in religion and society at a Christian university in Indonesia. I tracked women over a two- to five-year period in order to assess their long-term success in pursuing leadership goals and the impact of their resistance strategies. I conducted further research during 1995–96 at the Jakarta Theological Seminary and the graduate program of the South East Asian School of Theology, and again in 1998 at the Indonesian Consortium of Theological Schools in north Sulawesi.

Long-term involvement in the university setting offered access

---

2. Pseudonyms are used, except for those whose scholarly work is cited in conjunction with the narrative.

to the dialogue about religion, power, and gender among Christian intellectuals in Indonesia. Learning the language, developing cross-cultural understandings of gender issues, and noting resistance strategies in a setting geared to intellectual and religious discourse proved to be invaluable in accomplishing research objectives. Male faculty members and students augmented the study with their perspectives on gender relations in Indonesian society and at the university. Reviewing journal and newspaper articles continued the dialogue between men and women about the roles and status of women, bringing Indonesian feminist views and counter views into the study.

The Indonesian Context

Indonesia presented an ideal context for investigating those issues. This Southeast Asian agrarian nation is known for its cultural diversity. Anthropological studies of Indonesia describe indigenous cultures with kinship systems that reflect a gender equality considered to be unmatched in other parts of Asia (Atkinson and Errington 1990, 3). World religions have influenced indigenous cultures, beginning with the incursion of Hinduism and Buddhism in the eighth and ninth centuries and proceeding through the arrival of Islam to that of Christianity, making Indonesia a nation of religious plurality. Dedication to one's own religion is expected, yet freedom of religion is a constitutional right. Women's struggles for emancipation have spanned nearly a century, and their political rights were secured at the birth of the nation in 1945. The complex of gender ideologies and the layers of religion found in Indonesia provide a pluralistic environment in which the value of gender equality can be assessed across cultural and religious differences. The turbulent history that resulted in this diversity will be explored in chapter 2.

Conditions in Indonesia lend themselves to the rise of new ideas that empower women and lead them to engage the public worlds of politics and religion. Economic growth and modern birth control techniques free middle—and upper-class women from total involvement in survival and child care. Freedom from colonialism and political emancipation foster a sense of responsibility for public affairs.

Education opens doors to self-understanding through the study of history and indigenous cultures while exposing women to ideas about gender from outside Indonesia.

While globalization has brought new industries and development to Indonesia, the demise of the Suharto regime in 1998 resulted in economic hardship and political conflict. Nonetheless, the growth of cities, international travel, and television and computer technologies continues to bring new ideas and conflicting values into this traditional Southeast Asian Muslim society. Islamic universities have proliferated in the last twenty years. In addition, higher education for Christians brings new theologies to the country's Protestants (making up 6 percent of the population) and Roman Catholics (3 percent).[3]

Traditional gender ideologies vary among Indonesia's thirty-seven different cultural and language groups, a topic that will be explored in chapter 3. Despite anthropological studies that assert relative gender equality based on different gender ideologies in areas described as Centrist and Exchange Archipelagos in Indonesia (Atkinson and Errington 1990, 39), Indonesians claim that their society is strongly patriarchal.[4] Loyalty to father figures—the president, the CEO, the neighborhood leader, the family patriarch—is a central value for Indonesians.

At the same time, ideas of gender equality arise both in some traditional Indonesian cultures and from Western influences of democratic and feminist values.[5] Although none of the Western cultural

---

3. Of the population of 206,611,600 people, 87 percent are Muslims (Famighelli 1996, 774).

4. Women students and colleagues interviewed all agreed that patriarchy was the dominant ideology in Indonesia. Political leaders claimed allegiance as father figures. Matrifocal cultures in Mingakabau and Javanese areas participate in patriarchal values. Norma Sullivan, in her study of urban Javanese, argues that despite matrifocal patterns in Javanese society and modern descriptions of the role and duties of women in national development, "the positions of men and women are not equal, that their relations are characterized by male dominance and female subordination, an arrangement which does not give women high status" (1994, 8).

5. The Minangkabau in Sumatra, the Manado in northern Sulawesi, and the Torajan people in central Sulawesi are examples of indigenous societies with elements

studies of gender in south and Southeast Asia related the topic of "women" to contemporary feminist theory before 1990 (Atkinson and Errington 1990, 3), lively discussions in the Indonesian press during the 1980s and 1990s contrasted Indonesian feminist and patriarchal values.[6]

As a result of those influences, some educated women in both Islamic and Christian communities are moving into theology and pastoral work, traditional domains of the father figure. The Satya Wacana Graduate Program in Religion and Society seeks qualified women to pursue this goal. Chapter 4 discusses the challenges women face at the university: the daunting task of studying alongside men who are older and have higher status, the necessity of formulating strategies to accomplish the task of doing a thesis on a topic of concern to women, the demands of social etiquette that shape diffident women who defer to dominant men, and the need for support and bonding among women.

Navigating between traditional ascriptive and modern achievement systems of authority at the university presents challenges. Multiple tasks are necessary: balancing old and new ideologies, breaking into new areas of knowledge, practicing egalitarianism, and honoring old forms of status and respect. Since preserving harmonious relationships has high value in Indonesian society, finding ways to accomplish this task without open conflict requires sensitivity and tact.

Embarking on a life course radically different from those of one's peers requires strong convictions and independence. The women re-

---

of gender equality in their traditions, creation myths, and practices. Clifford Geertz noted that sexual differentiation is played down in Bali (1973, 417–418 n. 4), and Jane Monnig Atkinson and Shelley Errington note that Barbara Ward (1963) credits bilateral kinship structures with the relatively greater equality of women and men in Southeast Asia compared to South Asia (1990, 3). Further discussion of this issue shows that the complexities of gender interactions in Southeast Asia reveal that no simple criterion of high or low status and power of women can be used cross-culturally (Atkinson and Errington 1990, 2–7).

6. *Kompas*, an independent newspaper that was periodically shut down by the Suharto government, and *Femina*, a woman's magazine, were two popular forums for this discussion.

sponded to this challenge with an array of resistance strategies, discussed in chapter 5, which included claiming inclusion in the leadership pool by appealing to the authority of religious experience, resisting social expectations that marginalized them as leaders, and modeling Christian leadership.

The women developed support networks and everyday practices that strengthened their resolve, directed their activities, nurtured their spirits, and deepened their relationships with others who had chosen a similar course. Those everyday practices have the potential either to spawn new interpretations of religious meaning or to deter women from reaching their goals of leadership. Chapter 6 situates and analyzes everyday practices of offering hospitality, creating beauty, and honoring relationships.

Issues of Theory and Method

Ethnographic research in another culture to understand the reasons for and results of religion-identified resistance offers particular challenges in the postmodern era. The role of religion in world construction, the situatedness of religious institutions and their subsequent legitimating power, and the embeddedness of the researcher in the project are a few of those issues.

Part 2 of this book examines these and related issues in depth. It outlines a contextual-relational theory of social change and explores the methods that using the theory entails. That theory posits a contextually contingent development and use of theories, a perspectivalism that is influenced by the researcher's experience, an action-related notion of social change, and a valuing component to theory itself.

The goals of research, the involvement of the researcher, and the ability to discuss meaning across cultures are addressed in chapter 8. The importance of those issues in my engagement with social theory, the sociology of religion, and social ethics is traced through my own journey as a North American Christian feminist scholar. How humans form their worlds of meaning and are shaped by those worlds, how one understands one's own identity in a social and religious context, and how values are formed and change through time, action, and interaction with others are motivating questions of this study.

Chapter 9 addresses a methodological issue that presented itself not only in this study but also in teaching the sociology of religion and social theory in Indonesia. How applicable are theoretical models to different contexts than the one in which they developed? Do Western theories order and prioritize issues or veil crucial aspects of a unique context? Using the moral development theories of Lawrence Kohlberg, Carol Gilligan, and Hubert and Stewart Dreyfus provided a test case for the application of Western theories to non-Western contexts.

Feminist theorists also struggle with whether and how to apply a strong conviction of gender equality in societies that differ from their own. Chapter 10 explores the tension between feminist theory and advocacy and offers a hermeneutical approach to navigating the process of exploring and honoring difference while maintaining the centrality of gender equality.

Findings

1. A postmodern conversation across cultures is possible, and Western theories of moral development, agency, and social change, as well as universally held ideals of gender equality, can be part of that conversation. Employment of the contextual-relational theory and the narrative methods that partner with it disclosed a partial usefulness of the application of Western theories to the Indonesian context. The technique revealed some parallels between Indonesian and North American women's experiences of the pressure to conform to traditional gender roles and demonstrated the usefulness of studying practices as agents of social change in other cultures.

2. Conflicting ideologies create space for social change. Despite indigenous and government-supported gender ideologies and Western Christian theologies that do not espouse gender equality, aspiring women Christian leaders became convinced of the value of gender equality and pursued it.

Contradictions in Indonesian gender ideologies augmented the sense that change was possible—that the dominant gender ideology was not a fixed or "natural" way of doing things. In Minangkabau society, for example, a gender ideology of equality conflicts with practices that give men higher status (Krier 1995, 51–75). In Java, an ideology that gives men more spiritual potency and worth is contradicted by an underlying ideology of women's strength and capability (Brenner 1995, 19–50). Discussion continues as to which ideology should order the behavior of contemporary women and men (Geertz 1973; Sullivan 1983). Educated Indonesian women today have not experienced the monolithic view of women that the current dominant gender ideology depicts.[7] Their experience of conflicting views frees them to ask questions and to form new opinions about gender.

3. Religion-identified resistance leads to social change. Women resisted restrictive views of women's role in Christian religious institutions by claiming inclusion in institutional leadership roles based on an inner sense of religious calling. They resisted gender ideologies of female inferiority and relegation to private spheres of influence, developing a strong sense of moral agency that enabled them to choose a life course that made them appear strange to others. To resist social pressures hampering their development as leaders they used strategies such as embracing their own difference from others, choosing not to marry, living apart from extended family networks, and exposing the double standard of gender inequality in Christian institutions.

Anthropological research in Indonesia points to ways in which women challenge their subordinate position in Indonesian society (Sears 1996, Ong and Peletz 1995, Suleeman and Souk 1997). Studies of religion-identified gender resistance show that working from within the restrictive structures of institutional religion can provide

---

7. The Suharto government took a strong role in interpreting women's political emancipation, developing an interpretation of their role as partners in development that emphasized women's role in child raising and caring for home and family (see chapter 3). This ideology combines with a strong ideology of the father as dominant in family and societal life and a religious view of women's *kodrat*, which relates the meaning of a woman's life to marriage and childbearing. Those views combine, resulting in a dominant gender ideology that secures a woman's role in the family as a top priority in her life.

women with a measure of freedom to act without sacrificing the gender-based care provided them in patriarchal institutions (Brink and Mencher 1997). Speaking out from within those structures can serve as an indirect challenge to oppression (Kuipers 1998). Successful protest, however, can sometimes reinforce women's subordinate position (Krier 1995). Further study is needed on the complexities of gender relations in Indonesia and the possibilities offered by religiously based resistance.

4. Everyday practices can foster women's development as leaders. These women made choices that strengthened their sense of agency as subjects. They developed everyday practices that in some cases furthered their work, enhanced their identity as leaders, and nurtured their relationships and spiritual life. Even without articulating a meaning of particular practices, women were sustained by the ongoing practices of hospitality, honoring relationships, and creating beauty. While everyday practices hampered some women's ability to pursue their goal of leadership, others found empowering modes of exercising and interpreting these practices.

5. Reflecting on everyday practices can generate new understandings of gender equality. Some women reflected on those practices, interpreting them through more positive indigenous gender ideologies and feminist interpretations of Christian theologies, to create new theologies of gender equality. In this way new social constructions of reality enter the cultural nexus of ideas.

6. The process of choosing a different lifestyle, developing everyday practices, and reflecting upon them generates concentric circles of change in communities. Changes in the women's sense of identity occurred as they made choices and developed practices that sustained them. Changes in relationships occurred as women readjusted priorities and found support among other women. Changes in their communities occurred as they modified their roles and modeled leadership. Changes in their religion occurred as they articulated new theological interpretations of the meanings of everyday practices.

Through religion-identified resistance that claimed inclusion and resisted marginalization, through exercising agency in new ways within religious institutions, and through developing practices that sustained them in their choice of resistance and then interpreting those practices in ways that led to new theologies, women created social change that fostered gender equality.

2

Indonesia
Unity or Diversity?

My first months in Indonesia were filled with language study and getting to know colleagues and neighbors. I learned, along the way, about etiquette—the ways of politeness and appearance so important to Indonesian society.[1] During the second semester I started to teach in the graduate program in religion and society at Satya Wacana Christian University. I also began advising students on their thesis projects. Before long, I began to encounter confusion and misunderstanding arising from the cultural diversity there.

One day Yolanda, a young woman from Irian Jaya, spoke to me about wanting to study *adat*, the system of customs and social arrangements in her indigenous culture.[2] She wanted to identify patriarchal beliefs and patterns that could be modified now that her

---

1. Forms of politeness are considered part of morality among Indonesians. It is not only an embarrassment to lose one's temper, for example, it is considered uncouth and wrong. Harmonious and refined behavior is a moral good, while impetuous or uncontrolled behavior is considered morally reprehensible.

2. Each cultural group in Indonesia has a system of informal rules that order societal interactions and govern behavior. Those rules are related to the various primordial religions in the history of that culture. In West Timor, for example, *adat* laws are based on the household structure. The position of each member of the extended family is tied to beliefs about how power is "naturally" distributed. The father is at the center of this system, with less powerful figures organized around him. Each relative has a distinct status, invested with certain rights and duties. Even the physical structure of the house itself reflects this order. Although the region is now Christian, the customs that grow up around *adat* remain influential in the lives of the community.

group had accepted Christianity. She saw Christianity as a liberating influence, softening if not overcoming the male-dominated customs of her people. We struggled through this conversation with a combination of my rudimentary Indonesian and her faltering English. Then Yolanda left my office.

Ida entered next. She too had a project in mind. What had the church done to her Manado culture? Christianity was supposed to bring life and freedom, yet since Dutch Calvinist missionaries brought Protestantism to north Sulawesi in the mid-nineteenth century, women had become more oppressed and men more dominant. How could this be? Didn't Christianity teach equality between men and women? Ida wanted to study contemporary attitudes toward women's leadership in the church in her area and to attempt to resolve some of those issues.

After Ida left, I felt confused. I knew how indirect communication could be in the Indonesian language. I wondered if I had misunderstood one of the women, since they seemed to be giving contradictory accounts of the impact of Christianity on Indonesian society. If I had misunderstood, whose account had I misconstrued, and how? Yolanda saw the coming of Christianity to Indonesia as a breakthrough, a step up for women. Ida indicated with some frustration that the church brought oppression to women.

The incident was repeated by Fatima from Toraja, Connie from Sumatra, Nora from Java, and Jane, a Chinese student from Jakarta. Each told a different story of women and the influence of Christianity. I started to pay attention.

There were daily reminders of Java's cultural diversity. Five times each day the Muslim call to prayer announced that Islam was practiced in this Christian enclave. I passed a Chinese Buddhist temple every time I went to the theater downtown. Sleep was frequently punctuated by the sounds of gongs and loudspeakers used in all-night village performances of *Ramayana* stories. I heard rumors that fires were flaring up in hillside villages, started by the spirit of a young girl who was killed when a house burned down nearby. I did not realize, however, how multifaceted this diversity was, and how deeply it affects Indonesian society.

I did know that there were more than thirty-four major culture groups and more than 450 distinct languages in Indonesia, in a chain of over thirteen thousand islands stretching from Singapore nearly to the Philippines (*Index on Censorship* 1997, 2). Regional languages, cultural styles, indigenous religions, mores, and habits coexisted beneath the surface of Bahasa Indonesia, the common language of the nation. How did that cultural and ethnic diversity affect women's assessment of Christianity's influence upon those cultures?

Plurality, Colonialism, and Women's Roles

One of the keys to solving the puzzle of seemingly contradictory accounts of the influence of the Christian church on women's roles is an understanding of those indigenous cultures from which these women came. In Yolanda's community in Irian Jaya, the authority of the father was a prominent feature of the unwritten mores of her culture group. Women's subordination was clearly delineated in this society. Ida came from Manado, where indigenous culture designated women as leaders who commanded respect in the public life of the community. Nora was Javanese, a culture in which the word for "wife" meant literally "the one at the back of the house"; the kitchen was at the back of the house, and the wife was expected to be in it. In Sumatra, Connie's homeland, the Batak women were strong and central to family life. Nevertheless, a strong stream of patriarchy in Batak society kept even hardworking, assertive women in positions of economic deprivation and low status.[3]

Upon these and other culture bases, different forms of Christianity were established. The Dutch formed a colony in Ambon, part of the Moluccas in the eastern part of present-day Indonesia. With the

---

3. A number of the women mentioned wrote thesis projects on these indigenous cultures, returning home for a number of months to gather data about religions and women's roles in indigenous religions and to document the changes that colonialism brought to their islands.

Dutch came new forms of government, new codes of dress and conduct, and new religious beliefs. Dutch Reformed Calvinism spread through the Moluccas and north Sulawesi. Finding themselves at the center of a vigorous economic life, the Ambonese became heavily influenced by the Dutch.

At the same time, the Portuguese colonized Flores and Irian Jaya, both Catholic areas to the present day. At that time the islands of Java and Sumatra were less affected by the process of Western colonization, remaining staunchly Muslim in character. Hinduism flourished in Bali and continued to provide a cultural base in other islands, especially Java.[4]

Yet Dutch power reached into those islands too. How The members of the Batak Church grew strong in Sumatra, their new religion and practice of eating pork setting them apart from members of the surrounding Muslim communities. Reformed Protestantism made inroads into Java. In the twentieth century, Dutch Reformed churches were joined by American Presbyterians, Catholics, Lutherans, and Assemblies of God churches in Java, forming yet another layer of cultural diversity.

These Christian denominations brought to Indonesia a variety of theologies concerning women's status and roles. Although those theologies did not affirm women's equality, Christianity did bring expanded opportunities and roles for women in cultures where patriarchal hierarchies thrived. On the other hand, in cultures where women held power, particularly in the indigenous religion, Christian authorities curtailed the roles open to women, silencing or subordinating them.

The differences resulting from these influences interact within the broader context of Indonesia as a religiously and culturally plural-

---

4. *Wayang Kulit*, the popular, all-night shadow puppet plays frequently held in villages in Java and other islands, feature Indonesian versions of the Hindu *Ramayana* and *Mahabharata* epic tales. Children grow up with these stories. Adults enjoy the modern additions, political jokes, and spiritual lessons added by the *dalang*, a story teller who is a wise and respected figure in the village.

istic society.[5] Before Christianity came to Indonesia, waves of Hinduism, Buddhism, and Islam swept through the islands, each in turn being incorporated into the society, overlaid upon the indigenous religions already present.[6]

Over centuries of influence, Hinduism established a deep cultural base, providing myths, affecting attitudes, and establishing mores that are still very much present in Indonesian society.[7] Villages throughout Java celebrate Hindu holidays, markets display batik paintings featuring scenes from the *Ramayana* and *Mahabharata* stories, and traditional Javanese gamelan orchestras perform haunting music in villages as well as in grand hotels.[8]

The other religious traditions join Hinduism in their acquiescence to fate and traditional attitudes of tolerance. Religious ceremonies of major religions combine with rituals from indigenous religions to banish evil spirits, to acquire *samangat* (life force), and to preserve the souls of the dead from harm.[9] Death is accepted with

---

5. I follow my mentor, Robert N. Bellah, in understanding religion and culture to be part of the same arena of social life, coterminous in societies before the advent of world religions. Religion and culture carry the ideas of what is most ideal and sacred. Those ideas define the parameters of meaning and socially constructed reality in a given society.

6. A graduate student in one of my sociology of religion classes suggested that all four kinds of religion in Robert N. Bellah's evolution of religion scheme coexist today in Indonesia (Bellah 1973). Indeed, a megalithic culture was photographed on the island of Nias in the early twentieth century. Animistic beliefs and rituals of sacrifice combine with Hindu, Christian, and Islamic formal religions. For an intriguing and brief historical account, see *Indonesia* (Oey 1989, Nias photo, 18).

7. The first signs of both Hindu and Buddhist influence in Indonesia date back to the early fifth century C.E. Borobudur and Prambanan, the Buddhist and Hindu temple complexes in central Java, were erected in the eighth and ninth centuries respectively (Oey 1989, 21–23).

8. See *The Folk Art of Java* (Fischer 1994) to see batik paintings in folk art. Gamelan music is made with brass gongs on a twelve-tone music scale, creating music that is delicate and intense by turns.

9. Those rituals, lodged in ancient *adat* customs, are brought into celebrations of major religions such as Hinduism in Bali, Islam in Java, and Christianity in Sulawesi (see Oey 1989, 78–85).

equanimity, as Hindu beliefs are integrated with indigenous world constructions and modified to incorporate Islam. From time to time, students on campus join together informally to do trance dances, especially the popular horse dance, which is performed by young men.[10] Attention to appearances and conduct, along with a strong emphasis on harmonizing conflicting viewpoints, especially in Java, also shapes Indonesian mores.

Buddhist influences also appear in contemporary Indonesian society. The magnificent temple of Borobudur stands as a symbol of the presence of Buddhism in Java in the eighth to ninth centuries C.E. Chinese traders have been coming to the archipelago since the second century B.C.E. Many Indonesian Chinese Buddhists today worship at temples scattered throughout the islands (Oey 1989, 19). Personal meditation, an important part of traditional Javanese culture, is also practiced in Buddhist forms.[11]

Islam, the major religion in Indonesia today, has nearly 170 million adherents.[12] As the fourth most populated nation in the world, Indonesia has more Muslims than any other country in the world. Government relocation programs have moved Muslim families to Bali, Ambon, and other islands where another religion is predominant.[13] While attempting to live together peacefully, political unrest

---

10. It is not uncommon to see groups of students on the campus roadways watching a few others enacting this ritual with stick horses and deep in trance.

11. *Kebatinan,* a Javanese form of disciplined meditation, is practiced in order to amass personal power that can be used for one's own growth and also in public situations. It enables one to assume authority without appearing aggressive, resulting in a seemingly effortless ability to direct events in an authoritative way.

12. Statistics vary. *Index on Censorship* (1997) puts the population of Indonesia at 197.6 million, with 85 percent as Muslims.

13. Under Suharto, relocation was offered by the government to people in overpopulated Java, in order to even out the population and to provide poor people with land to cultivate. It was usually Muslims who were relocated to Christian or Hindu areas. Christians speculated that a hidden agenda of the relocation program was the Islamization of culture, an attempt to unify the nation under Islam without abolishing freedom of religion. Christians in Ambon resent the presence of mosques, with their loudspeakers calling Muslims to prayer five times a day. A participant in a major recre-

and economic disparities among religious groups sometimes foster tensions.[14]

Islam in Indonesia is characteristically moderate, although there are pockets of conservatism, especially in west Sumatra and parts of central Java.[15] Traditional *adat* views are still held, and respect for spirits is observed among Muslims.[16]

In accordance with the Indonesian value of harmony, efforts are made to honor all religions. Holidays of each major religion are observed. Intermarriage between followers of different religions is tolerated. Extended families often meet for both Christian and Muslim holidays when followers of both religions are family members.[17] Goodwill characterizes these celebrations in Java, where religious pluralism is most evident and accepted.

Many contemporary social customs arise from Islam. Women are expected to dress modestly, covering their bodies from shoulder to knee or ankle. School uniforms and Western dress have become ac-

---

mation ceremony in Bali in 1994 told me that Hindus in Bali consider Muslims *kafir* (crudely irreligious) because they go about their everyday work on Hindu holy days.

14. Economic hardship has increased since 1998, when the value of the Indonesian rupiah dropped from two thousand rupiahs to the U.S. dollar to fifteen thousand to the dollar. While the rupiah has stabilized since then, interreligious tensions have continued to plague areas where Muslims and Christians have coexisted peacefully in the past. Ambon, Halmahera, and Sumatera are examples. Sometimes these tensions arise because of the economic success of Christian Chinese, which is resented by Muslim neighbors. In other cases, Christians instigate violence because they resent the presence of Muslims who have transmigrated to their area from Java.

15. Devout Muslims who, because of economic or physical constraints, cannot travel once in their lifetime to Mecca can make a pilgrimage to Demak in central Java, once the center of a sixteenth-century Muslim kingdom. Kudus, a nearby city, is also a center of conservative Islam, as is Aceh in west Sumatra.

16. While walking by the river with a teenage girl from a neighboring Muslim family, Nani rather boldly suggested to me that we stay well away from the riverbed since it was noontime and the spirit of the river, who was resting, would be displeased if we went too near (Salatiga, April 1992).

17. The Muslim husband of Ibu Isminah, a Christian woman who worked in my home, described with some pride the family's peaceful participation in both Islamic holidays and Christian celebrations (village near Salatiga, December 1993).

ceptable for young people, but tight-fitting blouses or short skirts are still considered immodest.[18] A quiet decorum in women's behavior is also evident. Although women and men are not expected to separate in public places (as in Pakistan, for instance), women are expected to be unassuming, accommodating to men, hardworking, and dedicated to their families. Young girls may choose Arabic as a class in school. Many wear head coverings with their school uniforms as a sign of their devotion to Islam.

Many men are nominal Muslims, often quietly indulging in, rather than refraining from, certain practices forbidden by Islamic law, such as drinking alcohol and promiscuity. Some men are devout, however, regularly attending the mosque for prayer or taking time out at their workplace or in the open fields to bow toward Mecca five times each day.[19] Evidence of daily devotion and praise to God shows in the tolerant and tranquil faces of many older Indonesian Muslim men.

Besides these personal effects, Islam heavily influences societal mores. Although men are legally permitted to have up to four wives, the emphasis on devotion to family and religious practice keeps some men from overextending their economic resources by having more than one family.[20] Not only is atheism seen as incredible by most In-

---

18. One is less likely to notice modesty in women's apparel when visiting Jakarta, a city of more than eleven million inhabitants. A few Indonesians told me with embarrassed smiles that "Jakarta is not really Indonesia." This was their way of apologizing for dress that they considered unacceptable by Indonesian standards of etiquette.

19. One of the clear prescriptions of Islam is the practice of ritual prayer five times daily. While some attend the mosque for prayers, many men recite prayers at their workplace. A small prayer mat is laid on the floor and the ritual bowing and chanting of prayers is done facing Mecca. All hotels, even the simplest ones, have an arrow near the ceiling of each room, designating the direction of Mecca. The call to prayer is announced over loudspeakers from each mosque. Although some mosques provide a side room for women, in Java women usually pray in the privacy of their homes.

20. Men who are pushed by economic pressures to work in the cities, leaving their families in villages, sometimes participate in two households. This forces many village women to support their children alone. The second "marriage" is often an informal arrangement, leaving those "wives" no legal recourse for financial support if their "husbands" leave. A group presentation by five students in my summer course at Persetia, the Indonesian Consortium of Theological Schools, argued that informal sec-

donesians, it is also forbidden by the government. A dedication to Allah is understood to result in right action. *Pancasila,* the Indonesian statement on public ethics, asserts as its first tenet "belief in one God."

Politics and Religion

Pancasila expresses the political and social ideals that Western-educated Indonesian leaders brought to the islands. By the time Sukarno proclaimed Indonesian independence in 1945, his unifying philosophy, which combined Islamic, Marxist, and liberal democratic ideas, was hailed with enthusiasm by the people. With independence, a new government bound the islands together. Bahasa Indonesia, the trade language of the archipelago, was chosen as the national language, and "Unity in Diversity" became the nation's motto. As in every society, however, powerful groups order and dominate social structures as well as economic and political life. In Indonesia, the Javanese constitute that powerful group. Although the Indonesian Chinese wield much economic power, they are controlled by political forces mainly comprised of Javanese leaders. The larger islands—Sumatra, Kalimantan (Borneo), and Irian Jaya (West New Guinea)—are not nearly so populated or influential as the smaller, slender island of Java. This central island is populated by seventy million of Indonesia's more than two hundred million inhabitants.

Although national life for many years in Indonesia appeared unified under Suharto, the East Timor movement for independence, which reached the international press, was not the only dissatisfied group. Centralization of power and wealth in Java bred dissatisfaction in poorer, less economically developed areas throughout the archipelago.[21] Since political pressure forced President Suharto to step down from power, other dissatisfied groups have made their voices

---

ond wives should have legal rights to support from their male partners. The group was made up of two Muslim men and three Christian women students (Tomohon, Sulawesi, July 1998).

21. In Irian Jaya, for example, profits from the rich gold resources were used to build golf courses and high-rise hotels for international corporate executives and

heard. Economic reforms and El Niño hurricanes brought devastation and increased poverty to Sulawesi, Irian Jaya, Halmahera, and other eastern islands. Recent political unrest and conflict between Muslim and Christian groups in those areas show the difficulty of maintaining the ideal of unity in diversity upon which Indonesia was founded.

Since 1965, when an alleged Communist takeover plunged the nation into violence, Indonesia's government has closely monitored affairs of religion. Today, every citizen is required to be affiliated with one of five major religions listed by the government. These include Islam, Protestantism, Catholicism, Hinduism, and Buddhism.[22] Indigenous religions, although they have followers, are not considered official religions. Practitioners of *kebatinan,* a Javanese form of personal meditation that is centuries old, have unsuccessfully tried to get it approved as a religion by the government. Although one may practice *kebatinan* or any other indigenous religion, a citizen must still choose one of the official religions as his or her formal affiliation. In many localities one religion predominates: Islam in Java, Protestantism in Ambon and parts of Sumatra, Catholicism in Irian Jaya and Flores, and Hinduism in Bali.

Although freedom of religion is the official policy, it sometimes appears that Muslims are favored. "Islamization of culture" spreads Muslim ideas and practices seemingly in order to produce greater harmony among the people.[23] Fewer and fewer government leaders

---

wealthy Javanese partners in the industry, while poverty and malnutrition among poorer classes remained basically unchanged.

22. Islam is strongest in Sumatra and Java, Christianity is scattered across the islands, Hinduism flourishes on Bali, and Buddhism and Confucianism are practiced mainly among the Chinese. Statistics vary widely, depending on whether they are put out by the government or by religious groups themselves.

23. Government support of Islamic ideas, practices, dress codes, and leaders is generally considered to be part of an intentional program intended to homogenize the population without declaring an Islamic state. Margot Cohen reports that while Islamic separatism is seen as a threat to national unity, since the late 1980s Suharto has "encouraged Muslim think-tanks, publications, banks and schools. Trade links with Muslim countries are growing. This has all fostered a national atmosphere of Islamic

are Christians.²⁴ More and more women wear Muslim head coverings.²⁵ Christians claim that many more mosques are built than churches.²⁶ Transmigration programs move Muslims from crowded areas of overpopulated Java to Bali, Ambon, or Irian Jaya.²⁷ Consequently, more and more mosques are springing up in Christian and Hindu areas. When I toured Ambon, a church leader mentioned the large number of new mosques in the city. "Hearing loudspeakers from so many mosques gives the impression that this is a Muslim area," he said. "It is not. We are Christians here."²⁸

Tensions inevitably arise. If dissension between religious groups, or even among churches, arises, the government sometimes steps in.²⁹ Christians resent what they consider to be government interference in their internal affairs, and some worry that the government

---

pride, displayed in bumper stickers such as 'Islam is my blood' and 'Islam is the truth'" (1997, 39 f.).

24. By 1994, nearly all Christian members of the national parliament had been replaced by Muslims. This may be merely coincidental, although many Christian leaders believe it is intentional. It does appear that it is the more outspoken Christian members of Parliament who have lost their posts.

25. In Java, Islamic women wear white or pastel-colored head coverings that leave the face open and reach to hip level. During the 1990s head coverings as part of school uniforms became increasingly popular.

26. In 1994, a Chinese Christian pastor from Semarang in Java told me that he estimated that the government gave land for ten mosques for every Christian church that was approved. Christians become discouraged because they lack room for expansion. For example, from 1991 to 1996 in my university town, there was only one Catholic church. Mass on Sunday was restricted to two services. At the 6 A.M. mass, chairs filled the entire yard behind and alongside the church. Worshipers arriving after 5 A.M. had to sit outside, rain or shine. In the wet tropical climate of central Java, mornings often brought downpours to this mountain town.

27. Land is at a premium in overcrowded Java. A government offer of land in one of the outer islands encourages Muslim families to move to less densely populated areas.

28. Ambon, a center of clove production, has become a predominantly Protestant area since Dutch colonization of the "spice islands" in the seventeenth century.

29. For example, when the Batak Church in Sumatra could not agree on a new leader in the early 1990s, the national government stepped in and appointed one of the candidates. Rather than settling the issue, this caused a division in the church itself.

will institute an Islamic state. Muslims are spurned in localities that are predominantly Christian or Hindu or ridiculed because their religious practices differ.[30] Since 1997, the year of the national election of parliament, more frequent news of church burnings and violence against Christians has reached Western news agencies.[31]

The political situation of the Christian Church in Indonesia increases the pressure that women encounter as they enter church work and the study of theology as professions. Male church leaders already feel besieged and discriminated against. Competition from women for leadership positions is often resisted as one more attack on their authority.

Prevailing Gender Ideology

As colonization and, later, nationalization made their way across the archipelago, economic and political factors influenced changes in gender ideology, that is, organized and legitimated understandings of culturally constructed ideas about the differences between males and females and the appropriate tasks designated to each. Today, despite the multilayered pluralistic nature of Indonesian society and the various kinship network systems in different areas, there is a prevailing gender ideology that stresses home and family roles for women.

Women are expected to get married, bear children, and take care of home, children, and husband. This includes doing housework, shopping, cooking, caring for children, performing school obligations, and meeting the husband's needs as he wishes. Income-producing work among village women or managing household help

---

30. Proceeding to the river to procure holy water during a Hindu celebration in Bali, a woman pointed to Muslim women washing clothes in the river on the holy day. "They are crude and understand nothing," she said to me vehemently.

31. Media coverage reached both religious and secular presses. See "A Nation out of Control?" *Christianity Today*, 3 March 1997, 50–52, and "Restive Indonesians Find Little Hope in Vote," *New York Times*, 29 May 1997. International economic sanctions and a change in national government have increased interreligious tensions between Christians and Muslims.

among middle-class women is also expected. Today, many middle-class women work outside the home. In addition, women fulfill many social obligations within extended family and neighborhood networks.

These neighborhood obligations include frequent visits to neighbors, regular gift-giving, and *Selamatans*, which are life-passage celebrations at birth, graduation, and other important events. In our university housing complex, neighborhood meetings and organization of common responsibilities, such as paying dues, organizing communal workdays, and planning holiday celebrations, are held and run by women. The husband of the coordinator, however, holds the leadership title and receives public recognition for the work.

According to government statements on gender roles, women's primary role as "partners in national development" is to support men in their work and public roles and to raise future economic contributors through good parenting.[32] The double burden that this creates for women increases in agricultural settings, as factory jobs take men to the cities for a large part of the year. In middle-class families, increasing work pressures keep men out of the home for most of the week. Working women, subjected to the same pressures, must also manage the household.

Ibu Rita, a Javanese colleague and full-time faculty member, explained her daily routine to me: getting the children off to school, teaching at a seminary until early afternoon, collecting the children at school, and returning home to care for them and the house. On some days, required evening meetings or lectures completed her daily schedule.

Her husband, a pastor, was "too busy to help" with these family chores. If Rita were to complain or to fail to do these tasks, she would be considered a bad mother and a poor wife. If the husband participated in these chores it would be considered generous to a point on his part. Too much participation would be seen as neglect of his work

---

32. The government has established formal women's groups to develop programs to facilitate these domestic roles (Murdiati 1985). An analysis of government policy on women as partners in development will be presented in chapter 3.

as a pastor. He might also be considered henpecked or dominated by his wife, and thus an uxorious husband.

Norma Sullivan explores the issue of power in Javanese families and concludes that while women manage the household, they seldom hold real power in the family and even less frequently in the public sphere. What appears as gender equality on the surface actually covers a hidden power differential that gives men mastery over their wives, who must manage household tasks according to the husband's wishes (1983, 9). She claims that the "matrifocal pattern identified by several scholars (cf. H. Geertz, 1961; Koentjaraningrat, 1957; 1987), as a basis of high status and power for Javanese women is itself part of the subordinate familial-private sphere "(9).

Rita accepted her family obligations with apparent equanimity. Although apologetic that she could not meet with me on academic matters in the afternoons, she clearly stated her priorities. She had risen in the ranks of the faculty and, as one of the leadership team, was responsible for the financial administration of the seminary.[33] Rita was a gifted woman who managed her professional and domestic responsibilities extremely well. Since gender expectations were clear and acceptable to all concerned, the seminary supported Rita in her familial duties.

Things were not so clear for Alicia, a full-time doctoral student in the South East Asia Graduate School of Theology. Married with two children, she completed her impossible schedule by also serving as co-pastor with her husband at a Lutheran church in Jakarta. Alicia questioned the fairness of her double burden at home and in her professional career. Nonetheless, she believed that the family orientation of Indonesian society was preferable to what she termed "American

---

33. Given the strong emphasis on the *bapak* (father) being responsible for all under his care, one might question how much Rita's power was a delegated and regulated one. Norma Sullivan's research shows that male authority is definitive among urban Javanese, both in the public domain and in the household. In the private sphere, however, limited authority is delegated to women. Women's derived authority, as opposed to genuine power, is limited to managing a particular terrain under the direction of men, the real power holders (1994, 9).

individualism."[34] She not only managed her household, but also juggled her time working as a pastor with studying for her doctorate. When asked to coordinate the English-speaking service at her church on a regular basis, she felt she could not refuse. As her doctoral studies adviser, I saw her studies suffer under the weight of familial and social responsibilities.

Economic factors add to social constraints to keep prevailing family-focused roles for women intact in Indonesian society. Financial needs keep village women working in the fields and the markets. Lack of accessibility or use of birth control methods keep them bearing children and caring for the home. Child care demands and other responsibilities tie them to their homes and villages, keeping them from more lucrative markets (Smyth 1992, 41). Income of market petty traders is routinely spent on household necessities, children's school fees, and social contributions to neighbors and relatives.[35]

The same is true of middle-class women, whose social networks demand both time and financial contributions. Often young people from the extended family come to live with relatives who live in the university town. The economic burden this presents can be heavy, since university lecturers and their wives do not earn large salaries.

Patriarchy in cultural forms also supports women's traditional roles. Along with government pressure on women to express their "partnership in development" through a homemaker's role, *adat* customs among indigenous religions support the same view.[36] In Indonesia, Islam's view of women places them firmly in the private

---

34. Alicia did not seem to notice the individualism that men enjoy in Indonesia. Their position as head of the household, their freedom to come and go as they like, and their emphasis on amassing personal power through attention to their inner life result in a strong sense of agency and an ability to make independent decisions.

35. It is also common for small shopkeepers or market women to extend credit to villagers, even when they are not financially able to do so (Krisnawati and Utrecht 1992, 61).

36. *Adat* systems of informal rules define relative positions of women and men in family and social life in indigenous cultures. Even in matrifocal societies, such as the Minangkabau (Krier 1995; Blackwood 1995) and the Javanese, women's roles as child bearers and homemakers are clear (Sullivan 1994; Brenner 1995).

realm. Even attendance at the mosque is dominated by men, since women's attendance is relegated to a side or back room. Views of the other major world religions present in Indonesia are also used to argue that women's "place" is subordinate to men and must be exercised in the private sphere of the household.[37]

Indonesian culture manifests a complex, multilayered diversity of ethnic groups, indigenous cultures, economic strata, world religions, and modern influences. This pluralism offers opportunities as well as obstacles to women longing to develop their potential and to express their equality in contemporary society. At the same time, Indonesian society, in striving for unity in political and social realms, displays a strong view of family-centered roles for women. Women are pushed to accept that traditional role through economic, governmental, social, and religious pressures. They find themselves embracing, willingly or unwillingly, the double burden of work in the home and the workplace. In the next chapter we will look at the gender ideologies that lie behind these contradictory expectations.

---

37 Rita Gross argues that each of the major world religions supports patriarchy, although their rituals and texts can be reinterpreted to support equality between women and men (1996).

3

Gender Ideologies
Crisis or Opportunity?

As influences from the West converge with Indonesian traditions, gender ideologies meet, conflict, and reshape one another. As we saw in chapter 2, although culture groups in Indonesia differ in some aspects of gender ideologies, there is a prevailing ideology that affirms women's centrality in home and family affairs. When that centrality is threatened, those who have lived their lives with the traditional gender ideology react vigorously.

An elderly woman who lived down the lane in my Jakarta *kampung* (small neighborhood) watched my comings and goings from the little house at the end of the lane where I lived alone. The frequency and odd hours of my forays into the city distressed her. "Ah, going out again?" she would remark as I left. "Oh, you have been away again?" she would greet me on my return. Her life seemed to consist of sweeping the dirt path, hanging out the laundry, culling the chaff from baskets of rice, and tending her potted plants in the narrow lane. Seeing her grow more concerned over my habit of going out, I explained to her about my travels to the university in central Java and something of my life in Jakarta, which included not only teaching but also evening gatherings, chorus rehearsals, and weekend excursions with friends.

These explanations did not forestall a growing disapproval from the old woman. Her remarks and attitude increasingly showed that she believed a woman should stay at home, especially if she did not have a husband to accompany her when going out. This woman's own world was bounded and defined by home duties and limited by her social status as a widow. She rarely went beyond the boundaries of her small home. She dressed in traditional Javanese *kabaya* and sarong—dress appropriate for her place in society.[1] I, by contrast, sometimes wore a dress suit and sometimes went out in more casual attire. One day, when the *Ibu* saw me leave the lane wearing blue jeans, she called out disapprovingly, "What? Are you trying to become a teenage girl again?"[2]

Flexibility in lifestyle or dress is unknown to many older Indonesian women who have not been exposed to Western education or styles of dress. Departing from traditional ways can cause misunderstanding and result in criticism by those who have known no other way. Because customs seem like real imperatives of civilized life, departing from them can result in consternation and conflict.[3]

A greater tolerance toward different ways of dressing and different habits of living is necessary before an ideology of gender equality can be integrated into Indonesian society. The Javanese, like many sophisticated civilizations, see their ways as the best ways.[4] Contact with other indigenous cultures and Western civilizations now fosters

---

1. This attractive attire consists of a form-fitting lace blouse, a solid-colored cummerbund, and a batik cloth wrapped as a full-length skirt. Blouses were a European addition to the simple hand-dyed cloths that covered the body from the waist down. Older women in small villages still sometimes dress without the blouse.

2. In Java, an older woman of any class, culture, or religious affiliation is called *Ibu*, which means "mother." It is a term of respect, used as "Mrs." might be used in English. Although not as old as the woman in the lane, I too was old enough for this designation, and my neighbor thought I should dress accordingly.

3. See Peter Berger's three-phase theory of how societies create themselves and are in turn created by the social worlds that they construct. Reification of socially constructed practices occurs during the second stage of objectivation, when humanly created customs and mores come to be seen as absolute and natural in and of themselves (Berger 1969, chapter 1).

4. The Javanese notion of a civilized adult is synonymous with being Javanese. *Orang Jawa* (Javanese person) has the connotation of a civilized person. A common rebuke to a rude young person is "Belum orang Jawa?" (Are you not yet Javanese?).

a recognition of the acceptability and even richness of other ways of life. That recognition allows notions of gender equality to be implemented increasingly in Indonesia.

Guests in a society contribute to the process of mutual understanding by displaying different lifestyles while, at the same time, showing goodwill and moral uprightness. Their very strangeness can be seen as a gift that can open the local community's attitude toward change.[5] Becoming more aware of differences without feeling threatened by them enables people from both cultures to bring aspects of their lives and social interactions into the realm of consciousness and choice.[6]

Ideology and Role Conflicts

Conflicts occur during a time of gender ideology transition, not only between those who practice different lifestyles because of cultural differences, but also among women who are in the midst of the transition from a hierarchical gender ideology to an egalitarian one. That transition is acute in the Republic of Indonesia today.

Women's equal status, equal opportunity, and equal responsibility for national development have been part of the political platform of the Indonesian government since independence from Dutch colonial rule and Japanese occupation was declared on August 18, 1945.[7] In-

---

5. Anthony Gittons uses the metaphor of gift exchange to describe the interchange between the foreigner and the host culture. The local group offers hospitality to the stranger and the guest gives the gift of strangeness itself (Gittons 1989, 123).

6. Chapter 5 will explore how religion-identified resistance results from a heightened sense of agency, and chapter 6 will trace resistance theologies—religious ideas that spring from practices growing out of a strong sense of moral agency.

7. The Indonesian resistance movement took the opportunity to announce independence when the Allied troops declared the end of World War II. The constitution was developed during the first year (1945–46), while the revolution was actually being fought. Strong women involved in the liberation movement contributed to the constitutional rights achieved by women citizens of the new republic.

donesian women today are enjoined to work at all levels of economic and social life to build the nation. That new ideology has enabled dynamic changes in women's status and self-perceptions. Better-educated, more assertive women are finding their way into leadership in businesses, educational institutions, and religious organizations.

At the same time, prevailing gender ideology clearly delineates separate social roles. According to a study of gender in Southeast Asia, the various societies that make up Indonesia share a deeply rooted idea that women and men are innately different in their abilities and psychological traits. Only through marriage can male and female traits be complemented, allowing people to reach their full potential (Manderson 1983). Because that role division is based on naturalistic explanations of abilities and understandings of marriage, it is very firmly entrenched. The social roles that spring from that gender ideology seem to be at odds as well with the roles demarcated by the gender ideology of equality purported by the Republic of Indonesia.

As women attempt to act out of conflicting ideologies with competing value systems, ideological confusion occurs. Choosing among the responsibilities of home, neighborhood, job, and religious life, when one is expected to fulfill duties in all of them, exacts a price. Feelings of inadequacy arise, as a woman cannot fulfill all of her social obligations. Some values must be underplayed in order to act on others. As roles conflict, often it is personal and professional goals that give way to serving the needs of family and neighborhood. How did this situation arise?

An Ideology Is Born: Women As Partners in Development

Nyai Achmad Dahlan, a prominent nationalist during the long struggle for independence, said in her last public message in 1946, "The Dutch who have colonized Indonesia are driven away, but the Japanese occupation forces have posed an even greater danger. However, thanks to the nation's struggle, Indonesia has gained her independence. And it is the duty of all of you to foster and maintain what has been achieved so far through that struggle" (as quoted in Murdiati, Sabekti, and Sabarish 1985).[8]

Her statement emphasized what had been declared in the Indonesian constitution only a few months before that: "Without any exception, all citizens shall have equal position in Law and Government, and shall be obliged to uphold that Law and Government" (Republic of Indonesia Const., article XXVII).

According to the Department of Information, "The constitution thus grants Indonesian women and men equal political rights, equal pay for equal work, in fact, equal status" (Murdiati, Sabekti, and Sabarish 1985, vii). The responsibilities inherent in those rights are also carried by the women of Indonesia.

Thus, a new gender ideology was born with the founding of the nation. Since 1945, various organizations and government institutions have been commissioned to implement this new understanding of women's role in national life.[9] The *Guidelines of State Policy* demand total citizen involvement in development. The policy states, "Overall development requires maximum participation of men and women in all fields. Therefore, women have the same rights, responsibilities, and opportunities as men to fully participate in all development activities" (Murdiati, Sabekti, and Sabarish 1985, vii).

In this way, the original vision of equality and participation became more closely defined and linked to economic development. By 1983, women were considered *mitra pembangunan* (partners in development).

---

8. Nyai Achmad Dahlan (1872–1946) was a devout Muslim and nationalist who worked for better education for girls and independence from colonial rule. She played a prominent role in Sopo Tresno, the first Indonesian women's movement (1914–1923), was active in the Muhammadiyah Congresses, and advised Indonesian leaders on how to face the Japanese (Murdiati 1985, 116–19).

9. Examples include the PKK-Family Welfare movement, Dharma Wanita, the Office of the Minister of State for the Role of Women, and the government policy for fair distribution of the benefits gained from development, the "Eight Paths of Equity"(Murdiati, Sabekti, and Sabarish 1985, viii).

Are Women Actually Partners in Development?

When I spent two days with a coordinator for women's development from Irian Jaya, I heard a very different story. Government education programs for women on that island centered around basic health issues and home skills. The materials used for teaching management techniques to women were based on executive management programs but were applied solely to family management. Women in Irian were not well educated. Nor were they situated in executive positions that might reflect the phrase "partners in development."[10]

That information corroborated views expressed by religious leaders speaking to the national press. Aisyah Aminy, chair of the First Commission of the National Parliament and vice president of a section of the Muslim Political Party (PPP) in Indonesia, said in an interview with *Kompas* newspaper, "We are still in a situation of oppression, both in cities and in villages. If we are still busy finding food, we are not those who long for democracy. Women are especially vulnerable to exploitation.... Because of the connotation of being a woman," she went on, "we cannot hold leadership positions. Even though I sit on the commission, it is still a 'man's world' " (Aminy 1993, 2).

According to Abdurrahman Wahid, head of the Nahdatul Ulama and a prominent Muslim spokesperson, religion bears some of the responsibility for the fact that women have not achieved equal status as partners in development. "Men are still dominating women a generation later," he claimed. "It is not enough for religion to speak of moral ideals, we must have a concrete plan for beginning change, and a good attitude toward equal life together" (Wahid 1987, 1).

There are dissenting voices, however. "There isn't any longer a problem with women's emancipation in Indonesia," Endry Agoeng claimed only a year later. According to Agoeng, there may be structural problems in organizations or difficulties because women must

---

10. This section is taken from interviews held in Jakarta on December 28 and 29, 1994.

take leave after giving birth. "Another problem," he said, "is that women don't work hard enough and men end up being 'minders' to insure that they do their work." But even with such an attitude, the fact of women's inequality cannot be evaded. The interview concludes: "When asked if men ever exploit women, Agoeng didn't respond immediately. Then he laughed and said, 'Why not? It is clear to me that this happens. If the men are foolish...!'" (*Pembaruan Minggu* 1988, 1).

Despite political emancipation, a rising literacy rate, and more opportunities for women, "partnership in development" in Indonesia still seems like an impossible dream. The prevailing gender ideology is part of the reason for the continuation of women's inequality.

Laurie Sears suggests that the government promotes a view of women's role as mother that stifles the differences many Indonesian women wish to express (Sears 1996, 8). Norma Sullivan's research shows "how state-official discourses, augmented by older Javanese ideologies, help to disguise and perpetuate women's subordination while acclaiming their social equality and the critical importance of their role" (1983, 11).

Ideology and Innovation

In the West, the word *ideology* usually refers to a rather simplistic system of thought, centered in moral commitment and spread with impassioned rhetoric. But in Indonesia, ideology is viewed in a nonpejorative sense, more in line with recent understandings of the perspectival and evaluative dimensions of human knowledge.[11]

Clifford Geertz examines ideologies as "systems of interacting symbols, as patterns of interworking meanings" (1973, 207). Those symbols create a cultural system that orders action in everyday life. "It is through the construction of ideologies, schematic images of social order, that man makes himself for better or worse a political animal," writes Geertz (1973, 218). Action for the good of the community is

---

11. For an overview of the development of the notion of ideology, see my article "Political Ideologies" (Adeney 1994).

demanded or encouraged on the basis of a "right way of thinking" about what is good for society, that is, the right ideology.

During times of societal stress and transition, new ideologies arise as a response to instability. Geertz claims that when social reality becomes chaotic, ideologies proliferate, creating maps of social reality and matrices for the creation of collective conscience (1973, 220). Notions of the "good life," visions of a better world, and ideas about how to fulfill that vision then justify and motivate political action.

But it is not only a response to instability that spawns new ideologies. Practices that develop in times of transition, new ways of responding to situations that become habitual, may also be formulated into new ideas about how things "ought to be." [12]

The years of struggle for independence in Indonesia were a time of societal instability. As the resistance movement fought against colonial domination, it envisioned a new order. The notion of women as equal actors in society was linked to a vision of a free and just society for all. At the same time, women revolutionaries had been demonstrating their equality through their practices of political action. The gender ideology fostered by those practices in turn motivated other women to join the revolutionary movement, risking their lives and the lives of their families in the cause of freedom. After independence was won, the ideology was instituted in the constitution, to be supported and implemented in the new era.

That new ideology then motivated further social change. "A motive is both something that justifies and something that carries along," writes Paul Riceour, discussing ideology as a theory of social motivation (1981, 225f.). The new gender ideology provided vision, gave direction to action, and, when included in the constitution, legitimated values of equality and responsibility for women. In that way, the constitution helped to integrate societal meanings by formalizing the ideology that had motivated much action in the cause of independence.

Ideologies, then, structure and pattern social meanings. They ex-

---

12. Chapter 6 will explore this dynamic in the lives of women in Indonesia through describing everyday practices that help women pursue leadership goals.

plain practices that at first may seem contradictory to social expectations. They give energy and provide ideals for establishing polity. They provide motivation to seek and use technical skill, emotional resilience to support patience and resolve, and moral strength to sustain self-sacrifice and incorruptibility. Such motivation comes from a "vision of public purpose anchored in a compelling image of social reality" (Riceour 1981, 229). When women begin acting as equals and articulating a vision of equality, they build up their abilities to implement their dream of society. Ideologies, then, are meant to describe the best possible social reality and to enjoin people to act in accordance with that vision.[13]

This was the case with the new gender ideology in Indonesia. It both came out of social practices and contributed to new practices. But an ideology must be integrated into existing ideologies and their manifestations in social life. Since ideologies are something we think *from*, rather than something we think *about*, a new ideology often lags behind current social practices (Riceour 1981, 227). People continue to act out of the former ideology while purporting to accept the new ideology.[14]

Dissimulation begins to occur when the new ideology becomes a threat to the self-understanding of the group. The new ideology somehow cannot be reconciled with the old. An intolerance results which resists the direction that the new ideology has set. The old *Ibu* on my lane exemplified this intolerance and the anxiety that produces it. When such tensions occur, more established ideologies reassert their dominance with the force of an already legitimated system of in-

---

13. While this is the intent, ideologies do not always succeed in mapping out the best possible vision or bringing it about in society.

14. Agoeng's remarks earlier in this chapter are an example of this. He saw no problem with women's emancipation. At the same time, he suggested that women didn't achieve equality because they were too emotional, they needed leave after having children, and they didn't work hard enough. Traditional notions that women are overemotional, physically weak, and less capable than men are given as reasons why the egalitarian ideology is not implemented.

stitutions.[15] Confusion occurs as opposing ideologies result in contradictory social practices. The struggle with the older, more established ideology dampens the energy for creative change that the new ideology brought to the transitional phase of societal life.

The Double Burden for Women in Indonesia

The social motivation generated by the new gender ideology of equal participation for women encountered the resistance of traditional gender ideology in Indonesia. Strong and well-entrenched ideas of women's "place" in the home and neighborhood sphere were used to deter women from new roles in economic development and political leadership. At the same time, women's energy and talents were needed for development. Many people supported the new agenda of greater independence and freedom for women to pursue goals outside the private sphere. In an attempt to ameliorate this conflict, the Indonesian government stressed the traditional gender ideology alongside the new gender ideology.

Statements about the maximum participation of women in all fields were combined with specific injunctions to women to give their familial tasks the same attention as they had under the traditional ideology. Government spokespersons declared, "The role of women in development does not mitigate their role in fostering a happy family in general and guiding the young generation in particular, in the development of the Indonesian people in all aspects of life (Murdiati, Sabekti, and Sabarish 1985, vii).

The attempt to integrate the new gender ideology of equality of participation in public life with the traditional ideology of the woman as center of home and family resulted in a double burden for women. Mely G. Tan, in speaking of women intellectuals in Indonesia, states,

---

15. It is this tendency that Abdurrahman Wahid addressed earlier in this chapter. He encourages Muslim religious leaders to foster better understanding and attitudes of equality rather than to reassert traditional notions of male superiority fostered by religious institutions in Indonesia.

"Accounts related by those involved in the field state that the bulk of Indonesian women who achieve leadership positions in education, particularly in higher education, have to arrange their work alongside of their tasks as wife, mother, and supporter of the neighborhood" (1991, xiii; translation mine).

Many women have become aware of the importance of their contributions to public life. Yet a strong traditional emphasis on family and neighborhood relationships prevents many from giving themselves fully to their careers. When offered a company-sponsored scholarship to the United States, a research scientist for Indonesia's state-owned Pertamina Oil Company turned it down. " 'I really wanted to go so that I could realize my potential,' Ria recalls. 'But I felt my first responsibility was to my family. I had to decide in favor of my husband and my son' " ("Battle of the Sexes: Paternalistic Societies Are Challenged to Give Women a Break" 1993, 22).

A Core of Traditional Gender Ideology

Indonesia's pluralism makes discussing gender ideology for all of Indonesia a formidable task. Sears argues that "To speak of 'Indonesian women' is an impossibility" (1996, 4). Some scholars attempt to look at each ethnic or cultural group separately without making comparisons. Others see commonalties in geographic areas. At the national level discussions of gender usually focus on a view of women as primarily family-oriented and men as public-oriented persons. Despite differing views on gender ideology in various indigenous Indonesian cultures, that traditional view remains a dominant ideology.

A recent analysis of gender ideology in the Malay Archipelago suggests that there is a Centrist Archipelago tendency to "view male and female as basically the same sorts of beings." In this area, which includes Java, gender differences are played down. In the Exchange Archipelago, consisting of eastern Indonesia and parts of Sumatra, gender differences are emphasized and accentuated. Male and female are seen as "paired opposites" (Atkinson and Errington 1990, 39).

So, although cultures differ, some general traits of gender ideologies in specific geographic areas can be seen.[16]

In traditional, upper-class Javanese society, part of the Centrist Archipelago, girls were socialized to be soft-spoken, polite, and pleasing to behold. A princess at the royal court in Surakarta explained that she was taught manners and discipline by her aunt: "She taught me . . . to show deference to my elders, how to dress and wear my hair, and so on."[17] Traditional customs curtailed the activities of girls, and a period of total confinement to the house was not uncommon for teenage girls.[18] Men were considered more important in public and spiritual realms, and women were under the care of their fathers, receiving adult status only when married. Even after marriage a woman was under the care and authority of her husband.

Islamic religion dovetailed with Javanese hierarchical social patterns. Men held considerable power and were favored by divorce laws, social customs, and economic realities. Although modernization and the establishment of the republic have improved the situation, many women still suffer emotionally and economically under this system. Although the Qur'an was a liberating document for women in its day, interpretations of its teachings about women have not continued to improve women's status in Indonesia.[19]

16. Women with whom I worked from each of these geographic areas, however, agreed that a traditional ideology of women as weaker than and subordinate to men was prevalent in Indonesia. It was that traditional ideology that revolutionaries attempted to change in declaring political emancipation and partnership in development for women in 1945.

17. This account is taken from the story of a daughter of one of Mankunegoro V's sons (William 1991, 31).

18. Raden Ajeng Kartini (1879–1904), celebrated pioneer of women's rights, was confined to the grounds of her palatial home during her teenage years. Her attempts to study abroad in Holland met with failure when her father promised her in marriage to Bupati Rembang, and her life ended tragically with the birth of her first child (Haryati 1990).

19. Asghar Ali Engineer argues in "Islam and Social Liberation" that Islam was revolutionary in its time, espousing the acquisition of knowledge as the right of all men and women, the radical equality of women, and the demands of distributive justice

Rather, the combination of Javanese culture and Islamic religion works together to insure a traditional view of Indonesian women as central to the private sphere while remaining insignificant and ineffective in public life. Although a few women in Javanese court life wielded great power behind the scenes, this was the exception rather than the rule (Carey 1987, 32).

Further, even in traditionally matriarchal societies, such as that of the Minangkabau in west Sumatra and the Minahasa in northern Sulawesi, women's power is relegated to the domestic sphere. According to studies in Minangkabau, life in the world outside the home gives men freedom and the desire to achieve, while women are the keepers of the well-ordered home life (Postel-Coster 1987, 231).

A research study on the roles of women in contemporary Minahasan society indicates that the majority of contemporary women understand women's role in the home to be the *kodrat* (will of God) for women. Bearing and raising children is, in this view, the central life-task of a woman. Over 90 percent of the men interviewed agreed with this view. They described the woman as "queen of the home," although the importance of that role was secondary, since woman's overall position is below that of the man (Tangkudung 1994, 22).

In comparing *adat* customs in various Indonesian ethnic groups, Nunuk Prasetyo Murniati, a psychologist from Yogyakarta, remarks, "From Sabang to Merauke, many women are not treated fairly"(1993, 8, translation mine). Murniati gives the example of the bride price, a custom common to many Indonesian indigenous cultures, to illustrate her point. Originally intended to protect and respect women's rights, that custom now gives the impression that a woman can easily be bought and sold (1993, 8f).

Nasikun, a sociology professor at Gadjah Mada University in Yogyakarta, also sees commonalties in traditional *adat* systems, which not only locate women predominantly in the home, but do so in an oppressive manner. He suggests that "The phenomena of the treat-

---

(Asghar 1992). Marwah Daud Ibrahim states that "In the jargon of the Islamic religion, the principle is well known that tomorrow must be made into something better and of more excellent quality than yesterday" (Marwah 1993, 8).

ment of women in East Timur, Nusa Tenggara Timur, Batak Toba, and Lampung can probably be used as an indicator that indeed the rights of women are not respected as they should be. Their position in the *adat* already points to the strong domination and dominant position of men. Violent and unfair action of men toward their wives at home is not yet considered 'domestic violence' " (quoted in Murniati 1993, 10, translation mine).

The *adat* customs in these non-Muslim areas emphasize a pattern of family relationships not dissimilar to those found in Java. Although practices vary, the central position of women in family life seems to be a common denominator. It is a popular subject of novels and stories, both traditional and contemporary.[20] It is a common assumption in magazines and newspapers. It is a central tenet of traditional Javanese culture.

The government's emphasis on women's role in the home reflects that common traditional ideology. The government-sponsored women's ten-point program explaining how women can work toward modernization in Indonesia includes the following: creation of good family relations, correct child care, hygienic food preparation, care of clothing, care of the home, care of total family health (physical, mental, and moral), effective household budgeting, efficient housekeeping, security and tranquility of the home environment, and development of family attitudes appropriate to the modernization process.[21]

Implementing the New Gender Ideology

Ibu Nyai's charge to citizens of the republic to foster and maintain the gains of the revolution showed a new recognition of the deci-

---

20. Of book reviews of novels about women in Indonesia from a class of thirteen students from various islands and indigenous cultures, only one included concerns of profession or career. The others focused on women's struggles in love, marriage, and family life. This is not atypical ("Women and Modernization," Satya Wacana Christian University Graduate Program in Religion and Society, semester 1, September-December 1993.)

21. Government statement from Kelompok Pelaksana PKK 1977, 5–7; Cambang Tingkat Pusat PERTIWI 1978, 4 (quoted in Sullivan 1983, 154f.).

sion-making power of women, their independence, and their potential to act in the public realm. But the government's ambivalence about women and their roles in society is not surprising, given the pervasiveness and history of traditional gender ideology in Indonesia. Strategies for implementing the new vision of egalitarianism inaugurated with the constitution have been a topic of some concern in Indonesia.

Perceiving and developing women's abilities became important to many political leaders after the revolution had been won. A new focus on education for women was one response.[22] Throughout this century, active groups of women have brought their concerns to religious and governmental institutions. Communication with Europe, Australia, and the United States brought notions of democracy and human rights to the dialogue about women. The need for talents and willing workers in the struggle for independence also brought women to the fore. These forces combined to bring about a dynamic change in perceptions of women and an awareness of the necessity of education for girls and women.

Another impetus for implementing the new ideology was the rediscovery of historical accounts of women's rights and privileges in various *adat* traditions.[23] Accounts of women as queens in Java, of matriarchal societies that gave women prestige and honor, and of communal organizations in which women played a central part became examples for contemporary women to follow.[24] Marianne Katoppo states, "If women stayed at home in such a [matriarchal] context, it was because at the time the home was the center of power.

---

22. Dewi Sartika's Sekolah Istri, founded in West Java in 1904, became an example of progressive education for girls in Indonesia. (Murdiati, Sabekti, and Sabarish 1985, 109–13)

23. See Marianne Katoppo's discussion (Katoppo 1980, chapters 1 and 2).

24. Clare Fischer, sociologist of religion and frequent visitor to Indonesia, spoke to me of the powerful effect a central Javanese myth can have on contemporary people after she accompanied women on a ritual visit to the palace of Ratu Kadul: Queen of the South Seas, near Yogyakarta, Java. See "Ratu Kadul: Queen of the South Seas" (Fischer 1994).

It was definitely not the marginalized sphere it has become in many patriarchal societies, where it is the place women are confined to so that they may devote their whole life to the nurture of men and children" (1980, 15).

Intellectuals such as Marianne Katoppo embody the new ideology, describing independent, intelligent, and dynamic women, free to choose their lifestyles, free to engage in work in the public sphere, free to become future leaders of Indonesia. Martha Tilaar notes that Indonesian women have since earliest times held high positions both in the home and in society. She encourages women to participate in a "silent revolution" that will bring them into prominent positions in society in the twenty-first century (1991, 64–73).

Conflicts of Transition

The conflict between the old and new gender ideologies is deep and complex. It shows up in the discrepancies between accounts such as Naikun's and Murniati's of women as limited and hurt by their position in the home and assertions such as Tilaar's that women have always held high positions in Indonesian society. It appears in the frustration felt among women that, although they have the freedom to excel, few have reached society's higher positions of leadership.[25] It arises in the everyday struggle of career women to do well, as business persons, teachers, or religious leaders *and* as caretakers for their husbands, parents, children, and neighborhood affairs.

The conflict is powerful, in part, because it is so often hidden. One study of the economic role of petty traders in Lombok showed that although female traders made higher and more constant incomes than male traders, that income was invisible:

---

25. According to government statistics, in 1978, nearly thirty-five years after equal rights were established, less than 2 percent of women held public offices at policy—or decision-making levels (Murdiati, Sabekti, and Sabarish 1985, 76). Mely Tan reports that in 1990, only 120 Indonesian women had become doctors or professors with Ph.D. degrees (Tan 1991, xiii).

> This is because their incomes are immediately spent on routine household expenses, such as food, kerosene, and laundry soap, as well as on their children's school fees and on social contributions. Belonging to the category of social contributions are: regular payments to the ward organization (*banjar*), weddings, circumcisions, funerals of neighbours or relatives, and traditional as well as religious ceremonies (*Maulud, Selamatan, Puasa*). The magnitude of all these routine expenditures in relation to the low profit margins makes it difficult for small scale traders to accumulate capital. In the majority of cases, the volume, range and scale of their business remain stationary. Some have even seen their profits steadily decline; some have been forced to cease trading. (Krisnawati and Utrecht 1992, 61)

The necessity of such support of others within the social framework is masked by idealizing traditional paths as noble choices. Contemporary novels often show modern women who are independent in decision making but, when forced to choose, will put parenthood before career (Postel-Coster 1987). Women with professional careers continue to attend neighborhood meetings, to provide hospitality for extended family members, and to do household tasks such as cooking, cleaning, and washing clothes for the whole family. One hears only praise for the mother who arises before dawn and works until well past bedtime for other family members. While women's professional careers are downplayed by themselves and by others, failure to uphold traditional customs would result in censure by the community.

While living in Indonesia, I also experienced the inner conflict resulting from attempting to achieve success within both gender ideologies. I lived in a neighborhood community made up of families of professors at the university. During my first two years, I faithfully attended the monthly *ARISAN* (the neighborhood women's group). I wondered why the two or three other women professors in the neighborhood did not attend regularly. As my workload increased, I began to understand. Increasing work pressures and out-of-town conferences soon made it impossible for me to attend. Every month I received the invitation. Often a conflicting work commitment kept me from attending.

Results of conflict of this kind are twofold. First, a sense of failure to adequately fulfill one's responsibilities arises. The impossibility of fulfilling both roles is sometimes not evident. The feeling that one should fulfill societal expectations is deeply engrained, especially in the socialization patterns for girls.[26] One hopes that the next time one will be able to do that good thing which was neglected this time. Second, the neighborhood support network, traditionally sustained by women, suffers disintegration. Those family and neighborhood networks provide economic, social, and psychological support to families and individuals, enhancing the quality of life for people in communities. The modern career woman feels torn between neglecting her professional work and neglecting an essential dimension of the life of her community.

Conflicts also arise as children and household affairs demand attention. If both parents spend most of their time out of the home, children may suffer. Although many professional families in Indonesia can afford in-home child care and help with housework, the quality of care varies. Live-in servants also present special needs for medical care or school fees, or may have emotional problems that require time and energy.[27] Giving attention to children and keeping a household running smoothly takes time away from professional pursuits.

Another area of conflict arises between the stated agenda of women as partners in development and the hidden agenda of those in power who wish to hold onto that power. In Javanese society, power is ideally expressed through polite and refined ways of relating, ways

---

26. I treat this issue in the Indonesian context in "Kemitraan Gender Dalam Gereja Kristen di Indonesia Ini: Akibat Dua Faktor Sosiologis, Yaitu Ideologi Gender dan Sosialisasi Anak-anak" (Gender partnership in the Christian church in Indonesia: The effects of two sociological factors—gender ideology and socialization of children) (Adeney 1995a).

27. In the university community where I lived in central Java, it was considered very bad form to dismiss house help. Whatever problems they presented, the family, by hiring them, had become their patrons and must work out the situation within the household itself. The woman of the house was responsible for organizing work and keeping peace among household help. Often other family members of the workers required medical attention, needed school fees, or would even move in with the family.

that exert control without appearing to control. In this view, power to control one's environment is gained by concentrating power in the inner self (Anderson 1990, 28). The need to demonstrate one's power is understood as a lack of inner strength. It is also considered legitimate to use power to overcome a weaker power. Because of the sophistication of this style, women may feel that they are being encouraged to move ahead but feel frustrated that their progress is slow or seems nonexistent. Unless the power games are unmasked, women may blame themselves for a lack of leadership qualities, when they are actually being prevented from advancement by their male colleagues.

The social structures of power that are already in place inevitably favor and legitimate the status quo. Women's failure to advance according to the rhetoric of the new ideology may be a result of power-seeking male colleagues.

Strong hierarchical structures that legitimate male power also resist change. At a typical meeting of small-town leaders in central Java in 1989, the women prepared the food, served the men, and then ate separately in the back room. When they entered the front room where the men were seated on the floor, they came in on their hands and knees so that their heads would remain lower than the heads of the men. Some of those women held high positions at the university and were also neighborhood leaders. But the ancient Javanese customs continue to be practiced alongside of and sometimes in disregard of the more equal status achieved by women in their professions.

Revising Gender Ideology

The role conflicts produced as gender ideologies conflict and social structures resist change can produce debilitating effects. Or, those conflicts can reinforce new and creative social practices that can integrate the new ideology into societal life. Innovation from nontraditional sources, such as women, requires more than a new gender ideology. Actions that put those ideals into practice by demonstrating new ways of interaction between women and men can begin to change those hierarchical structures. As new practices develop from these tensions, a revised gender ideology will become an integrative force in Indonesian society.

The time of transition between traditional and new gender ideologies offers an opportunity for a conscious revision of social practices. While some Indonesians worry that a new gender ideology may put women first, equal human rights for women and men better reflects the goals of those who established equality for women when the nation was founded. Fostering equal human rights may enable women and men to question the traditional assumption that men are more important and worthy than women in social life. Public discussion of gender in the framework of human rights can help balance inequalities while showing continuity with accepted values.

Changing practices that make impossible demands on women's time is another step. The Javanese custom of fathers carrying their babies or walking with young children in the early morning or late afternoon is one existing practice that could be utilized more extensively. The refined notion of power for men allows them to show affection in family life. This aspect of male identity could be incorporated more intentionally into the new gender ideology, thus aiding a restructuring of family life necessary for women's advancement. Encouraging men to be more present in the home as fathers could be part of a program to develop strong national leadership for the future. At this time, while strong government programs encourage women to care for their families, I know of no such programs for men.

As hierarchical social structures become more egalitarian, women's voices can be heard. Political agendas that focus on the vast needs of women, who are still far behind in educational qualifications, salaries, and opportunities for advancement, can be developed. Reinterpretations of religious traditions that allow for contemporary understandings of women and men as equal in dignity and ability can be developed. Economic changes that foster women's advancement can be devised.

Recognizing conflicts between traditional and new gender ideologies sets the stage for developing new practices and more egalitarian ways of understanding partnership between women and men in Indonesia. Many students and professors with whom I worked at the university struggled with these issues, both in classes and in their personal lives, a topic explored in the next chapter.

4

The Challenge of University Life
Inclusion or Exclusion?

Using religious and intellectual discourse as a mode of resistance to gender inequalities presents unique challenges. An essentialist view of women's inferiority presents one obstacle to women entering university life. The dominant gender ideology in Indonesia clearly sets women's intellectual abilities below that of men's. In addition, spiritually, morally, and socially, women are considered beneath men. It is therefore considered "natural" and right that women defer to men (Brenner 1995, 21).

These evaluations of women's capacities are particularly damaging to women in their pursuit of intellectual excellence. Not only are women considered less able to reason and use their intellect, but they are also thought to be more inclined to emotional and physical excesses.

Akal (reason) is an important part of the faculties of a mature adult as defined in Indonesian society. Reason not only aids one in thinking clearly and utilizing one's power, it also helps a person control "base passions." Lack of reason is linked to excesses, wild emotions, and a general loss of self-control.[1]

This crucial capacity is lacking in women, according to tradi-

---

1. Reason is distinguished in Indonesia not so much by type, as Aristotle understood the distinctions among theoretical, practical, and technical reason, but by amount. As one matures and becomes more civilized, one gains reason. The balance is tipped when reason outweighs the emotions typical of children. Reason then guides and controls the passions.

tional gender ideology. Building on various indigenous views, Islamic interpretations of the Qur'an have augmented this notion in popular consciousness in Indonesia: "Although men as well as women have natural desires that threaten to overcome them, it is believed that men have greater rationality and reason (*akal*), which enables them to suppress those desires and to hold fast to the guidance of the Qur'an" (Brenner 1995, 30).

Dutch colonial influence contributed to this ideology. Ann Laura Stoler, in her article "A Sentimental Education," argues that in 1884, access to European-equivalent status in the Indies included a legal requirement of suitability for European society defined by "training in European morals and ideas." Candidates were required to sever the "invisible bonds of shared history and the attachment to native society" (1996, 73). Women and men were expected to quell their emotional attachment to Indonesia in order to be considered civilized.

Western views that sever reason and emotion and place a high value on empirical studies have augmented these attitudes. Indonesian universities today value the natural sciences more than they do areas of study that focus on the affective domain, for example, the humanities, psychology, and theology.

Christian theology as an area of study is affected by this attitude. Since majoring in theology at the undergraduate level is considered less difficult than majoring in one of the hard sciences, it is a popular major at this level. Students who are not qualified to go into physics or chemistry may choose a field in the humanities. Even among the humanities, theology is considered a less difficult major. It is not surprising then, that women, who are socialized to see themselves as less intellectually able, choose theology as a major and are welcomed there. This does not mean that they will be welcomed to practice their training as pastors or Christian educators.

Young men, by age seventeen, are encouraged to be serious and articulate, and to see themselves as knowledgeable adults.[2] By con-

---

2. College students have a unique status in Indonesia. They are believed to have a prophetic voice in an almost mystical sense, and their political views, often expressed in the form of protests, are taken very seriously. Whereas I have seen many young men

trast, socialization has taught young women to be retiring in the presence of males. Their speech is often tentative, even questioning, and laughter to hide embarrassment is a common response to engaging them at the intellectual level. Whereas a few women have broken through these stereotypes to excel in their studies, the majority reflect these learned patterns of behavior.[3]

When I was teaching at Jakarta Theological Seminary at the undergraduate level, about half of my students were women. A few excelled. Many seemed to feel intimidated, rarely spoke in class, and declined opportunities to lead small group activities. In 1995, when two women received awards for the second—and third-highest grade point averages at graduation, the student body responded with embarrassed laughter.

Reasons for these attitudes are complex and diverge from one subculture to another. One factor may be that, for some women, education has been more connected to status than to achievement. Sita van Bemmelen's study of education and elite formation in Toba Batak society claimed that a well-educated woman was valued because she mediated the social status of two groups through marriage (van Bemmelen 1992, 160). If a woman's educational gain is primarily social esteem, achievement is not the goal. In Dani society at about the same time (mid-twentieth century), only boys were sent to school (Devries 1985, in van Bemmelen 1992, 29). Girls' interaction in the market economy was restricted and passive. Apparently their need for education was considered less urgent than that of boys who were active in the market economy. These examples are not given as explanations but only to point to the many possible interpretations that spring out of the multiplicity of subcultures in Indonesia.

Graduate study remains a rare opportunity for Indonesians. Many professors teach for years with a bachelor's degree. There are occa-

---

emulating this prophetic role, undergraduate women do not seem to see themselves in this way.

3. An exception is a young woman who, despite opposition from professors at her Christian seminary, did her senior thesis on Muslim views of women under my direction.

sional opportunities to do graduate work in theology in the Netherlands, England, and the United States. Graduate programs in theology at the Jakarta Theological Seminary and the South East Asia Graduate School of Theology provide master's level training in Indonesia for a few select students. Most graduate work is done overseas, however, and men have usually been the students.[4] Women, married or single, are expected to stay nearer to their homes. A few programs of graduate study in Indonesia have begun to include women students, partly in response to pressure from the Southeast Asian accrediting agency. The graduate program in religion and society at Satya Wacana University in central Java, where most of the women that I discuss in this chapter did their studies, is a pioneer program, linking the fields of sociology of religion and ethics in the Indonesian context. It is also unique in its active recruitment of qualified women students.[5]

The program began in 1991 as the second graduate program of the thirty-four-year-old university. The first, in economic development, provides courses in economics, political thought, and problems of development. The second program offers contextualized education in sociology of religion, social ethics, and Christian theology. This combination of studies is offered with the expectation that if influential religious leaders better understand political and social structures, religions, and ethical theory, they can better serve both church and society.[6] Women as leaders were part of the original vision. Later

---

4. It is considered improper for a woman to leave her family and go to another place to study. The ones who do are usually exceptional women with supportive spouses and sponsoring institutions. Satya Wacana University has a progressive policy concerning women faculty. During my time there, the director of the School of Psychology, a wife and mother, returned from two years' study in England. The chair of the Economics Department was also a very competent woman.

5. The director of the program not only recruited women but also supported them in their programs, encouraged study of many women-related topics, and looked for postgraduate career opportunities for women who completed the program.

6. This goal may sound strange to Western ears because the ideal of free inquiry into all ideas is augmented by the goal of service to others by religious people. In Indonesia, however, those goals are understood to be complementary rather than oppositional. Most institutions of higher learning are affiliated with religious bodies.

the plan expanded to include Muslim women and men as religious leaders. The university was already training a religiously diverse body of undergraduate students: 50 percent were Protestants, 25 percent were Catholics, and 25 percent were Muslims. Religious tolerance and a strong sense of the importance of national unity among people of diverse faiths characterized this educational institution.

The new program faced the conflict of traditional and egalitarian gender ideologies head on. Eight out of the first twenty students were women. Courses on women and modernization and gender ethics were offered. Summer programs in feminist theology became part of the regular program of study. Despite the tensions engendered by this radical shift from traditional theological studies, men and women participated together in these courses, which specifically addressed issues of gender in Indonesian society.

Women Take Up the Challenge

By their very presence, women arriving on campus to complete a master's degree in this male-dominated field have already broken through gender stereotypes. In order to succeed, they need to continue to do that. They need to act in different ways than they were socialized to act.

Fatima came to the university after successfully completing her undergraduate work in theology. She had taken a number of years after completing her bachelor's degree to live at home and help her extended family. She was now returning, a poised, articulate woman in her thirties.

Diati was married, had two school-aged children, and was teaching English at a university in Sulawesi before she came to Java to work on her master's degree. She was used to working responsibly in a situation that gave her a good deal of authority. She came alone for her first year of study and was joined by her husband for the second year. Her children stayed in Sulawesi and were cared for by relatives.

Fatima and Diati worked hard to complete women-centered projects. Both were prepared by earlier life experiences to disregard the gender stereotypes that labeled them as inferior to their male fellow students. During their time in graduate studies, they each grew in their ability to handle delicate situations of gender tension, confident in their own abilities as moral agents and intellectuals.

Other women were not so well prepared. Yolanda, daughter of an important member of her indigenous group in Irian Jaya, was young and naturally shy when she entered the program. Jane, a Chinese student from Jakarta in her mid-twenties, was enthusiastic in her approach to her studies. But both Yolanda and Jane felt their lack of maturity and life experience in relation to the other students.

Many of the male students were in their forties and had years of experience as pastors or professors. The respectful demeanor women were expected to adopt toward these older men added to the sense of inferiority that younger women students had already developed through socialization in the dominant gender ideology. Yolanda said that she felt like a child in comparison to the older, intellectually mature male students. In Jane's case, the need to find acceptance as part of an ethnic group that was discriminated against in Indonesia added to her burden.

Yolanda took a bold approach, exploring patriarchal *adat* customs in her homeland and offering a Christian theological critique. Jane decided to study the Chinese urban family, steering away from a more focused investigation of women's status. Both accepted their role as younger students while pushing ahead in their personal development. Both successfully completed the program. During their time at the university, their studies of gender and involvement in the women's group enabled them to grow beyond their internalized attitude of inferiority based on gender.

Some women students steered completely away from gender— or family-related projects. Donna, a sophisticated and soft-spoken Javanese woman, wrote a biography of a famous male Indonesian intellectual. Sabariah worked on public ethics in the context of the new political structure of the Indonesian nation. These choices allowed both women to focus on their studies without experiencing the tensions that gender-oriented thesis projects generated at the university.

Men Struggle with Gender Ideologies

The struggles were not all on the women's side, however. Women students presented a challenge for male professors as well as male students as graduate education began to include women. Prejudices needed to be overcome, new ways of interacting with women needed to be developed, and different styles of communication needed to be understood.[7] A few examples may help illumine these struggles.

Women as Leaders

The idea that women are intellectually inferior bolsters the male ego and results in patronizing behavior toward women. Becoming aware of this attitude and changing it is not easy.

During the inaugural year of the program, faculty-student meetings were held to discuss curriculum and direction. Pak Otto, an older professor from another university who had come as a student to work on his Ph.D., took a role in these meetings that was somewhere between a faculty member and a student. As an older, qualified professor and church leader, he spoke as a voice of authority. Yet he was not a faculty member in the program but a student, given leave by his university to do further study. Indonesian etiquette required a high respect for Pak Otto's opinions, although they were not policy statements by a faculty member.

At one of the first of these gatherings, Pak Otto voiced a concern that women were pushing their way into church leadership. With some finesse, he described women as intellectually unqualified for the work and unmannerly in their approach to change. In Pak Otto's opinion, their disruptive behavior was lamentable.

I mention Pak Otto's ambiguous yet authoritative role in the

---

7. Deborah Tannen's work on gender differences in communication styles has some applicability to educated women and men in Indonesia. According to her, men tend to discuss facts and solve problems; women tend to share experiences and listen empathetically (1990).

meeting because certain indigenous cultures in Indonesia purport to have an ideology of equality while subordinating women through patterns of male authority. This seemed to be the situation in this case. Women students were accepted on an equal basis in this program. But Pak Otto's remarks formed a complaint that women dared to go against structures that were firmly in place in the Indonesian Protestant Church. His reasons for voicing this criticism had to do with women's supposed lack of intellectual ability and, in his view, their disruptive ways of intruding upon the orderly patterns of church organization. Jennifer Krier argues that "dispute narratives," in the form of protests by women against the inequalities that they experience, actually serve to reinforce the social structures that foster that inequality.[8] Pak Otto's comments substantiate her conclusions.

His remarks were particularly significant because they were made at a meeting of the new program, a program that encouraged and had accepted several women. Those women would be trained as church leaders. In the presence of other church leaders, professors, and students in the program from throughout Indonesia, Pak Otto reiterated the consensus that women were prohibited from entering top echelons of church leadership. Yet he was polite, soft-spoken, and did not attack any women in particular. In fact, in personal interactions he was quite supportive of women students. Even his presence in the program with them could be construed as an affirmation of women in leadership. But his remarks served as a reminder to faculty and students alike that the women in the program would not be welcome in church leadership after graduation. The implication was that women may study, they may protest inequality of opportunity, but in the end, they would remain as powerless as women who had created "disruptions" in the past.

Two years later Pak Otto made another set of remarks about women in church leadership that showed he had struggled with the issues surrounding women's intellectual abilities and qualifications as

8. See Jennifer Krier's analysis of Minangkabau structures of authority in "Narrating Herself: Power and Gender in a Minangkabau Woman's Tale of Conflict" (1995a, 51–75).

church leaders. The setting was a class in gender ethics. It was the second course on gender in Indonesia that Pak Otto had taken. This time he commented on the incredible resource that women presented in the Protestant Church in Indonesia. He stated that with encouragement and liberalization of church authority structures, women could aid the church tremendously by providing much-needed local and regional leadership. Rather than lament women's "disruptive narratives" about unfair treatment, Pak Otto now lamented the limiting theologies that had kept women from the leadership roles that they were qualified to practice.

Pak Otto came to the university holding traditional views about women's intellectual and leadership capacities. Openness to new ideas, study of women's leadership in Indonesia, and interaction with women professors and students had changed his attitudes and had become the basis for a larger vision of the church and women's participation in it. Pak Otto modeled for younger men a new path for male leaders in the church. Rather than a spirit of criticism and competition, he displayed an attitude that fostered acceptance and positive social change.

Honor and Status

Expectations about who receives honor is another obstacle to women's acceptance as leaders in university and church life. Tradition requires that older males receive deference from younger males and women of a similar social status of any age. These gender-oriented prestige structures give the ordering of human relationships a sensible and forceful character and are experienced as legitimate ideology (deVries, in van Bemmelen 1992, 119). At the university, it is considered highly improper for women to hold higher positions than men, to receive invitations to speak that would make them appear more important than men, to lead men, or to hold authority not delegated by men.[9]

---

9. Even in the matrilineal Minangkabau society in Sumatra, men hold positions of authority and must be recognized in their leadership capacity. Women who hold rights

But by its own standards, the university system challenges these prestige structures. Authority is to be based on achievement; academic qualifications should determine position. The national ideal of women as partners in development also lifts up an achievement model of authority, although government interpretations of the constitution have reduced the impact of this ideal. The university itself, where intellect and achievement form the basis for status distinctions, thus becomes a prime location for gender ideologies in transition.

The difficulties that arise from this situation are not minor. Men in authority are torn between following the old ascriptive pattern, giving older males position and power whether or not they have earned it or can manage it well, and the achievement-oriented path, which requires at times that younger persons direct older ones, or that women have authority over men.

As the only woman on a six-person faculty, I could empathize with the dilemmas the director faced. How could he send me to a prestigious conference to give a paper and neglect a male faculty member? How could he send a male professor to the conference in an area of expertise that he did not have, when he had a woman faculty member who was qualified to give the paper? How could he honor me by putting me in a position over older male colleagues? Yet how could he not put me in a position commensurate with my education and experience? Qualifications clashed with ascribed status on many occasions.

A concrete example of this dilemma occurred when my expertise was needed on the committee of a male doctoral student who was a prominent leader in the national church. At the meeting in which the student defended his proposal, the responsibility of the chair was to decide which suggestions made by other faculty members the student must follow in his doctoral work.

Although given the position of chair because of my knowledge of the subject, I was not asked by the director, who moderated the

---

to the land may lose their land if they are challenged by male authority through the legal system (Krier 1995a, 56).

meeting, to make an evaluation of the suggested changes to the student's program. To make that evaluation I would have to render judgment on the opinions of other male faculty members. But, not making that evaluation left it unclear as to which suggestions the student had to implement.

Both the director of the program and I were put in an awkward position. This situation was satisfactorily resolved when I asked to speak at the conclusion of the meeting. In this way, the director was able to satisfy the demands of Indonesian etiquette, honoring the older male professors and the student, and I was able to fulfill my responsibilities as chair of the committee by requesting an opportunity to make an evaluation of the suggestions made during the meeting. The student received both input and clear direction. Had I not understood the conflictual demands of ascribed and achieved status faced by the director, I might have taken offense at the lack of recognition needed to fulfill my task as chair of the committee.

Service

Besides the issues of leadership and honor, an interrelated issue of who should serve whom often arose at the university. While women students were "equal" to men, they were frequently asked to organize conferences, to run errands for male faculty, or to provide other socially oriented services. In these instances they were called upon to act more as women who served than as students whose main task was the pursuit of knowledge.

It was inappropriate for students who were asked to serve in these ways to refuse. Although there were no formal work-study programs at the university, students were expected to help their professors with everyday organizational tasks. This was the result partly of an apprentice-disciple model of learning, and partly of the unspoken but very real obligation incurred by students who had received university tuition remissions.

Men students also worked for their professors without remuneration on many occasions. But women students got a larger share of the burden, especially when it came to secretarial work or tasks of hospitality. It was difficult for men in authority to pass up the opportunity to get work done efficiently and, instead, to begin giving women students more opportunity to focus on their work and excel in it. Old ways die hard.

Women Struggle with Gender Ideologies

Women faced similar dilemmas as they attempted to act on their belief in gender equality and to become qualified leaders in the church and in the society.

Javanese requirements for politeness demand that women be soft-spoken, reticent, and accommodating in their views. Those valued "feminine" qualities seem incompatible with the task of graduate students to communicate clearly in class, to express opinions boldly, and to develop new lines of inquiry. A soft-spoken, polite, and intellectually malleable young woman will have a difficult time excelling as a graduate student, and a more difficult time fulfilling her duties as a professor or church leader after completing her studies.[10]

On one occasion a woman student presented her research project in a barely audible tone to a group of forty students and faculty members. The tropical heat became oppressive as windows were closed to block out noise from the streets. Some students quietly moved their chairs a bit closer to the front. Even so, much of her presentation was inaudible, and it was hard to remain attentive throughout it.

This example shows a certain incompatibility between Javanese etiquette for women and behavior that will lead to success in the academic world. Not every Indonesian culture has such stringent protocol for women's behavior. In Manado (northern Sulawesi) and Ambon, women develop independent leadership skills. In Toraja (central Sulawesi) and Batak areas of Sumatra, women are more outspoken. Nonetheless, in general, compared to women in the United States, Indonesian women are encouraged to be extremely subdued.

---

10. For an analysis of the cross-cultural and ethical issues brought up by these behaviors, see chapter 10.

Family Relations

A married woman doing graduate studies at the university may become the subject of gossip because her family relationships appear unusual. Diati, one of the few married women students, provides an example.

There was talk when Diati came. A woman from Sulawesi, she was married with a husband and two children. What was she doing at the university in Java? Her husband did not have a master's degree. They both had teaching jobs at a university. Why was he not coming first to get his higher degree? And how could she abandon her children like that?

Diati, a smiling, practical, hard-working woman in her forties, seemed blissfully oblivious to the gossip going on around her. She set to work on her first three courses. In the second semester of study, she came to me with a project proposal.

"I want to study the impact of Christianization on the women from my culture," she said. "Although we have many women pastors, it seems that women are not considered equal by either men or women in the church. Has Christian influence actually harmed women? And if so, why? And how?"

Perhaps it was the cultural difference that shielded Diati from the impact of the gossip going on around her. Women from this cultural group in northern Sulawesi are more independent than women from Java, despite the fact that Javanese wives traditionally hold the family purse strings. Traveling alone, leaving her children in the care of her husband, working on an advanced degree before her husband had achieved one—these actions may have been seen in a kinder light in her indigenous culture than they were in Java. Javanese poet Saraswati Sunindyo writes about a city woman with a university degree. In the poem she laments the equation people make between a woman's education and abnormality, and the connection between working far from home with prostitution ("City Garbage from the Nongo River," in Sears 1996, xiii-xvi).

Diati studied hard. A year later her husband, David, joined her in the graduate program. There were titters about her being a year ahead of him. Again, Diati, and her husband as well, remained undaunted. Chiding remarks, a mention of competition between them, teasing about women who get ahead of their husbands—all were met with a smile.

It was, however, harder for David to get into the groove of study. Plagued by financial worries and a lack of self-confidence, David's first and second project proposals failed. But eventually he did succeed. He finished his work the year after Diati had returned to her post at the university.

David and Diati are both back in Sulawesi now with their children, teaching at the university again. Diati dreams of doing doctoral work in the United States. Given her persevering spirit and the mature attitude of her husband, she will probably reach her new goal of studying abroad.

Occasionally one sees people like Diati and David who swim upstream seemingly effortlessly. Armed with positive attitudes, they press on through social censure, their inner strengths and confidence carrying them through. In addition to those qualities, Diati had an agreement with her husband. It was a pact they made before she agreed to marry him. She said, "I love study and learning. The man I marry must support me in my goal of furthering my study and becoming a scholar." David agreed and has kept his agreement.

Doubtless there is a price. David's inability to make much progress during his first year may have been related to psychological and social difficulties he encountered upon entering the program after his wife. Having a lower status than one's wife is definitely considered unmanly in Indonesian society.

Diati told me that she and David did not converse much about things that really matter, which is common in Indonesian marriages. Married women and men often live very separate lives, finding their closest companions in same-sex friendship rather than in marriage. Indonesians pose a different, but not necessarily inferior, view of what a marriage is about.

David and Diati did depart from social expectations in other ways. Perhaps most significant was Diati's leaving of her children to go to university for two years. Although it is commonly accepted for husbands and fathers to leave the family for long periods of time, her behavior was definitely considered abnormal by many Indonesians. For David to remain at home with the children was no less strange. Added to this was his allowing his wife to surpass him educationally, another practice that diverged from the norm.

These behaviors reflect a gender equality that holds promise for the future in Indonesian society. Together, Diati and David changed the blueprint for marriage, molding it to fit their particular needs and dreams, becoming part of a new social construction of equality.

Thesis on Gender Equality: A Test Case

The most serious dilemmas for women arose around the content of their studies. The first oral exam on a gender-oriented thesis project presented a test case for how serious the university was about gender equality.

Magdalena's project was controversial from the start. One of the first women students to join the program, Magdalena, a strong, capable woman from Minahasa, decided to study women in the church.

Although the church in Minahasa currently has strong women leaders, Magdalena felt that on the whole the status of women had declined in comparison with their status in the indigenous religion. Dutch colonizers in the seventeenth century were more interested in acquiring cloves for export than in the religious beliefs of the people.[11] Nonetheless, Dutch Reformed Christianity took root in the spice islands. Eventually the area became predominantly Protestant.

Magdalena believed that this change in religion had hurt Minahasan women. She explained that the theology of gender relations brought by the church emphasized women's submission. In her view, this contradicted the creation narrative in Genesis that gave women

---

11. Until the twentieth century, evangelization of the Moluccan people was forbidden by the Dutch government.

and men equal status and dominion over creation.[12] Although many women were active in church leadership at the local level, women were not seen as equals by the church. Magdelena argued that the theology of women's submission supported the dominant Indonesian gender ideology, leaving women feeling like second-class citizens. She wanted to test her theory by interviewing men and women in the church.

When Magdalena presented her project idea to me, I cautioned her. This research addressed the issue of women's status in the church at the theological level. It could easily draw fire from church and university men who preferred that the issue of women's equality not be addressed at all. To use theological arguments would confront the issue of women's equality at a basic level. For one thing, while women studied theology as an undergraduate major, men developed and articulated theology. Further, male theological interpretations of the Bible were understood to be inviolable. For a woman to reinterpret "the word of God" was a risky business. I pointed this out to Magdalena and asked if she was willing to face ostracism and perhaps even failure at the exam.

Magdalena heard me out and made her decision. She wanted to proceed with the research. She did her theological work at the university and returned to Minahasa to do her research, combining sociological and theological approaches. First, she studied the traditional *adat* laws concerning women's *kodrat,* or destiny to bear and rear children. Next, she interviewed women and men in the church about their beliefs and practices with regard to how the idea of *kodrat* fit with Christian theological views of women's roles and status. Then, using passages from the Bible, she made her own theological appraisal of gender roles.

Magdalena's interview findings were intriguing (Tangkudung 1994). While over 75 percent of both women and men thought women were equal, men were more active in suggesting ways that

---

12. Creation stories are numerous and influential in Indonesian indigenous cultures. Going back to origins to find meaning and order for society is a common practice.

women could act upon that equality by taking leadership in the church. On the other hand, most men and women in the church saw the care of children and husband as a woman's responsibility, part of her God-given role.

Magdalena's theological study argued that the gender equality suggested by the creation narratives should override specific Pauline injunctions to women's silence or submission. Overall, Magdalena's paper presented a strong argument for women's equality in the theology and life of the church.

As students and faculty assembled for Magdalena's oral defense of her thesis, Magdalena's calm exterior could not hide her nervousness. Her short introduction and the questioning of the first professor went well. Then a second professor began his examination. He held up a copy of her paper. "There is not one sound idea in this paper from the first word to the last," he began. He objected to Magdalena's method, her research content, and her conclusions. Magdalena addressed each question with quiet confidence.

After nearly an hour of questioning, that professor asked his final question: "Are you trying to dismantle our whole way of life?" After a long pause, Magdalena answered in a quiet voice, "No, I only want to be considered a human being."[13] There was a long silence. Then both Magdalena and the observers were dismissed, and the examining committee began their deliberations.

The faculty committee discussed Magdalena's project behind closed doors for nearly an hour. There was disagreement. There was tension. But finally consensus was reached. Committee members let go of their diverging views to present a united decision.[14]

13. Oral defense, March 19, 1994.

14. Consensus (*musyawarat*) through discussion (*musafahat*) is an important traditional pattern for resolving issues in Indonesia. The leader, in this case the director of the program, hears all sides of the issue. He then states a position that is usually a middle way between opposing viewpoints. The group then assents to his decision, thus reaching compromise. The ability of the leader, a clear father figure, to facilitate a peaceful resolution through finding a position that all can agree on is crucial to both his continued leadership and respect by the group. The others in the group may assent without really agreeing in order to maintain group harmony and respect for the leader.

Nervous students congregated in the hall outside. The significance of this examination was clear to all. Would the committee pass such a bold project? Not only Magdalena's future, but also the future of other students doing gender-related projects hung in the balance. Magdalena passed—a great victory for women and a mark of honor for the university that she did so. It was not easy for a woman student to stand against criticism from an older male professor. It was not easy for other professors to agree to pass a student who had been so criticized. Magdalena had accepted the risk and had defended her research. After the grade was announced, many students surrounded Magdalena, congratulating her on her fine defense. Women students were encouraged by her example and were impressed by the fairness of the university.

Significance of the Exam and Thesis

By handling the situation in this way, new ground was broken. The first thesis project at a Christian university in Indonesia that directly addressed the issue of women's equality had been successfully defended.

The transition between traditional ways of life and modern influences in Indonesia can be clearly seen at the university. A Western system of education, with Enlightenment ideals and individualistic competitive values, operates in a Southeast Asian country, with Eastern ideals and cooperative ascriptive values. Unavoidable clashes between these ideals and values occur. Magdalena's exam was one of those clashes.

Traditional Indonesian ideology prohibits public questioning of norms and social structures. Traditional gender ideology forbids going against male authority. Traditional Christian ideology denies women the prerogative of developing new theologies. Magdalena's work confronted each of those traditional ideologies.

On the other hand, university ideology values free inquiry, unhindered development of new ideas, and quality performance, regardless of research findings. Honoring people because of their age, sex, or social stature or finding ways to harmonize disparate viewpoints without conflict are not prominent values of university education.

The clash was not a minor one. The peaceful resolution of the conflict shows that ascriptive and achievement orientations, as well as traditional and egalitarian gender ideologies, can be successfully blended. The university stood by its values of free inquiry and rewards for achievement. By reaching consensus, the examining committee also upheld the traditional values of respect for authority and social harmony. The opposing professor reached consensus with professors who saw value in Magdalena's egalitarian ideas. Agreement within the faculty examining committee was reached, despite theological and cultural differences. No professor lost face or remained in competition with the others. The student received appropriate credit for work accomplished. The difficult situation was resolved with traditional and university values intact.

Finding Support: The Graduate Women's Group

Overcoming gender stereotypes and internal barriers until patterns of perception and behavior actually change takes a great deal of effort. Magdalena and others doing the difficult work of effecting societal change need support. Much of that support comes from other women.

In Indonesia, same-sex friendships are strong. Women look to each other for advice, consolation, and help. Time for relationships is freely given, often taking priority over other tasks. Through informal visiting and sharing meals together, women students began to develop friendships. Studying and working on papers together became a common occurrence among the women students. It was not long before informal networking among women in the program developed into an official group.

The Graduate Students Women's Association sponsored monthly four-hour meetings. Women students and faculty wives were invited. The program began with informal chatting and snacks. It took about an hour for the fifteen to twenty women to arrive.[15]

---

15. Here is another example of Indonesian finesse at harmonizing different cultural practices. It is a custom in Indonesia to arrive "fashionably late" for a social event that includes a meal. University functions start punctually. Since these meetings in-

When all were assembled the formal program began: worship and a lecture given by a student or woman faculty member or community leader. Since there were only a few women in the latter two categories at the university, student lectures were frequent. Discussion followed the lecture. Then the group shared a dinner together, which was organized and prepared by the students. When the meeting was over, cheerful goodbyes were exchanged, and the few with cars drove the others home. All were satisfied. Intellectual, spiritual, and physical food had been served in abundance.

This seemingly benign graduate women's group did not function without controversy. "What were the women discussing?" male students wanted to know. "How could women justify forming an exclusive group, a group that excluded men?" one queried.[16] The two married women were escorted to the group by their husbands. The husbands soon asked if they could sit on the porch and wait during the meetings, then join the group for the dinner. They needed to wait for their wives and take them safely home. As long as they were there, food, at least, could be shared, they claimed.

As the faculty sponsor of the group, these complaints came to me. I stated frankly that graduate study presented unique challenges for women. Meeting together to discuss those issues was a good thing. Perhaps the men might try it themselves, I suggested. Surely there are special concerns that men shared as they worked on their graduate degrees. Many were far from home and family, some faced financial difficulties, others saw job opportunities fade as they took time out from their careers to study. Perhaps a men's group might be something that could support *them*, I suggested.

---

cluded both types of activities, it was not clear whether one should adhere to official punctuality or to social "rubber time." Many jokes were made about this, but the solution to the dilemma was to devote the first hour to informal socializing. When everyone had arrived, the formal meeting began. All this was carefully planned so that no one would be embarrassed.

16. One common objection by male students to thesis proposals that focused on women's issues was that such projects were invalid and divisive because they excluded men.

The male students did not form a group. One claimed that men did not need such support. But pressure to participate in the women's group continued. Rather than give direct advice, I encouraged the Indonesian women students to work out an acceptable resolution. By the second year, men were joining the group for dinner. By the third year, men were attending the meetings and participating in discussions after the lecture. Not only the few husbands, but also other male students attended the meetings.

I was disappointed with this outcome. The group remained a women's group in name, but the ethos of the group changed. In Indonesia, as in other settings, men tend to dominate discussions, stating their opinions strongly. Women tend to defer to men and to seek their approval. Topics shifted from dissatisfaction with the system or fears of being dominated by men to discussions of partnership and how to keep everyone happy with the way things were. Men were not asked to lead activities in the group, but that too seemed a likely possibility for future meetings.

Other Support Activities among Women

Women found other ways to support each other on the campus. Gender topics were sometimes presented at all-campus lecture events. At one such lecture, a lively discussion ensued among undergraduates about women's and men's differing expectations of the opposite sex. I noticed that while the young men insisted that women were more immature and emotional, they were quite agitated while making these assertions. The women, by contrast, seemed more reasoned in addressing issues of gender inequality and were more adult in their behavior.[17]

---

17. "Women and Men: What to Expect," lecture by *Ibu* Konta, chair of the Economics Department, May 1993. These observations about behavior confirm Suzanne Brenner's research, which documents a subordinate ideology exhibited through practices that contradict the dominant gender ideology of male superiority (1995). Although gender stereotypes insist that men are more rational and in control of their emotions, in practice, the reverse is often the case.

Some of the students from our program helped form a campuswide women's group. Women faculty from all departments, along with the graduate women, sponsored lectures, discussions, and dramatic events on campus. For two years the theme of these meetings was violence against women.[18] There was no lack of courage or creativity in addressing this volatile issue. Besides campus presentations, a support network for women who experienced domestic violence was set up, including small sharing groups and a telephone hotline.

A local discussion group of Christian women was also formed during this time. This group focused on theological issues and linked up with a regional group of church women in theology.[19] Again, domestic violence became a major theme, and Christian responses to violence were frequently discussed. This group had international contacts and began seeking funding for a women's center.[20]

Another significant group on campus was the Research Center for Women. This group, comprised of women faculty and a staff of researchers, investigated village life. Concerns of women in the villages were explored, for example, health and birth control, economics, and care of children. As consultant to this institute, I saw a consistent focus on finding ways to improve women's situations and to educate women about health and social issues. At the same time, significant research into the context and problems of village women in Java was ongoing.

Besides participating in formal campus women's groups, students in the graduate program found encouragement in personal re-

---

18. Domestic violence has only recently been recognized as a justice issue among Indonesia's educated elite. In general, it is assumed that a wife "belongs" to a husband. Men are in charge of the family. Traditionally, a husband's violence against wives or children is not seen as criminal. (Information from student and faculty discussion of violence and women in Indonesia, April 1994.)

19. EATWOT sponsors a network of Christian women that meet regionally in various parts of Indonesia. It also sponsors the annual National Meeting of Women Theologians.

20. Because of their lack of economic independence, abused women often feel they cannot leave their husbands. Domestic violence is not confined to the lower classes but occurs in middle- and upper-class families as well (Women's Regional Discussion Group, EATWOT, Salatiga, Indonesia, September 1993).

lationships. Some sought counsel from faculty members, some formed strong friendships with other women, and some worked together in church or social service. Many found support in relationships with extended family or in church fellowships. The single women remained single; the married women continued to relate to their families, carving out time for study in various ways.

Despite the struggles, both women and men found ways to complete their work, juggling their lives and wending their way through conflicting gender ideologies and expectations. Decisions about how to act and what lifestyle to develop as students had an ongoing effect on their subsequent direction. Some women, even while in graduate school, remained focused on traditional gender ideology. Some developed strategies of resistance, launched into new ways of acting in their world, and became advocates for an egalitarian gender ideology.

The next chapter will examine that religion-identified resistance: the ways that women demanded inclusion in their religious institutions, how they resisted the confining views imposed upon them, and the sense of moral agency that grew as they continued to develop as leaders.

5

Strategies of Resistance
Independent Agents or Followers of God?

In order to thrive at the university, women discovered ways to resist ideologies and attitudes that confined or subtly subjugated them. They found a space to develop their sense of agency and a way of establishing authority on egalitarian terms by using religion as a site of resistance and growth.

Ratna, a refined woman of mixed Javanese-Torajan ancestry, studied for her master's degree during a turbulent time in her family life. Although her parents said that they needed her at home to care for a young child and later an ill mother, she stayed for four years at the university. Her parents' ambivalence about this arrangement manifested itself in repeated invitations to come back to her home city for extended visits. As Ratna asserted her independence, the calls became more urgent: a divorcing sister needed her counsel, her mother's illness demanded her care, the family was gathering for a special celebration. In order to focus on her studies, which were lagging because of frequent trips home and lengthy visits from family members, Ratna stopped communicating with her parents altogether for a period of more than one year.

While family structural arrangements in both the cultures of the father (Javanese) and mother (Torajan) have been viewed as unmarred by gender bias, this was not Ratna's experience.[1] Despite

---

1. Both Java and Toraja in central Sulawesi are part of the Centrist Archipelago, characterized by bilateral kinship systems that have been understood by Western anthropologists to offer greater equality of women and men because a child is considered

parental pressure to stay at home or at least live with another family, Ratna chose to live alone. Her parents wanted her to marry her boyfriend, whom she had known for eleven years. Ratna chose not to marry. Her father, a prominent Christian leader and seminary professor, wanted her to study Christian theology. Ratna chose to do her thesis on women's roles in Tuluk, the traditional Torajan religion.

According to Ratna, the inner strength she needed to make these choices came first from a strong religious calling and second from a growing sense of her own independence. This chapter explores those themes in the lives of women who made choices that defied social convention in order to pursue leadership in the church.

Religious Calling and Institutional Structures

Religion might be defined as "that discourse whose defining characteristic is its desire to speak of things eternal and transcendent with an authority equally transcendent and eternal" (Lincoln 1999, 395). By invoking the power of the divine to sanction their actions of pursuing leadership in a human institution that denies them access to that leadership, women participate in the process of constructing gender and religion (Brink and Mencher 1990, 60). They demand inclusion in the power centers of the religion.

While in many Protestant churches women were technically allowed to become pastors, few attained those positions. Fewer still gained access to the education that would allow them to rise in the ranks of denominational power. A "call" lent weight to many women's claim to embark on the road to leadership. By utilizing the idea of "calling," a concept fraught with notions of divine power, the

---

equally related to both its parents (Atkinson and Errington 1990). Ratna clearly indicated, however, that parental expectations were that she remain in the family home until marriage. The strong role of women in the indigenous Torajan religion (Kobong 1995) and the custom in some eastern Indonesian societies to send young people to extended family members who lived in university towns for their education may have contributed to the decisive stance that she took in pursuing university studies in another city.

women gained entrance to the leadership track usually reserved for males. It was noted in chapter 2 that in certain Indonesian indigenous cultures, Christian notions have expanded women's freedoms, since the *adat* laws were more restrictive. More often, however, Christian views of women as subordinate to men and unfit for church leadership have flourished in Indonesia. Dutch Reformed views of the order of creation and the importance for all people to fulfill their God-given role in society kept women from establishing themselves as church leaders in some areas. In others, Roman Catholic practices of limiting priestly functions to men curtailed women's leadership roles.[2]

Theological arguments that support women's subordination invoke the authority of sacred texts. The man as head of the household, requiring submission from his wife, is one such interpretation from the letters of the apostle Paul in the New Testament (1 Cor. 11:3, Eph. 5:22–24, 1 Tim. 2:11–14). A related view relegates women to secondary and dependent status because Eve was said to have been created from Adam's rib.[3]

A parallel notion that has influenced views of gender in Indonesian society is that of *kodrat*. In this understanding, woman's destiny is to bear and raise children. The God-given reason for a woman's life

---

2. The United Protestant Church in Indonesia is predominantly Reformed. Catholicism was brought by the Portuguese to eastern parts of Indonesia: Irian Jaya, Flores, and East Timor. It too spread to Java and other islands.

3. The first creation story in Genesis 1 includes both man and woman, created together as equal caretakers of the earth. This order of creation argument is based on the second creation account in Genesis 2. In this story, Adam, after naming the animals, could find no counterpart to himself. According to this account, God then put Adam to sleep, and, taking out one of his ribs, created a woman. The emphases of her likeness to Adam, her sameness, and her ability to be an equal partner with him are lost in the interpretation that Adam had authority over her because he was created first, and woman was made from him. The apostle Paul partly supports this traditional interpretation in 1 Corinthians 11, with some qualifications. Unfortunately, in his first letter to Timothy, he ignores those qualifications (1 Tim. 2:8–15). They have generally been ignored in the church since, and women's subordination has been a standard part of Christian theologies for many centuries.

is to provide this service to society. While the idea of *kodrat* was brought to Indonesia with the Muslim religion, Christian theologians, as well as governmental interpreters of the role of women in Indonesian society, have built upon this notion (Marwah 1993; Murdiati and Sabekti 1985; Tan 1991; Tangkudung 1994). The force of religious authority is here added to arguments from nature and custom.

By speaking out about their sense of calling to leadership work in the church, the women resisted the religious authority that supported the confinement of their roles in society and in the church. Such internal resistance strategies, if recognized in feminist discourse, could broaden connections among communities of women struggling against gender oppression (Fulkerson 1999, 146).

The women also called upon their experience as a source of authority in their lives. Rather than rely on interpretations of sacred texts that traditionally reserved power for males (Brink and Mencher 1997, 60), the women drew on their subjective experience of God as a source of their conviction that they should embark on a road to leadership. In doing so, these women align themselves with feminist Christian theologians from the two-thirds world, as well as those in the Euro-American context who make this a basic tenet of feminist methodology (Chung 1990; Daly 1994; King 1994).

The appeal to a calling as a source of motivation for action also reflects trends in the West. Belenky, Clinchy, Goldberger, and Tarule speak of women's reliance on subjective intuitive knowledge as a way of knowing (1986, 15). In her study of women's religious imagination in contemporary North American settings, Mary Farrell Bednarowski points to women's growing trust in the authority of their own experience and the immanence of the divine as major features of women's religious understandings (Bednarowski 1999, 84).

The appeal to experience indirectly criticizes a traditional Protestant idea that authoritative theology comes directly from the divinely inspired text of the Bible. While using the Bible, interpretations of the role of women by male theologians in Indonesia have mirrored the notion of *kodrat*. By appealing to their experience of being called by God, women muster a counterauthority that supports gender equality.

It is worth noting that both of these forms of resistance—the appeal to calling and the reliance on experience—can be done without directly challenging male theologies of women's roles in the church. This indirect use of power adapts itself to the strong cultural ideal in Indonesia of exerting power calmly and indirectly (Anderson 1990; Atkinson and Errington 1990, 5f.).

Similar resistance strategies were undertaken by nineteenth-century American Christian women who felt called to preach. They responded by acting within the institutional structures of the church, creating a place for themselves as deaconesses or lay preachers. Some were able to expand the scope of their public work by gaining the favor of male leaders who supported them (Hardesty 1984). Others worked independently, leaving the religious institutions that rejected their leadership while maintaining their sense of call to public Christian work (Andrews 1986). These strategies of resistance make use of openings in institutional power structures or, alternatively, work outside of those structures.

Because a sense of calling arises from the authority of experience and requires resistance from within the religion itself, the struggle to decide how to respond can be intense. In Indonesia today, if Christian women do listen to and follow an inner call to leadership, they encounter resistance from church authorities and their theological interpretations of women's role in the church. This resistance is allegedly backed up by "the voice of God." But if women resist their sense of calling to a religious vocation, they encounter resistance from their inner spirit that calls them with "the voice of God."

Following a Call: Ida and Marlene

Women make various choices when faced with the dilemma of reconciling the authority of the church and the social pressures it exerts with their inner experience. Without a strong sense of moral agency, a woman may doubt her own convictions and will conform to the expectations of family and social pressures. Some women, however, do listen to that inner call and take steps to follow it in their lives. The following stories will illustrate the various directions a woman can take when she decides to follow a call to a religious life.

From the time she was about twelve years old, Ida knew that she was meant to be a pastor when she grew up. Her mother was a strong role model for her and supported her choice of theology as her college major. After graduation, Ida married a Lutheran pastor in Jakarta. This church allowed copastoring, so she and her husband worked as a team.

I asked Ida about her sense of calling. She said she never wavered in her commitment to become a pastor, believing that God was calling her to this work. She was a *Peranakan* Chinese, an ethnic group that consists of people of mixed Chinese and Javanese descent. She had grown up in Jakarta, where she interacted with people of many ethnic and religious backgrounds. As a Chinese Indonesian and a Christian, she was used to being the "other," the different one, the one who stood out as strange. She was also accustomed to hard work.

After becoming a pastor, however, she did realize that women were discriminated against in that work. She felt that women were overworked because they were expected to perform the duties of a pastor's wife as well as fulfill the responsibilities of a pastor. Even if a woman succeeded in these multiple tasks, her husband would have more authority in the church, receive more honor, and have more freedom to choose parts of the vocation that he liked best, leaving the rest to his wife. Free from the responsibilities of child care and maintaining a home, he could also find more time for study.

As Ida's adviser for her doctoral work at Jakarta Theological Seminary, I listened to these concerns, since they were part of Ida's attempt to understand Indonesian women's psychology. She chose feminist studies as a concentration, focusing on feminist interpretations of Freud's Oedipal complex theory. The mother of two, she was interested particularly in the psychological dimensions of mothering and how girls' early sexual development differs from that of boys.

Ida was a good thinker and tried very hard to excel in all areas. But her huge workload severely limited the time she could devote to her studies. She found it difficult to say "no" when the church asked her to take on extra work. For example, she was asked to organize the monthly English-speaking service during the first year of her doctoral work. She was already heavily involved in the church and in raising two school-aged children. Since she had added doctoral studies to her schedule, she felt overwhelmed. Yet her sense of calling to the pastorate and her sense of duty to traditional gender roles combined to pressure her into taking on yet another task. Her studies suffered, but she remained faithful to her sense of calling to the pastorate, giving that work top priority.

Marlene also grew up in a Protestant church in Jakarta. During her teens, she experienced a sense that God wanted her to become a Catholic sister. Both her family and her church reacted strongly against this idea. Nonetheless, Marlene visited a few monasteries in Java. When she spent time at Gedono, a women's Trappist monastery in central Java, she had a deep sense that she belonged there.[4]

The vocation of the sisters at Gedono is to pray for the unity of the church in the world. They choose to remain cloistered, leaving the compound only a few times during their early years and remaining committed to that particular community and the Benedictine practice of prayer for the rest of their lives.

Sister Martha, the abbess at Gedono, heard Marlene's wish and advised her to return home and attempt to find a Protestant group that she could join. After a year of looking, Marlene was still convinced that God was calling her to Gedono. She wrote again to Sister Martha.

That letter began a long series of visits to Gedono and discussions with family and church elders. Marlene did not rebel, going against the wishes of her family and church because of the strength of her calling. Instead she chose to work with those who opposed her,

---

4. I met Marlene when she was visiting the monastery, and we talked about her sense that God was calling her to that place. Two years later, after Marlene entered the Trappist order, Sister Martha, the abbess, told me the whole story. Her account was confirmed in Marlene's own words through a written, open-ended questionnaire that served as an interview. After taking her vows, Marlene was prohibited from conversing with outsiders.

confident that if God was calling her to Gedono, those whom she loved and who had authority over her would eventually be convinced of the rightness of her choice.

Marlene's patient work brought success. After two years of dialogue she entered the monastery, not only with the blessing of her family, but also with the support of her Protestant congregation. Her church held a special service of dedication, sending her on to her new vocation. Later, when Marlene officially joined the Catholic Church, her Protestant congregation approved.

This was most unusual. Misunderstandings between Protestantism and Catholicism, seeded in their European colonial histories, have remained strong since the mid-sixties, when the Indonesian government declared Protestantism and Catholicism to be two separate religions. In many places relationships between Catholic and Protestant churches are often strained or nonexistent. By working within the bounds of social expectations and family commitments, yet pursuing her dream, Marlene made an impact on ecumenical relations in Indonesia.

Religious Vocations and Gender Ideologies

Ida and Marlene each attempted to honor traditional gender ideologies. But their sense of calling to vocations in the church made them break with societal expectations at a certain point.

Ida married and cared for her husband and children. Although she felt that it was unfair that her husband was more privileged and benefited at her expense in their church work, Ida dutifully fulfilled her family responsibilities. At the same time, she followed her sense of calling in becoming a pastor, unlike most women in her social group. When making difficult choices about the use of her time, her vocation as a pastor came first. Yet she pursued doctoral studies in feminist thought, attempting to educate herself and others about injustices that were being perpetuated in the name of Christian theology and gender ideology in Indonesia.

Marlene's sense of calling to a religious vocation enabled her to resist societal expectations of getting married and bearing children.

Yet she did adhere to societal expectations as much as she could, believing that understanding could overcome the denominational divisions that prevented her from entering the monastery.

Each woman worked from a strong sense of moral agency, acting self-consciously toward the good as she understood it. Each evaluated her life and chose a direction that differed from the norm but was true to her inner longings. Along the way, each made choices that were consonant with social norms that were important to her. Yet a sense of calling by God to a particular life strengthened the resolve of each of these women to depart from social expectations when necessary to fulfill that calling.

Analyzing Moral Agency and Resistance

In following that resolve these women and others in this study, intentionally or unintentionally, resisted the social constructions of religion and gender in their social milieu. They developed new practices: of study, of preaching, and of pastoral counseling. Those in the monastery developed practices of daily communal prayer, study, and private devotion to God. In following their religious callings, their practices modeled a new gender ideology of choice and purpose for other women.

The growing sense of agency that encouraged Marlene to continue to work toward acceptance by the monastery and enabled Ida and Ratna to stay the course of university graduate work presents a complex phenomenon. Societal social networks, issues of context and historical location, understandings of identity, and socioeconomic status contribute to an individual's sense of freedom to act.

The women in this study who were selected to pursue graduate studies were all privileged economically and held high status in their cultures. However, they differed widely in their social locations, history, and maturity. The youngest, who called herself the graduate program's mascot, was twenty-three years old, while the oldest boasted more than fifty years of age.

In order to make comparisons and find common behaviors that strengthened their choices to become leaders, three models of moral development were used. By using Lawrence Kohlberg's hierarchy of moral development, Carol Gilligan's relational scheme of women's moral decision making process, and Hubert and Stewart Dreyfus's model of ethical action developed through practices, a more nuanced understanding of the actions of resistance of these women came into focus. The appropriation and limits of application of those models is discussed in chapter 9.

Analysis showed that women who completed their graduate studies demonstrated a high level of independence in decision making (Kohlberg 1984), along with a focus on relationships with others, especially women who were sympathetic to the life choices they were making (Gilligan 1982; Gilligan, Ward, and Taylor 1988). They developed practices that reinforced their choices and enhanced their skill in maintaining those choices (Dreyfus and Dreyfus 1986, 1992).

These actions fall into the category of moral agency, using that term in the broadest sense to indicate actions geared to good ends (Aristotle 1952; Niebuhr 1963). It is a subject that acts. Agency itself, in a feminist framework, is a good end, since actions that enhance the subjectivity of a woman can be considered moral acts. Those actions may be oriented toward moral principles or relationships, but they are always located in particular contexts and life narratives. It is in that narrative context that the meaning of those acts resides (MacIntyre 1981). An ability to make strong evaluations about one's actions shapes identity for people in contemporary modern societies (Taylor 1989). Educated Indonesian women respond, not only to their indigenous cultures, the religions brought by colonial powers, and the gender ideologies in society, but also to this modern zeitgeist of which Taylor speaks.

Moral agency for Indonesian women spans a wide swath of behaviors considered to be mere etiquette in the West. Modesty, refined manners, and gentle acquiescence to authority figures are part of morality for most Indonesian women, even those in societies in the Exchange Archipelago (Sumatra and parts of east Indonesia), which allow relatively more assertiveness in women's comportment (Atkinson and Errington 1990). Achieving independence in a society that defines morality in terms of social conformity challenges women who are struggling for a different kind of life to break out of those systems, even as they live within them.

Resistance Strategies

Becoming Other

In veering from the norm, a woman that chooses more independence will encounter resistance from family, peers, and social structures. Many forms of indirect pressure keep individuals in line with societal expectations and mores. A woman who steps out of those bounds will find many obstacles in her path. Her sense of self-worth will be under attack, she will be barred from acceptance in many arenas, she will have to endure being misunderstood, and she may come to feel unwelcome in her own milieu.[5]

Marianne Katoppo, a native of Indonesia, describes this process in her book *Compassionate and Free*. "I have always been the 'other,' " she remarks. "The only Manado among Javanese, the only Christian among Muslims, the only girl among the more serious students" (Katoppo 1980, 14). Katoppo goes on to describe the effects that childhood experiences of being the "other" had in her life. She became more able to articulate who she was and what she stood for. She became stronger and more independent. She learned what values she was willing to assert and at what cost.[6]

The women I worked with resonated with Katoppo's sense of otherness. Many came from cross-cultural families, with parents orig-

---

5. Women's changing roles have become a heated topic in the popular press. Yayasan Bina Darma, an institute attached to Satya Wacana Christian University in Salatiga, Java, Indonesia, has compiled two volumes of newspaper clippings on topics of women's emancipation, work conditions, marriage, and related rights issues. The first deals specifically with issues of gender ideology (Kajian Perempuan: Dari Kodrat Hinqqa Iptek [Women's philosophy: From fate to independence] 1992).

6. Katoppo spoke to me of her practice of having male guests into her home as an older single woman in a Muslim Jakarta neighborhood as an example of a practice that would be misunderstood but, nevertheless, was worth doing. See chapter 8.

inating from different ethnic groups.[7] Some had parents who practiced different religions. Children in such families are forced to deal with identity issues that other children need not face.[8] Their sense of self is complicated. Sometimes they experience rejection because of one parent's background. As they near adulthood, they must choose which religion to follow, which ethnic group to identify with. The ensuing struggles can lead to a stronger sense of self, a resilience in responding to new situations, and a more empathetic relationship to others who do not fit neatly into society's categories.[9] Or, alternatively, those struggles may result in a lifelong sense of ostracization, rigidly held views of right and wrong, combative attitudes, and a sense of victimization.[10]

Women who choose a career in theology encounter a sense of otherness, whether or not they experienced it when they were younger. Their decision to move into public life as a pastor, a theologian, or a religious sets them apart from other women with similar age and status.

---

7. Examples of interethnic marriages of parents of students in the graduate program included Manado-Javanese, Torajan-Javanese, and Chinese-Javanese.

8. Chinese face discrimination and limitations of their rights. Although economically favored by the government, their cultural rights are limited. They are required by law to change their name from their traditional Chinese family name to an Indonesian name. They are prohibited from using Chinese script on their places of business or on cemetery headstones. Public celebrations of holidays such as Chinese New Year are prohibited. Systematic rape of Chinese women in Jakarta during the political upheaval in 1997–98 brought discrimination against Chinese to a level of extreme violence. For these reasons, young people may deny their Chinese heritage. This is possible in *Peranakan* (mixed-race families), and in Chinese families that have been in Indonesia for many generations. However, it is less likely if the family is open about its ethnic background and practices Chinese Buddhism.

9. For a discussion of the family as a source of resilience in a rapidly changing world, see "The Concept of Family Resilience: Crisis and Challenge" (Walsh 1996, 262ff.).

10. Walsh notes that "many ongoing, recursive processes involving each individual, family, and larger social environment interact to influence whether vulnerabilities give way to resilience and a successful life course or whether they intensify, resulting in dysfunction and despair" (1996, 267).

Choosing Not To Marry

A major difference arises from a common choice among these women to delay or forego marriage. Marriage is an institution that is held in high esteem in Indonesian society. Both boys and girls are expected to marry. In the villages young people marry in their early teens, and in middle-class, more urban settings, couples marry at least by their early twenties. The polite question *"Sudah kawin (menikah) atau belum?"* (Are you married yet, or not?) must be answered repeatedly in even the most informal social situations. Failure to find a mate by age thirty is considered a tragedy in a young woman's life.

After marriage, children naturally follow. A woman who chooses to marry but does not bear children soon becomes an object of pity.[11] Parents are disappointed. Friends want to know reasons for this failure. Questions are asked. If the couple has intentionally decided not to have children, they are considered abnormal. Children follow marriage, and the couple then begins a new phase of social life in the extended family and neighborhood.

Few of the women students in the graduate program followed the usual path of marrying and bearing children in their twenties. Most chose not to marry.[12] The stated reason for this choice was that if a woman marries she can no longer follow her calling into the pastorate or professional world. She must follow her husband to his place of work. She must care for his professional interests and physical needs. Choosing to remain unmarried causes problems, to be sure, but it leaves women basically free to pursue studies or to work in the churches.[13]

---

11. *Bhima Swarga*, a traditional Balinese tale, notes that although pitied, a childless woman is nonetheless punished in hell for not bearing children. Although it may not be the fault of a woman, it is still a sin and must be punished (Pucci 1992, 68).

12. Of twenty women students I worked with in the Graduate Program in Religion and Society, three were married. Another was widowed. The remaining sixteen were unmarried.

13. "The Challenge of the Single Life," a women's retreat for women in the Graduate Program for Religion and Society of Satya Wacana Christian University in October 1993, yielded this information.

Marianne Katoppo, an influential feminist scholar, chose to remain unmarried. Some students remained single, despite strong family pressure to marry. One student chose an even more unusual course. She married and had children but left home and family for two years in order to study at the university.

All of these women struggled with becoming the "other." Their choices had a deep impact on their relationships, lifestyle, and sense of identity. The way they made moral decisions changed in the process. No longer "in the groove" of following societal expectations, they had to forge a new path, choosing what seemed good to them despite disapproval by those around them. They were forced to analyze their moral principles. In doing so they made concrete decisions to live their lives on the basis of the principle of women's equality—a principle that their society at worst rejected and at best tolerated with ambivalence.

Exposing the Double Standard

A double standard for women and men manifests itself in many areas of public and private life in Indonesia, as it does in North America. One strategy of resistance is to expose that double standard where it appears, as Dora did in the church.

Dora was a shy, smiling young woman, whose anger did not show at first. She came to the university from Sumatra, part of the Batak Christian Church. Dora wanted to look into a problem that women pastors from her region faced. They could not seem to advance into synod positions of leadership. Traditionally, Batak women were strong and assertive. Male church leaders insisted that women could become pastors and leaders of the churches. However, only a handful of women had become pastors, and none had advanced to a position beyond leadership of a local parish.

Dora was convinced that internal contradictions and opposing expectations created a glass ceiling for women as church leaders. For example, she noted that single women were considered unfit for pastoring a church because they would have to counsel married couples. Without the experience of being married themselves, how could they counsel others? If a woman did marry, she was obliged to follow her husband in his career choice. If he was a pastor, she would have to move to his parish and cease her own work as a pastor. Co-pastoring by husband and wife teams was not allowed. Nor could he follow her to where she worked, since he was the "head of the house."[14] Here was a classic double bind that kept Batak women from moving into leadership positions.

Dora saw this and other obstacles to women's advancement being created by the church. Official church policy stated that women could hold any position in the church structure. *"Silakan, kau bisa"* (Go ahead if you can), male leaders said, smiling. Their smug attitude enraged Dora. She wanted to expose this doublethink that prevented women from rising in the ranks of church leadership.

Upon submission of her thesis proposal, an older white male, who was an American church historian on the faculty, objected. With years of experience teaching in Sumatra, he had built up credibility as an authority on the Batak Church. He argued vehemently that since only fifteen years had elapsed since the first woman pastor was ordained, it was too soon to analyze whether women were being prevented from taking high positions of leadership.[15]

Dora assumed a respectful submissive attitude during the proceedings. But she did state that, in her opinion, enough time had elapsed to note patterns that might prevent women from being appointed to positions of leadership. It was not too soon to analyze policies or informal dictums that would serve both now and in the future to prevent women from assuming their rightful place as co-leaders of the church.

Dora's efforts to expose the double standard in her church's

---

14. These views were confirmed by Pdt. N. M. Hutahaean, another woman pastor from the Batak Church (HKBP). According to Hutahaean, the patriarchal structure of Batak society was brought directly into the church, thus denying a voice to women and youth (1994, 126f.).

15. During the 1970s women were permitted to serve the church as elders and missionaries, but it was not until the 1980s that women were allowed to become pastors in the Godang Sinode of the HKBP Protestant Church (Hutahaean 1994, 127).

treatment of women who aspired to leadership proved to be a costly choice. Although her proposal did pass, her research project floundered, and she did not finish her program. However, her reasons for not finishing may have been related not only to the project itself, but also to other conditions and choices in her life. Her story reveals the complexity of assessing moral agency across cultures using models from the West. This issue will be taken up in chapter 9.

Avoiding Marginalization

What happens when societal or church structures prevent a woman from fulfilling a call that she senses has come to her from God? One can fulfill a life task only if one's community affirms that task and allows one to practice it.[16] A professor is dependent on the affirmation of her intellectual ideas in the community. A church leader is dependent on the recognition of her calling by the community. A woman with a call to church leadership may be thwarted if she cannot find that assent in her community.[17]

To lead women's ministries in the church is more acceptable for women in Indonesia than to lead women and men together at the regional or national levels. Becoming a theologian is even more difficult because of the power of authority that theologians hold—power to shape the life and doctrines of the church. Church leaders of every type are chosen by the community and are supported by it. Without

---

16. In part, the meaning of a statement or an act is determined by the response that the act elicits (Mead 1934; Niebuhr 1963; Smith 1982). If women act as leaders but are responded to as dependent followers, they cannot become leaders. In this way, community feedback and affirmation are integral to leadership development.

17. The social expectation in Indonesia that a leader calls forth salutations of honor from others illustrates this point. If a woman pastor, for example, cannot elicit respectful salutations and acts that honor her from the congregation, she is considered unworthy of the post of leadership. If the community, on its part, refuses to give these honorary tokens of respect because it does not truly accept leadership from a woman, the woman will not be honored, no matter how much respect her personal achievements deserve.

that support, women cannot reach positions of leadership, or if they do, they are subtly discounted and marginalized as leaders.

Resistance to marginalization may succeed as a strategy. Or, as Dewi's story shows, a lack of support by church and community can result in a failure to reach leadership goals. Though qualified, discerning, and amicable, Dewi has not been able to become the leader she is qualified to be.

Dewi was in a tough spot. A pastor from the Batak area of Sumatra, she was finishing her master's thesis on the family as an agent of Christianization in the program in religion and society at the university. It was a fine piece of work, and she was considering going on for doctoral studies. But the university was not quite ready for such a move and discouraged her, saying she needed to get more experience before going on to further study.

During her time at the university in Java, Dewi's church in Sumatra had been in turmoil. For two years they debated about who should be the new leader of the denomination. At length the Indonesian government stepped in and appointed a church leader. Those who were in favor of him were relieved. Those who were not dissented vigorously, claiming government interfere in church affairs.

The government's move effectively split the denomination in two. Dewi actively resisted the government's appointee, letting her voice be heard in the churches. When it came time to return to Sumatra, she was on the outside, a dissenter in her own denomination. Because of these church-government politics and the university's resistance to her further study, Dewi found herself pushed out of her vocation.

Dewi had chosen effective strategies for resisting marginalization and advancing her influence as a church leader. An effective pastor, she was supported by her home church to do graduate work at the university. In choosing her project, she was careful not to emphasize "feminist" issues.[18] Her thesis argued that women, in their central

---

18. *Feminist* is a word that carries negative connotations for many people, including Christians, in Indonesia. It is linked with the erosion of family values and Indonesian identity by modern influences from the West.

role in the family, were a major influence in the development of the Batak Church. Dewi told me that in reworking the thesis for publication, she would more forcefully assert the centrality of women in effecting positive change in church and society. But for the thesis she took a broader approach, rightly discerning that such a project would be more acceptable to both university professors and to the church supporting her in Sumatra.

In addition to her studies, Dewi had the opportunity to co-teach a course in Christian ethics in the undergraduate department of theology. That department, like most theology departments in Indonesian colleges, had an all-male faculty.[19]

Professors in the graduate program saw the imbalance in this situation. Women were graduating from the graduate program with a master's degree, yet finding no place to teach. When a male faculty member in the graduate program was asked to teach ethics for undergraduates, he suggested that Dewi be invited instead. The university, however, was unwilling to do this. So the professor agreed to teach the course on the condition that Dewi be allowed to co-teach with him. The university department agreed. But when the catalog came out, Dewi's name did not appear as an instructor of the course.

Here is an example of the power of social structures to maintain the status quo. Rather than inform the Western male professor that Indonesian women were not welcome as professors in the department of theology (too embarrassing for an institution well-aware of the issues of gender equality), the university simply ignored Dewi's involvement in the course. They succeeded in getting the male professor to teach without recognizing a woman's role in the course. Thus the all-male appearance of the faculty was preserved, and Dewi's professionalism was undermined.

A similar indirect approach was taken with regard to Dewi's desire to do further study. Dewi was mature, articulate, polite, politically savvy, and showed promise of becoming a fine scholar. Two

19. The one exception to this was a Western woman who served as chaplain to the university and taught undergraduate courses in theology on an adjunct faculty basis.

professors brought up her name repeatedly as a student who would be an asset to the doctoral program. One offered to raise scholarship support for Dewi's tuition during a trip to the United States. The faculty accepted that offer but suggested that the monies be raised instead on behalf of a male student, who was given the opportunity to pursue doctoral studies. Dewi was not invited to apply.

The situation was made more serious by the fact that because of the troubles in her church, Dewi had little chance of gaining a position of leadership in her denomination. Having declared herself as one who opposed the government's appointment of a leader, and being a woman, she was left with few options. Despite her experience, maturity, and qualifications for leadership, she returned to Sumatra to work in a parish—as she had before she did her master's degree at the university.

Recognition by accepted authorities is extremely important in Indonesia. Because of the tradition of *bapakism,* in which the father figure seeks consensus and expresses that consensus to the group, little advancement can be made without the affirmation of male leaders. In addition, a woman who establishes herself as a leader more powerful than most men around her is in a very tenuous position. Men receive the honored positions, particularly older men. If a woman for some reason is advanced above the majority of men in a particular group, reasons for lowering her status can be easily found.

An example from the political arena was the appointment of Sukarnoputri as leader of the opposition party in Indonesia in 1997. While she was officially appointed, some leaders in her party opposed her, stating that she was chosen not for her qualifications, but because she was the eldest daughter of the first president of Indonesia. When political issues with the party became tense, the Suharto government removed Sukarnoputri from her post as party leader. Party criticism and government action combined to strip Sukarnoputri of her position and her power. It was not until after Suharto's power was broken and his image as the father figure of the nation removed that Sukarnoputri rose to a leadership role as vice president and later president of the new government.

Women encounter invisible boundaries in establishing new paths and gaining recognition. Gender equality cannot become a reality without changes in customs and social structures that keep women from positions of leadership in church and society.

Resisting Stereotypes

Social controls take effect not only through an unwillingness to affirm women as leaders on the part of recognized authorities. Women are also kept from advancement by seemingly positive attitudes toward them.

One common stereotype in Indonesia is that women need protection. This was the attitude expressed by church leaders that I met with in Ambon in 1993. "Our women are strong and feisty, but they still need us men to protect them," stated one. A result of this paternalism is that women are considered unable to supervise work in the church in outlying island areas. Travel to remote islands during the monsoon season was considered too dangerous for a woman to undertake alone. Yet social custom frowned upon a single woman traveling with men, and most women pastors were single. Since visiting the churches regularly was part of the job of the regional director, these attitudes kept women from becoming regional leaders in the outer islands. "A woman traveling in a small boat alone during the monsoon season? How could a woman do that?" said one male leader.[20]

While in Sangir Terlaud a year later, I met a robust woman in her late thirties who managed to circumvent these protective customs. She was the first woman to be appointed regional leader of those northern islands. I asked her if it was difficult for her to travel to churches during the stormy season. "It's my job. I do it," she replied matter-of-factly. Her quiet self-confidence models a culturally appropriate stance for women breaking into new roles of leadership in Indonesian society. The example empowers other women and corrects

---

20. This comment was made by a regional church leader in Ambon during a discussion of women's roles in the church on December 5, 1992.

the reified attitudes of society that insist that women are weak and need male protection.

The notion of gender partnership itself can hamper women in developing as leaders. "Partnership" in church work, as "partnership in development," can be construed as women supporting men in their public roles as leaders. That is the model of partnership most evident in Indonesian society. "Women hold up the world," remarked a male church leader in Ambon.[21]

Because of the role differences implied by this view of partnership, women at the National Convention of Women Theologians of Indonesia in 1993 voiced dissatisfaction with the theme of "Women and Men in Partnership." One suggested that partnership had been a common theme for years, but little seemed to be changing in the church organizational structures to mirror the egalitarian notion of partnership that women in the church were advocating.

Recognizing the hidden agenda of apparently positive attitudes of men toward women is the first step in establishing that more egalitarian partnership. Jennifer Krier's study of "disruptive discourses" reveals that positive attitudes toward "strong women" may encourage outspoken behavior that ultimately undermines their power and demonstrates their marginalization (1995a, 69). In a research study of the financial arrangements between spouses in Java, Norma Sullivan found that the purported equality of spouses exhibited by women's role as "managers" of family finances masked a deeper reality of men as "masters" over women (1994).

Such studies signal the necessity of applying a hermeneutic of suspicion to attitudes and customs that appear to affirm women in situations where women do not seem to be experiencing the affirmation or equality that would result from those attitudes.[22]

---

21. This remark, made during the same conversation in Ambon with church leaders in December 1992, showed a respect for women's strength but gave no assent to women's ability as church leaders.

22. Elisabeth Schussler-Fiorenza suggests that women ask who benefits from particular customs or power arrangements rather than accepting without question that the reasons given for these arrangements are the true reasons. This "hermeneutic of

Modeling Christian Leadership

Resistance can be framed positively by modeling Christian leadership in ways that are acceptable to religious institutions. While participating in "acceptable" forms of leadership, strategies of resistance are combined and implemented.

Nancy L. Eisland researched resistance through modeling in the lives of women in a Pentecostal congregation in North America. She found that their strategies for creating niches for themselves in their male-dominated workplace included adopting familiar feminine styles and roles while nurturing the creation of women's spaces and female-centered support systems (Eisland 1997, 105).

A few Protestant women in Indonesia are modeling gender equality in the church in visible leadership roles at the national level. While living in Indonesia, I had the opportunity to work with two of these leaders. Each of them held an acceptable position, one as wife of the national leader of the Protestant denomination and one as national director of women's ministries.

I met *Ibu* Kartini while on a speaking trip to Sulawesi in 1995. Arriving tired after a long plane journey from Java to northern Sulawesi, I was met at the airport by *Ibu* Lena, director of the women's ministries division of the Protestant Church. She told me that *Ibu* Kartini, wife of a high official of the United Protestant Church in Indonesia, would be joining us on our trip north to the remote islands of Sangir Terlaud. When we arrived at the house, *Ibu* Kartini greeted us, having just gotten up from her afternoon nap.

She appeared to be in her late forties, a petite woman, but round in a soft kind of way. Her naturally curly hair framed a face that exuded warmth and gentleness, giving a most pleasing impression.[23]

Later I found that *Ibu* Kartini was not shy in any way. She shared

---

suspicion" can unmask hidden agendas and deceptive power arrangements that oppress women through seemingly acceptable attitudes and social structures (1983).

23. I give this physical description because *Ibu* Kartini's work and impact on women in the church was augmented by her personal appearance and style, important features for traditional Indonesian women.

generously of her life and struggles, and she listened just as generously. She was from Manado, the region of north Sulawesi where we first met. In contrast to the Javanese, women there are assertive, direct in polite ways, and ambitious. Many do college-level work and enter careers, juggling those tasks with marriage and child rearing.

Lena, Kartini, and I met in Manado for a specific purpose. Our task together would take us on an overnight journey in a small boat with six bunk rooms and a crowded deck full of passengers. Our first destination was Sangir Terlaud, a group of three very small islands at the northern tip of Sulawesi, not far from the Philippines. These islands were the farthest outpost of Protestantism to the north. We were headed there to speak at a regional Protestant women's conference that drew women from each of those remote fishing islands. We spent a fascinating week together traveling to and from the islands, speaking at the conference, and visiting informally with the women there.

On our return to Sulawesi, we went on to the annual National Convention of Women Theologians of Indonesia, held in Tomohon, Sulawesi. Here, churchwomen from many islands in Indonesia met to discuss theological issues of concern to women in the Protestant Church. The two conferences were very different; the Sangir Terlaud group consisted mainly of village women who raised families and did manual work, while the second group was made up of educated urban women.

Leadership Styles

During these weeks together, I had the opportunity to observe *Ibu* Kartini and *Ibu* Lena in those diverse settings. The ways they patterned their daily lives, the styles of conversation they used with women of different backgrounds, and the interaction between them and with me proved enlightening. As leaders of the Indonesian Church, they model for many women a new gender ideology that offers women opportunity and builds confidence in its assertion of women's competence and equality.

What kind of leadership did they model? What spiritual practices energized their lives? How did they navigate between traditional and modern gender ideologies? Although both were from Manado, the two women were very different. First, their roles differed. Lena held a formal leadership position in the church while Kartini filled an honorary leadership post as wife of the national director of Protestant churches. Second, their social status differed. Kartini had been married for twenty-five years and had two grown children and a very important man for a husband. Lena had chosen not to marry. She had achieved a high position in the church structure that challenged her and gave her significant authority and responsibility. Both were mature, confident, and articulate women.

During meetings, Lena had the more formal lecture style, covering issues of women in church and society. She offered a strong vision of women as church leaders and called the male hierarchy to accountability in their task of enabling women to fulfill this vision. Kartini's style was more pastoral. Through sharing accounts of her own life and struggles as a woman in the church, she offered hope and encouragement to women facing difficulties in their family and professional lives. Each emphasis was needed and welcomed by conference participants, both the well-educated leaders at the theologians' conference and the simple fisher folk of the outer islands.

Lena and Kartini differed too in their everyday practices, a topic that will be explored in chapter 6. Kartini, the quintessential mother, listened to anyone who had a trouble, noticed with gratitude even the smallest task done on her behalf, and spoke freely of the heartaches of mothering children. She offered a superb model for younger Christian women who longed to combine family life with a calling to church work.

Kartini not only gave freely, but also seemed at the same time to draw strength from giving. A vocation to nurture seemed to energize her as she followed its call. I remember clearly the morning we arrived at the bustling dock upon our return from the northern islands. Kartini had so many parcels that two men from Lena's family were needed to help her carry them. She laughingly described the contents of every bag and box—*makanan khas* (special foods of the region) for husband, children, cousins, and friends.[24] There were tropical fruit drinks, coconut cakes, a special type of yam, and, of course, dried fish. Kartini delighted in bringing these gifts back to those she loved.[25] And her acts of care fed her own spirit.

Since she was returning to her childhood home in Manado, Lena's daily life was filled with family visits during our stay. She also acted as a thoughtful host to me, Kartini, and another houseguest. She showed us around town, took us shopping for fabric, and then to her dressmaker to have the cloth made into special Manado-style suits.[26] In addition, she had numerous visits from church leaders and parishioners. She spent time discussing national and local church issues and offering individual counsel to those who came with personal problems. I wondered how Lena sustained her energy through this hectic schedule and still found reserves for making vibrant presentations at the conferences.

Frustrations of Leadership

When I asked her about this, Lena said that she did get very tired at times. But the work itself energized her. She felt that she was fulfilling

24. Each region of Indonesia proudly offers special foods of the region in the marketplaces. A common and delightful custom is for visitors to the region to buy those foods and take them home to family and friends in their own locale. Whenever I returned to the U.S. to teach, my house helper would give me large packages of individually wrapped peanut candy, the *makanan khas* of Salatiga, to take home to my friends and family as her gift to them.

25. Sharon Parks draws a link between the sharing of food and the sacredness of life, declaring that "whoever does the work of it becomes a priest, weaving the fabric of life as the sacred ordinary work of the everyday" (1988, 187).

26. Designs on plain cotton cloth are made by pulling individual threads out of the fabric and reweaving it with threads of other colors. This painstaking task developed, I was told, centuries ago, when Islamic law required women to remain in the house. Rather than do nothing, the women developed this creative and artistic embroidery style, called *karawan*. Today, modern suits for both women and men are made of this special cloth and worn for formal occasions.

a God-given task to aid women and to help the church develop its potential by enabling women to participate more fully.

At the same time, Lena expressed frustration that women were still so marginalized as she looked at the national church. Manado, her home in Sulawesi, was the exception. Women were active in church life, many following a call into the pastorate. At the national convention in Tomohon there were 150 delegates and another 150 observers—women from the Manado area who came to listen and learn. Many of these women were leaders in the Manado Church. Yet despite their active and competent leadership, men held the positions of higher authority.

The convention itself was opened by a procession of church leaders, most of whom were men. In Indonesia, formal events begin with opening ritual ceremonies performed by honored leaders. The highest church officials (all male) were present to inaugurate the conference of women theologians and to give their stamp of approval. At the same time, their presence clearly demonstrated who was in charge.[27]

Lena expressed dismay that international conferences of women theologians also seemed to neglect Indonesian women. The Philippines, Korea, and Singapore were well represented at these gatherings. "But why weren't Indonesian women given the opportunity to participate?" she lamented. This concern shows Lena's love for the women in the church in Indonesia.

It also reflects the fact that money from United States churches and organizations often funds international conferences.[28] People in the United States knew little of the significance of Indonesia until the economic collapse and the change of government in the late

---

27. Perhaps as a subtle form of protest, one woman theologian sitting in the front row read a book through the two-hour session of rituals and speeches by male church officials.

28. Other reasons include language and educational barriers, visa problems, hesitancy for women to travel "alone," lack of consistent networking with funding organizations, and the devaluation of the rupiah in recent years.

1990s. The massive changes and development that have occurred in the last fifty years have not been totally lost, however, and the bold advances that women are making in this unusual society are significant.[29] As interaction with organizations in the West increases, Indonesian women's opportunities to share on an international level will also increase.

Kartini, too, faced frustrations. She had been working on her master's degree at Jakarta Theological Seminary for years. But family concerns and the necessity of playing a supportive role to her husband when he stepped into national leadership sidetracked her studies. She longed to finish her degree. Yet, she said, she was getting older, and she wondered if the hard study was worthwhile for her, as she herself held no professional position.

Calling and Gender Ideologies

Beneath the stated frustrations of these two Indonesian leaders I sensed a weariness with the struggle of breaking old ways and forging new paths. To talk of "women's oppression" was not their style. Perhaps they internalized some of that oppression and expressed it in the form of frustration with others or with their own work.

Each woman modeled a different kind of leadership. Lena made the move into the new gender ideology of equality. A dynamic leader and articulate spokesperson for women's rights and leadership capabilities, she embodied the new churchwoman emulated by younger, educated women.

Kartini modeled a more traditional figure. While active in church affairs and leadership, she fulfilled the role of pastor's wife, her speak-

---

29. Despite recent setbacks because of economic reforms imposed by the International Monetary Fund, the outlook for women's advancement in Indonesia is good. The formation of the Association of South East Asian Nations (ASEAN), which promotes economic opportunities and interchange with Western nations, the involvement of nongovernment organizations (NGOs) in women's welfare, and the increasing ties with international corporations improve the situation for women and create opportunities for their involvement in globalization.

ing opportunities tied to her husband's position. She also showed a way for family-oriented women to become church leaders. Her vocation of care giving and her motherly style made a good transition model for women who, by choice or life situation, saw themselves primarily as caregivers.

Each path can be affirmed, both in itself and in its value as a religion-identified strategy of resistance. A traditional caregiver model for women, while sometimes devalued in contemporary societies, is not less valuable than a career-oriented model. Choosing to spend one's time and energy in practical and pastoral acts of care, as Kartini did, may not be a sign of inequality or forced gender difference. Choosing to forego family life in order to devote one's time to building up women in the church, as Lena did, does not imply a devaluing of nurturing activities common to women's lives in Indonesia.

What is common to each of the narratives discussed in this chapter is the combination of a sense of calling and a sense of moral agency that each woman felt. Each of these women successfully pursued her calling and found a place in the church for living out that vocation. All developed a strong sense of themselves as subjects, making strong evaluations about what they deemed worthwhile in life. All resisted gender inequalities in their religious institutions with an array of strategies. How they sustained their resistance by developing and reinterpreting everyday practices in their lives is the topic of the next chapter.

6

Strategies of Growth
Everyday Practices or Feminist Innovations?

As women continue to pursue religion-identified resistance, they develop everyday routines that support their sense of agency and enhance their ability to continue on the path they have chosen. These practices are chosen, not to conform to or reject societal expectations, but to nurture life.

By practices, I refer to everyday activities, ordinary or ritual acts that, with repetition, become habitual. While myriads of practices could be studied, this chapter explores three everyday practices: offering hospitality, creating beauty, and honoring relationships. Those practices were chosen because they mirror practices of other women of similar age and status in the community.[1] Understanding how those everyday practices might be employed differently, understood differently, or have another effect on the community will help in understanding how those practices become strategies of growth for women leaders.

The community dimensions of those practices, whether done in religious services, in public forums, or in home life, have an impact on both individuals and on the community. Amanda Porterfield notes that "religious communities often play definitive roles in the development of individual life." She describes the transformative effects of religious rituals on shaping outlooks on the world, enhancing relationships with other people, and affecting a person's sense of pur-

---

1. A few examples from Hindu and Muslim women's lives show the usefulness of religion-identified practices in religions other than Christianity.

pose as well as her behavior (1998, 197). The practices explored in this chapter result in those kinds of transformations.

In chapter 4 we explored how women students struggled with finding time to study, gaining support for their academic work, and receiving affirmation for their research projects. They developed everyday practices that helped them reach those goals. Kartini and Lena, whose stories are told in chapter 5, modeled Christian leadership styles that included practices which deepened their lives and influenced their communities.

Chosen practices that are similar to activities of other women of a woman's social class may become deterrents to her goal of becoming a religious leader. Or, they can strengthen her sense of moral agency and facilitate her movement into leadership. Reflecting on those practices can also form a link to her theological conceptions. New interpretations of her faith and new images for God and humans can be envisioned.

A Story of Transformation

Hyun Kyung Chung, a Korean Christian theologian, describes this process (1990, 3–5). She had already chosen a path of theological study and had identified her anger at limiting, patriarchal views of women. Self-determination became her "burning desire" (1990, 2). Then she found out that a poor and powerless woman had given birth to her. When she discovered this family secret, the voice of her downtrodden birth mother became crucial to Chung's theology. Through honoring the relationship with her birth mother, Chung turned her angry, deconstructive theology into a life-giving theology of women's liberation. Both her conceptions of God and her ethical agenda as a Christian leader were transformed in the process.

The catalyst for Chung's new theology of Asian women's liberation was not a study of Christian texts, a comparative analysis of religions, or a reflection on her own tradition. Chung, as a theologian, did do all of those things. But the shift to a liberation perspective grew up between her sense of herself as a self-determining moral agent and her focus on honoring relationships, a practice endemic to her Korean culture. Traditional Christian theologies have silenced women's voices and minimized, if not denigrated, women's importance in the circle of life. Through the simple act of honoring her relationship with her mother, Chung broke through that silent space and gave voice to the passion of her identity as woman.

Some practices that are integral to a woman pastor's work show continuity with family-oriented activities of wives and mothers in Indonesia. Fostering religiosity in the family and helping children develop their spirituality is one of the social roles of women in general and mothers in particular. For a woman pastor, serving the spiritual needs of her community augments the traditional woman's role of teaching "private religiosity" to one's own children. The practices themselves are not dissimilar, but the realm of those activities is broadened to include the public and congregational spheres.

Practices that display continuity with traditional roles of women reveal a complexity that deserves attention. While nurturing others, these activities often bring joy or stimulate worship for the women taking part in them. Although performed by women who have resisted many stereotypes and social conventions, these practices do not contradict traditional gender ideology for women. Practices of gift-giving, providing shelter, sharing hospitality, caring for plants or pets, telling stories of one's family, creating beauty in home surroundings, and fostering relationships provide a bond to women in the community.[2] Moreover, they are not performed with the intention of developing theologies, enhancing spirituality, or creating social change, yet they have an impact on each of those areas of community life. At the same time, while nurturing women and fostering independent action, these practices can also deter a woman from reaching her goal of becoming a leader.

---

2. In a study at Harvard University, Elizabeth Dodson Gray analyzed the spiritual dimensions of those ordinary practices for women in the United States (1988). I am not aware of any studies by or about Indonesian women that make these connections other than this project.

Hospitality as a Link

How can the practice of hospitality form a link to new theologies, enhance or detract from personal growth, and influence the community? While in Jakarta, I became friends with *Ibu* Masooma, a teacher at the Pakistan International School. Masooma was a wife and a mother of two, and her home was constantly full of Pakistani friends and neighbors. Nearing her house, one could catch glimpses of chatting women attired in colorful Pakistani robes. One smelled delicious aromas of food cooking and heard the busy sounds of children reciting the Qur'an together.

Despite her hectic schedule of elementary school teaching and hospitality to her Pakistani neighbors, Masooma reached out to others. Her Indonesian servant's daughter came to live with the family for a number of months. Young college women from a dormitory next door were invited in to tea. She suggested that my adult children come and stay with her family on visits to Indonesia. A few times each week, one of Masooma's daughters would show up at my door with plates heaped with warm curries and rice. "We are family, are we not?" she would say when I protested. Although on a limited income, she offered food and shelter with joy.

Soon I learned the reason. "Food and shelter belong to Allah," Masooma told me. "I do not own them. It would be wrong of me to withhold them from others. They are given to be shared."[3] While not labeling this a spiritual practice, *Ibu* Masooma was very clear about the theology that motivated her actions. Although she modestly claimed she was not a devout Muslim, she was dedicated in practicing her theology.

---

3. The source of this theology can be found in the Qur'an, 16:69, 71: "From its belly [the bee's] comes forth a syrup of different hues, a cure for men. Surely in this there is a sign for those who would take thought. . . . In what He has provided, God has favoured some among you above others. Those who are so favoured will not allow their slaves an equal share in what they have. Would they deny God's goodness?" (Dawood 1997, 192).

Christians, Jews, and Muslims share the same ancient story of Abraham and Sarah, who entertained angels without being aware that they were messengers of God. Descendants of Abraham and Sarah are encouraged to offer hospitality freely, remembering that their first ancestors received the promise of offspring in their old age through the message of those angels.[4] Hospitality to strangers, although facing peculiar difficulties in modern urban societies, continues to be a strongly held value among all three religions.

Ibu Masooma's hospitality formed a bond between us, building interethnic and interreligious understanding. It also made an impression on others in the neighborhood. Indonesians saw the comings and goings of many friends and strangers, including Indonesian young people, from *Ibu* Masooma's house. They heard of and respected her provision for the daughter of her servant. Masooma's hospitality put her theology into action. It became a spiritual practice, reminding her of Allah's goodness and showing to others her continued faith in Allah's provisions.

On another occasion, receiving hospitality from Hindu women was a highlight for a family trip to Bali. Visiting a small town for a cremation ceremony, we found all of the hotels fully booked. A kind woman invited us into her home, where we slept and ate with the family. We were included in family preparations for the Hindu rites of cremation. After obtaining proper ritual clothing for us, they helped us dress and took us to the ceremony with them as part of their extended family. Other women explained to me the meaning of various ritual ceremonies in which we participated throughout the day. Such hospitality is a spiritual practice that grows out of religious convictions and enhances the lives of persons and communities of many faiths.

Hospitality as a Deterrent

Although hospitality can forge a link to new theologies and dynamic spiritualities, it can also distract a woman from her calling to Christ-

---

4. This story can be found in the Bible in Gen. 18:1–15 and in Heb. 13:1–2.

ian leadership. Without a strong sense of moral agency directing her choices, a woman can devote too much time and energy to hospitality. A loss of focus and an inability to fulfill her leadership goals or responsibilities can result.

Ibu Kartini, the wife of a prominent Christian leader in Java, whom we met in chapter 5, provides an example. While on a lecture tour in Sulawesi, Kartini gained personal satisfaction from gathering gifts for family and friends in Java. In this and other personal choices, she developed a lifestyle focused on caring for relationships in concrete ways. When she began graduate studies, her priorities and activities did not change to correspond with her new goal. She regretted that her husband's career and her college son's needs kept her from finishing her master's degree. While remaining a leader because of her husband's high office in the church, *Ibu* Kartini allowed the distractions of hospitality to keep her from pursuing her graduate degree.

Ibu Sabariah was also deterred by her commitment to hospitality. She had been married for many years to a professor when she entered the graduate program. Sabariah had spent her adult life as a homemaker and had raised three children. She, like Kartini, supported her husband in every way in his work. While he pursued doctoral studies, she did the marketing, cooking, and cleaning. She took time to chat with friends, to encourage younger women students, and to visit faculty wives. Her studies were often interrupted by visits from her adult children or by trips she made to see them.

Since her priorities remained focused on caring for family and community, *Ibu* Sabariah might have chosen a research project that related to her life experience as a mother and churchwoman. But she wanted to work with issues of political power in Indonesia at the national level. She began her project, but sufficient time to work on it eluded her. Her husband, a well-known seminary professor, was quite knowledgeable in both politics and national church issues. He frequently corrected or augmented *Ibu* Sabariah's viewpoints in informal conversation. That criticism, combined with a lack of depth in the field, left *Ibu* Sabariah feeling inadequate. She received more affirmation for her everyday practice of hospitality and caring for others, and it became dominant in her life.

Discovering one's voice and learning to use it is a difficult and costly process.[5] Sabariah's life pattern was set when she came to the university. Breaking into a second career in the same arena as her husband handicapped her in developing and expressing her own views. Participating in everyday practices that focused on family life and choosing a difficult area of study in which she had little background combined to hinder her progress.

Nonetheless, Sabariah's choice of a topic of national significance in the public realm revealed her yearnings to be heard. Sabariah's presence at the university and her discussions of her ideals contributed to positive change in the community. Her participation in the program and her husband's active support of her studies became an example for others. These actions gave Sabariah a voice at a critical time of transition between traditional gender ideology and a new pattern of gender equality arising in Indonesia.

Creating Beauty as a Link

Creating beauty can become a habit required by religious duties, or it can be a personal expression of creativity and joy. It can be a service to others who benefit from the order and tranquility that beauty offers. Beauty can be created by the way a woman dresses and how she arranges her home, her place of worship, her garden, or her mind.

The beauty of the everyday practices of Balinese Hindu women impressed me on several visits to Bali. On special religious occasions, such as the cremation ceremony I attended, carts and floats decorated with flowers process through the town. But even on ordinary days, daily routines of Balinese women are punctuated by creative artistry. Every morning and evening hotel workers leave delicate flower offerings on the doorsteps of guest rooms to honor good spirits and protect guests from evil spirits. Colorfully clad worshipers carry intricately designed fruit arrangements on their heads, bearing

---

5. An important study on this topic done in the United States, which has influenced my own work, is *Women's Ways of Knowing: The Development of Self, Voice, and Mind* (Belenky et al. 1986).

them to the temple for offerings. Those simple, everyday routines frame the women's lives with beauty and religious ritual.

It is not only the Balinese who make rituals of great beauty. In Java, a whole section of the local market is devoted to selling flowers. Market women gather and sell strongly scented white blossoms and red rose petals. On ordinary days and especially on religious holidays, Muslim women come to buy these blossoms. Accompanied by husbands and children, the women use the flower petals to adorn the pale blue headstones in their neighborhood Islamic cemeteries, remembering loved ones who have died.

Signs of beauty created by women are everywhere. Young Muslim women go to work or school with lovely white or pastel head coverings draped over white blouses and dark skirts.[6] Simple verandahs are covered with potted plants, and front yards are swept clean around well-arranged flowering shrubs. Many houses face the street at an angle, an arrangement meant to protect inhabitants from evil spirits while creating a delightful impression of bamboo, tidy walk ways, and flowering shrubs. Women create and care for this beauty. Maintaining an impression of order and tranquility in these ways becomes a spiritual practice.

Students at the university took opportunities to create beauty in academic settings. Fatima was asked to coordinate a World Council of Churches conference being hosted by the university. At the closing ceremony, she and other students created a *selamatan*, a ritual feast that marks crucial life passages. Held after a birth, a graduation, or other significant events, this ritual brings the community together in worship and celebration of life.

Fatima and her friends spared no cost or effort to bring beauty into the ceremony. Carefully prepared and beautifully arranged food, including the traditional cone of yellow rice, was served. Intricately

---

6. *Hijabs*, the Islamic headscarves, are worn with public school uniforms as well. This has not caused the problems that the same practice caused in France. Public institutions in France maintain a strict secular neutrality rather than allowing religious expressions in the public setting. To explore this contrast, see my response in "A Matter of Veils" (1999, 159–72).

beaded dresses and traditional formal wear, usually worn at weddings, were donned by the women and men who served the food. The ceremony itself was held outdoors, with a backdrop of green rice paddies and the peak of the volcano Mount Merbabu. Every song and reading of this worship service was orchestrated to add to the solemnity of eating together. It was a true cross-cultural Christian communion, combining Christian and indigenous features, Western and Indonesian customs. Grace and beauty marked the event.

Creating Beauty as a Deterrent

It is hard to imagine the creation of beauty as a negative or detracting feature. But it can be. Fatima spent so much time working on perfectly orchestrating the creative details of social events that she often became too exhausted to fulfill her academic responsibilities. Fatima's capability and willingness to provide this service, along with her careful attention to every detail, multiplied the tasks. Too much attention to creating ambiance and beauty can result in overburdened, tired women. Although the communities are bound together by women's creation of beauty, they forego forging new links with empowered Christian women.

To say that does not detract from the importance of the worship service created by Fatima and her friends. That service provided an aesthetic and culturally authentic experience of worship. Fatima's leadership role in creating the worship was present, if publicly muted. The service solidified relationships. Participants from the Middle East, Europe, North America, and Asia ate together in a ritual that demonstrated their bond across ethnic, cultural, and geographic distances.

Honoring Relationships as a Link

The practice of caring for relationships in everyday, concrete ways was important to the Indonesian women I worked with. Many saw relationships at the heart of their calling to Christian service. Some of those relationships were related to their work itself and to the process of attaining their goals of gender equality in the church. Despite busy study schedules, administrative responsibilities, and family obligations, however, these women spent time caring for each other.

The first retreat of the graduate women's group, described in chapter 2, demonstrated the importance of this practice. The students planned a weekend around the topic of the unique problems they faced as single women in Indonesia. Only one of the students attending the retreat was married. The others shared their stories of alienation from families, misunderstanding by peers, and uncomfortable encounters with strange men as they traveled. They talked about the difficulty others had in accepting their choice to be single: rather than being objects of pity or scorn, they were acting intentionally to fulfill their life dreams.

Hearing about others' life struggles, preparing meals together, learning folk dances from each other, and talking around candles until the wee hours of the morning brought a new sense of unity to the group. Each woman felt stronger in herself, more supported by others, and more convinced that the path she had chosen was the right one.

When we returned to campus, the women "hit the ground running." Two immediately met with their professors on their projects, taking bold steps to do what they had dreamed of doing. One told me that it did not matter if the male professors liked her idea or not—she would pursue it. Others met with women students who had not been able to attend, telling them all that had transpired.

The atmosphere on campus was charged. In their enthusiasm they put up a petition for other students and faculty to sign in solidarity with them. It rejected authoritarian notions of God as judge and lifted up the idea that God was with them in their struggles. It was a very different theology than what they had learned in their church traditions. After sharing their pain, they found courage to announce a new way of understanding God and forging solidarity with each other.

The emphasis on caring for relationships was also evident at the National Conference of Women Theologians in Tomohon, Sulawesi, in 1995. "Partnership in God's Work" was the theme. This theme brought together the national emphasis on partnership in development, discussed in chapter 3, with an interest in creation mythology and understandings of beginnings that are shared by Indonesians from many cultures. Speakers articulated a theology of gender partnership built around the Genesis 1 story of God's creation of the world and humankind.

While striving for equal status and opportunity, these church leaders stressed that they did not want to take over authority from men. Rather, they longed for a partnership in which both women and men could receive equal honor and bear equal responsibility. Much care was taken to make clear that these women wanted to work alongside men, as partners. Even as they struggled to rid themselves of oppressive theologies and church structures, these women were building a new theology of partnership by caring for relationships with those whom they confronted.

Their statements were backed up by their actions during the conference. The event was opened by a procession of leaders in the national church, mostly men. These men had the opportunity to inaugurate the conference and were actually the first speakers to have the floor. The six-day conference was closed with a panel discussion that included a number of prominent churchmen discussing the issue of gender partnership in the church.

Ceremonial rituals are extremely important in Indonesia, as they legitimate systems of existing power. Showing honor to those in authority, opening formal events with pomp and circumstance, and having the proper personages to make lengthy speeches at the start and end of a convention are important rituals. The wholeness of ritual speech, dense with meanings, can be used as a "veil" to exclude others (Kuipers 1998, 11).

Despite the danger of exclusion presented by asking men to perform these rituals, the planners took care to give those positions of honor to men who held authority in the national Protestant churches. In so doing they were caring for relationships and insuring a peaceable unity in the church. The women not only theorized about partnership, they practiced partnership.

Honoring Relationships as a Deterrent

These two examples show the importance of women building relationships as links between fulfilling their goals as independent moral agents and constructing new understandings of religious beliefs. It was exciting to see the solidarity that grew up as women shared their grief over the misperceptions of their choice of the single life at the retreat. The partnership embodied by the women at the national conference showed both wisdom and care. At the same time, each of these examples also shows how caring for relationships can deter women from realizing their goal of gender equality.

The solidarity formed in relationships during the single women's weekend retreat had two negative effects. First, the bonding that occurred set them apart from others in the program who had not attended. Second, the overenthusiastic actions of the group members when they returned to campus caused some faculty to question this "radical turn." No one showed public support of the declaration of God as a caring mother image. As important as developing relationships is the task of strategizing about how to present ideas of gender equality to others.

The attempts of women at the national theological conference to include men in the program as a way of preserving relationships also had negative effects. In order to lead, one must don the mantle of leadership. National women leaders of the Indonesian Church deferred to male authority. Consequently, even at a women's conference, men received the highest honors. Men legitimated the conference in the opening ceremonies. Men had the last word at the conference, evaluating women's work in the church in Indonesia and the world.[7] Giving men a prominent place in the conference undermined the theme of partnership between women and men in the

---

7. Not all evaluations were positive. One national leader claimed that women as a whole, not only Indonesian women, had done so little publishing worldwide that partnership with male leaders could not even be considered (Lokakarya Wanita Berpendidikan Teologi di Tomohon, May 28, 1995).

church and demonstrated that gender equality was not yet a reality in the Indonesian Church.

Reflection on Resistance Theologies

Reflecting on these everyday practices can result in new theological conceptions. New interpretations of religion that resist male-centered theologies and images for God and humans are envisioned.

Hyun Kyung Chung's relationship to her birth mother led to a life-affirming liberation theology. Her ritualized presentation, which used Korean spirit images, created healthy dissension when presented at the World Council of Churches convention in Canberra, Australia, in 1990 (Chung 1991). Her book *Struggle to Be the Sun Again* (1990) outlines an Asian resistance theology rooted in gender power.

Marianne Katoppo's spirit of independence brought her to the United States to study Christian theology. She published *Compassionate and Free* (1980), a theological work that presents God as nurturing mother, a theme found in indigenous gender ideologies and grounded in her family life experience. Highly criticized by her Indonesian male academic colleagues as "simply Western feminism," Katoppo's work presents an integration of Indonesian, Manado, and Christian feminist theological concepts.

Katoppo articulates a theology that grew out of her childhood experience of being "other." There is an emphasis on standing alone, being willing to be different, and following one's own convictions. Through *resisting social conventions*, she learned that social conventions and conventional theology can be challenged. She learned to think for herself in new and creative ways and to integrate disparate streams of culture that were part of her background.

The result was a new direction in Indonesian Christian theology, a direction that affirmed women's equality and importance in the overall scheme of life. She studied myths from her indigenous culture and from the many myths of mother figures, and she developed an appreciation for God as creator and nurturing mother. The resulting resistance theology grows out of Katoppo's practice of listening to stories from the past and integrating them with her experience of God in the present.

An Afternoon with Marianne

I learned a great deal about Marianne's everyday practices from a visit I made to her home on a particularly hot day in January of 1994.

I untangled myself from the *bejei* and looked around.[8] Mesjid Lane in this crowded section of Jakarta had not been easy to find, even for the seasoned cabdriver. But here I was at Marianne Katoppo's house. It was a low dwelling, enclosed at the edge of the dirt street with the usual iron fence. Plants suffused the house. A cat lounged on the narrow walk beyond the gate.

I rang the bell, moving mentally from the heat of the street behind me into the cool recesses of the house. She came out, dressed in a simple housedress, another cat in her arms. "Oh, come in," she said. "How good of you to come."

In Indonesia, it is an honor for a person to be visited at her home. Friends drop in unannounced between 10:00 A.M. and 1:00 P.M. or at about 4:30 to 6:30 in the afternoon. It is the obligation of the person with the lower status to drop in at the home of her superior: an older person, a teacher, a pastor, an employer. A small gift is brought, and hospitality, comprised of smiles and tea, is forthcoming.

I entered the cool house, handing my token gift to Marianne. As she thanked me, I glanced around the room with its modest furnishings and a few antique items. I noticed the walls, covered with photographs—groups, individuals, families, people at every stage of life. "What a lot of photos you have," I remarked. "Oh yes," she replied. "These are my family." And she pointed out her parents, her brothers, along with nieces, cousins, flitting from one photo to the next

---

8. When President Suharto banned *becas* (bicycle-powered conveyances to carry people) in Jakarta in the early 1990s, *bejeis* replaced them. They are comprised of a motorcycle with a simple metal cab attached for carrying people and goods. Noisy, polluting, and unsafe, these "taxis" provide transportation throughout Jakarta.

with confusing rapidity. Then we sat. Her houseboy came out, was introduced, and left again. Marianne herself went into the kitchen and put on the water for tea.

Then our conversation began. It did not take much to start Marianne talking. *Omong-omong* (chatting) is jokingly referred to by Indonesians as the national pastime. Completely unrestrained by a sense of hurry, Marianne delved into the delights and traumas of life on Mesjid Lane.

Her houseboy, she said, aroused suspicion in the neighborhood. How could she, an older woman living alone, possibly have a twenty-five-year-old male living under her roof? She did not care, she said. She was beyond fretting about her neighbors' gossip.

Marianne was very given to hospitality. She told of a visitor from India who had stayed with her not long before—how the neighbors also raised eyebrows at that one. "But what should I do?" she asked rhetorically. "Hotels in Jakarta are exorbitant in price. I have space—he is a friend. I've decided to have guests stay here whatever the neighbors may say." She paused. I thought in that moment of quiet how sensible her attitude was. At the same time, I thought how brave it was of her. Her sense of independent moral agency was strong, and her practice of hospitality enabled her development, in part by meeting resistance of this sort.

Hospitality opens some doors, although it closes others. Even while Marianne was criticized by some neighbors for having overnight male guests, at the same time, sharing her home with others resulted in friendships and an example of Christian care that endears her to friends, locally and internationally. It was part of her way of caring for relationships.

Certainly, relationships are important to a single woman living alone in Jakarta, a large and dangerous city. Strong social pressures push a woman to gain the "protection" of a mate. Marianne's allegations of gossip were undoubtedly true. Such a situation is considered nearly intolerable by self-respecting neighbors, be they Muslim or Christian.

Marianne is obviously not making her decisions based on social sanctions or community pressure. She has taken her own path, despite community disapproval. Her decisions are based on reason and practical considerations. She also says that it is not the community's concern in the first place to censor her.

The theology that results from these independent actions and everyday practices in conjunction with biblical themes and indigenous mythology is one that strongly affirms women as full human beings. Marianne depicts God as mother, although not exclusively female. She speaks of oppression of the poor and how Christians must act against societal conventions to liberate those who are oppressed. Reflecting on her own history, culture, life choices, and actions has given rise to an Indonesian women's theology of liberation.

Marianne's story, however, is not fully a success story. Although she continues to work on recapturing indigenous Indonesian cultures, she does not hold an academic post and has turned to editing to sustain herself financially. She feels that she has not been accepted by the academic community in Indonesia, and her sense of "otherness" has grown.[9]

In the transition from traditional to egalitarian gender ideology in Indonesia, as in any major societal transition, there are inequities and suffering. The first women to break through the patriarchy in Christian circles in Indonesia are not finding life easy. They struggle for recognition in a male-dominated field. Religion-identified resistance is not an easy road.

Yet in Marianne's case, one can see the direct impact of her struggle on her personal sense of moral agency. Rejected in some ways by the community, she became free of its strictures. She does not reify the customs set before her. She is empowered to chart her own course, to make moral decisions that seem good to her, and to develop practices that balance and enrich her life.

From this independent sense of agency, born out of her choices, come practices that result in new theologies that are more true to the

---

9. Her feeling was corroborated by a university faculty session a few months later. A suggestion that Katoppo be hired as a summer faculty person, although finally approved, was met with resistance by a number of faculty members. Reasons for that resistance centered around her "Western feminism."

intent of her religion as she understands it. Katoppo's struggles have made her into a prophet who does hold a certain power in the academy. Because her work is respected in the United States, she cannot be totally ignored among Indonesian theologians. As one with less power than male leaders, she has a certain freedom to speak out.[10]

Her very presence in academic gatherings marks a changing of the guard. It declares to uncomfortable men, "Things are different now. The academy is no longer a male club." Somehow, she, an individual who represents women as a whole, must be dealt with, incorporated, recognized, and at the very least criticized. In a culture that values smooth surface harmony, Marianne's presence is not only a statement, but also a goad, a reminder that things are forever changed.

I pulled myself back from reverie. The interview had only just begun. I noticed the beauty with which the photos were arranged and the simplicity of the furnishings. She had created an ambiance in her small dwelling that was built around her close-knit family.

After telling me about her family, Marianne showed me her verandah, full of potted plants—another part of her home that displayed beauty and care. Then she invited me back to her kitchen, where we continued the conversation over tea, rice, and fish. Her seven cats gathered for handouts.

One by one she picked them up, spoke to them, and offered them food. She told me where each had come from. Some were strays. One had been lost for months and then found again. Their life adventures were shared with gusto. The character of each cat was explained to me. They each had not only names but also distinct personalities. They were important to Marianne, and she assumed that because of that they would also be important to me.

A person who loves cats is not unusual, but I sensed here a link to Marianne's inner life, her spirituality. These cats were a symbol, it seemed to me, of how relationships ought to be. Her care for them,

---

10. More powerful persons in Indonesia are tightly bound by conventions of status and polite behavior. Those with less power, including women, have more freedom to go against social convention and speak more openly on sensitive issues.

and their reciprocation of affection, modeled what Marianne did not find in a community in which she felt like the "other." These small creatures of the kingdom were a safe domain in which exchange of care could happen without hidden agendas, manipulation, or status hierarchies.[11]

When the leisurely visit came to a close, I had a better impression of Marianne's life and how her theology was being developed through it. Independent choice, hospitality, a love for beauty and culture, and a care for relationships—these practices had led her to a view of God and the world that was unique and particularly suited for her as an Indonesian, a woman, and a theologian.

A Narrative of Personal Growth: Lucy

Marianne, as a single woman living alone, had time to study, to investigate indigenous religions, to write, and to travel for public-speaking engagements. Relating to her parents and brothers, entertaining international guests, spending time creating beauty in her home, and caring for her pets fostered a balanced lifestyle for Marianne.

Those same practices in another context may not help a woman to become a strong leader. Lucy, a graduate student, made choices that deemphasized care for others and resisted close family relationships. She did this in order to focus on study and to gain the independence that public leadership requires. Rather than foster relationships, the impossibility of serving both her own needs and the needs of a difficult family forced Lucy to develop practices of resistance that led to independence and maturity.

Lucy's family was close-knit. Moreover, her parent's needs

---

11. Katoppo was not articulating a theology here. It seems more like an example of Pierre Bourdieu's *habitus*. He argues that practical action changes the social construction of reality, sometimes in unarticulated ways. *Habitus* contributes to the production and reproduction of the existing social order "invisibly," without an individual's conscious awareness, even though the *habitus* exists only through those individuals' own actions (Roth 2000, 296).

worked at cross-purposes, leaving Lucy constantly feeling confused and guilty.

Lucy's mother wanted Lucy to be a traditional wife and mother. She complained about Lucy's ineptness at homemaking skills. When Lucy arrived home after a twelve-hour journey from the university, her mother would set her to work in the kitchen. Then she complained that Lucy could not even cook rice properly. (In Java, rice is eaten three times every day. Even a young girl can cook rice expertly.)

Lucy's father wanted Lucy to succeed in academic studies. Because no boys had been born to the family, Lucy, as the oldest girl, was chosen by her father to do graduate studies. She was intelligent and was expected to succeed in academic pursuits. Her father was an exacting taskmaster, frequently checking up on Lucy's progress by contacting her professors. He chided her for her slow progress in completing the degree program.

Those two parental agendas for Lucy's life conflicted at a basic level. It seemed that her father was grooming her to be an intellectual, and that constant striving toward this goal was a requirement of relating to her father. Her mother's criticisms, on the other hand, seemed to indicate that Lucy was a failure as a woman. Her mother could see no use at all in Lucy's intellectual pursuits. She had failed to marry. She failed again and again to perform well in the home. Her studies took her away from family responsibilities.

Caught in this tangle of conflicting parental expectations, Lucy's work suffered. Her feelings of obligation and inadequacy were augmented by the fact that Lucy was financially dependent on her parents.

Lucy's own talents also stood in her way. She related well to others, and hospitality seemed second nature to her. Her refinement and social grace delighted her friends. She was a good organizer and very responsible at follow-through. Despite her mother's low view of her homemaking skills, Lucy was an expert at planning social events. As a hostess, she was unparalleled at the university.

Using these talents gave Lucy great satisfaction. Her sense of loyalty to the program director also made it difficult for her to say "no" when requested to organize a conference, an anniversary celebration, or a student-faculty retreat. Lucy took on burdens of fostering hospitality, nurturing relationships, and creating beauty that added to the already considerable stress she faced in her life.

In addition, Lucy had a vision for a graduate student women's group. She helped to form and organize the group for more than two years during her graduate work. The sessions she arranged were always lively, consisting of a lecture, a group liturgy, and a celebration of eating together. Lucy included many women in the planning and executing of these group meetings. Through her contribution, women in the graduate program learned about women's issues and about developing openness and solidarity among women.

Because of her relational orientation and her multiple skills, the hardest task for Lucy was choosing one track and staying on it. Especially when time for herself, unencumbered by emotional trauma and free from serving the needs of others, was required, Lucy found it hard to keep the commitment to herself. It seemed that some family crisis or university event constantly demanded her time and energy.

Cutting out some of those activities in order to focus on accomplishing her task at the university was extremely difficult for Lucy. She suffered when she did not choose to focus on her work because her progress lagged and time seemed to be running out. She suffered when she did choose to focus on her work because she felt she was neglecting her familial or social obligations.

Coming to grips with these conflicting demands and finally making hard choices to distance herself from family needs and to focus on her studies caused Lucy to grow. Each time she chose to focus on her work, she went through a great struggle. But each time she succeeded in finishing a course or in completing another phase of her research, her self-esteem rose.

During the five years of her master's work, Lucy learned to choose her own path. She made hard choices between spending time with her family and pursuing her studies, between placating her mother and affirming herself, between succeeding for her father and accomplishing a task for her own sake. She learned to say "no" to overly demanding colleagues who appreciated her social skills more than her intellectual gifts. She learned the value of a project focused on women that integrated her own ethnic history, theological issues, and desire to do worthwhile, original academic work. She learned that she could not do all that she longed to do at the master's degree level.

When the time came to defend her thesis, a wonderfully poised, mature woman faced the committee. For the first time at the university, the examining committee consisted of more women than men—two out of three. The exam went well, and Lucy received well-deserved high marks. The struggles had paid off. Despite social pressure, family pressure, and internal pressure, she had succeeded in her chosen goal.

Comparison

Both Marianne and Lucy found themselves to be different from other young women. Beginning from this point of recognizing difference, each of these women pushed on to make choices about how to respond to becoming the "other."

Marianne, rather than minimize her difference, accentuated it, going to the United States to study Christian theology and returning to Indonesia as a "feminist theologian." Many of her everyday practices, however, followed traditional patterns. Her emphasis on hospitality, her nurturing of relationships, her creation of beauty in her home, her love of indigenous mythology—each served to balance her life and inform her theology. Yet Marianne lived alone and pursued a lifestyle that was unacceptable, according to her immediate neighbors. She made decisions about her lifestyle based on her own reasoning about the good and despite social sanctions. She moved her social network from the neighborhood, making friends in her field and traveling widely. Marianne maintained close relationships with her family while developing a strong, autonomous style of making moral decisions.

Lucy attempted for years to satisfy both societal expectations and her parents' demands upon her. She accepted financial help from her family to study at the university, further binding her to familial obligations. Even doing graduate study was a way, at first, of pleasing her father. Yet as she went on in her studies, Lucy found she could not satisfy everyone's wishes. Little by little she broke the parental bonds and pursued her studies for her own sake. By the time she graduated, Lucy had become more focused, more mature, and more able to say "no" to demanding familial expectations.

Each woman developed by making different choices about everyday practices related to her unique situation. Devotion to family provided a base for Marianne's radical departure from societal expectations as she developed a Christian feminist theology. Lucy's separation from close familial relationships and focus on practices of study and writing gave her freedom from exhausting emotional interactions with her family. Devoting time to caring for others aided Marianne but deterred Lucy, detracting from her ability to pursue her goal. Lucy developed practices of creating beauty in public arenas, while Marianne found strength in surrounding herself with the beauty of plants and pets at home.

It is clear that practices of offering hospitality, creating beauty, and honoring relationships can aid or deter a woman from reaching her goal of becoming a religious leader. The context and circumstances of the woman's life may require distancing or engagement in any one of these practices as an aid to her focus on the goal of leadership. Her attitude toward the practice itself and how she balances it with other activities such as study also influence whether the practice itself proves valuable on her journey to leadership. Reflecting on the practice and its meaning in theological terms can enhance its effectiveness in resisting theologies that hamper women and in developing new religious meanings that foster gender equality.

Assessing the influence of everyday practices on a woman's sense of agency and her use of practices in formulating resistance theologies raises crucial methodological issues. The role of a Western feminist scholar in a study of religion and gender power in Indonesia, the use of "universal" theories in identifying and assessing women's behavior and choices in new contexts, and the valuing role of the feminist researcher in her work will be topics addressed in part 2.

PART TWO Theory and Method

7

Introduction to Part Two
Parameters and Use of Theory

This study utilizes a contextual-relation theory and an interpretive methodology to identify and analyze social change that occurs through gender-based, religion-identified resistance. Three major components interact in this study: ethnographic research, the use of theories in a postmodern age, and the conscious valuing of feminist scholarship.

Ethnographic Research

The first component is the ethnographic research itself—a study of Indonesian women striving to become leaders in their religious communities. Doing research on religion in another society raises three issues: the role of religion in world construction, the historical situatedness of religious institutions, and the embeddedness of the researcher in the project.

The Role of Religion in World Construction

The importance of religion as a world-constructing activity in Indonesia cannot be underestimated. Everyone considers religion an essential part of life, be it indigenous practices or a major world religion. Most people combine religious practices from a number of sources. Western philosophy and science are highly respected academic enterprises, and higher education is valued. Often, Western viewpoints are held alongside cultural understandings, but much meaning construction occurs in the cultural domain (Berger 1969, chap. 1).

Religion plays a powerful role in Indonesian higher education. Most major universities are affiliated with either Islam or Christianity. Graduate work in religion and society at the Christian university includes studies in political theory, ethics, sociology of religion, theology, and gender studies. The goals and ideologies of religion influence curriculum, and the authority of those strong religious institutions legitimates those viewpoints. At the same time, university studies are modeled on disciplines and methods of Western universities that strive to avoid ideological posturing. That combination of religious and scientific legitimation gives Indonesian intellectuals and universities tremendous power to outline and define knowledge.

The Historical Location

The historical situatedness of university and religious institutions in Indonesia also affects how research on religion is carried out. To study the ways in which the defining influence of religious institutions affects women and engenders forms of resistance requires an understanding of Indonesian concepts of power and ways of combining the legitimating power of university and religion. Indonesians construe power as an inner strength that is held by an individual—a possession rather than a relation between two individuals or institutions (Anderson 1990). In addition, "secular" and "religious" domains of knowledge hold together or are coterminous, depending on whether one looks at Christian or Islamic institutions.

The Embeddedness of the Researcher

Participating in this education, however, are students and professors from many different cultures in Indonesia—cultures with unique indigenous religions and social customs. Add to this mix professors from the United States and Europe, and the complexity of evaluating the impact of the particularity of this context on the questions and findings of this study becomes apparent.

Understanding this context is essential for inscribing social discourse, yet that understanding itself is an interpretation (Geertz 1973, 15–19). Since the ethnographer is present in the situation and interprets from the outset, but often from another sociohistorical location of experience, caution must be exercised in making claims about changes in structures of legitimation in another society. In this study, the caution applies to analyzing changes in gender equality in Indonesia from the perspective of a Western researcher. The conversation among scholars from different societies and points of view can help clarify those interpretations in ways that reflect more fully the complexity of social change.

The involvement of the researcher begins at the start of the project and cannot be avoided. Russell T. McCutcheon asserts that "One does not have unimpeded access with which to understand issues such as power and legitimation. Nor, on the other hand, is the researcher 'utterly isolated from others' " (1999, 368). To address that issue, he recommends including a conscious autobiographical element in research studies (1999, 9). This reflexive stance acknowledges the assumptions and foibles of the researcher and highlights the interpretive and nonconclusive nature of the results. This project does take that reflective stance, by keeping the researcher in the picture as narratives are told and by including an autobiographical narrative in chapter 8 that explains how I came to do the research project in this way.

Use of Theory

The second aspect of this study grapples with the use of theory in a postmodern age. Many scholars reject the universalizing tendencies of the modern era and claim that all knowledge is local knowledge, bounded by experience, perspective, and social location. Theories that claim universal application must be reevaluated or reformulated in particular contexts. If theories are not modified in that way, they become rigid grids that narrow perceptions of complex social realities.

Rosalind Shaw elucidates the problem by drawing attention to the perspectival anomalies in Mircea Eliade's rendering of *Homo religiosus*: "How universal can this impersonal subject be when represented through such unabashedly gender-specific depiction?" she asks (Shaw, as quoted in McCutcheon 1999, 105). Universalizing a religious subject from a particular male Western perspective undermines the claims of universality.

On the other hand, if theories are relegated to particular contexts, conversation about human meaning can occur only within and not among those contexts. This study rejects the idea of incommensurability of discourse among different cultures. Instead, it advocates using theories as tools to enter and explore the meanings of others (McCutcheon 1999, 3). Used in this way, theories can be applied and revised according to historical situations.

Theories, as all knowledge, are mediated through perspectives—individual and communal. Cultural anthropologists have led the way in respecting other cultural forms and working to describe them accurately (specifically Geertz, Myerhoff, and Howell). This study uses a phenomenological approach, seeking understanding of lived reality, not attempting to describe ontological verities.

Conscious Valuing

A third aspect of the study is the conscious valuing that occurs within and outside of the study. The overarching value of gender equality as a critical standard sets the direction of change sought as women develop their potential. Values also influenced researcher involvement in the study itself. Besides using methods of participant observation and grounded theory, the study includes participant involvement. I participated in the community of the university, teaching, taking part in intellectual discourse, analyzing values, and encouraging women toward gender equality. My views influenced the women as their views influenced me during the time I lived in Indonesia.

A Contextual-Relational Theory of Social Change

Setting up the study and finding appropriate methods required employing a theoretical approach. Although that approach can be construed as an antitheory approach, it nonetheless forms a framework in which to do research. That framework consists of five tenets:

First, the theoretical approach in this book is contextual. Theory develops in a context, through observing and analyzing events and communities in a historical setting. Social scientists work in a rich cultural setting rather than in a controlled laboratory. That context provides the content to be observed and determines what facets of life are deemed important.

Rather than approach the situation with a theory, one allows the situation itself to call forth concerns and to determine directions. When I first went to Indonesia, I did not intend to develop an approach to social change that grows out of practices. It was working with students, noticing what was important to them, observing how they spent time, and watching their patterns of interaction that led me to a closer study of lifestyle choices of women, moral agency, practices, and their relation to theological reflection and changes in gender ideologies.

Second, the approach taken in this study is perspectival. As in any time and place, scholars engage in a conversation that compares ideas in contrasting settings. There is no overarching theory with which to compare this view. Neither will views in this study become an overarching theory by which others will definitively judge the process of social change for all communities in all ages.

My observations, questions, and analyses are each influenced by my own background and training as a North American scholar and as a Caucasian feminist woman raised in a large, middle-class family in the Christian and democratic traditions. While attempting to be open to Indonesian traditions, religions, family structures, and political ideals, I am rooted in Western values and traditions.

Acknowledging this "small" vantage point frees me to look in some detail at persons and events in another context. I find similarities and contrasts between my own views and attitudes and those I encounter in a different setting. I engage in exploration, speculation, and analysis as part of a global conversation of scholars attempting to understand religion, gender power, and social change in the contemporary world.

Third, the research focuses attention on action. Social change occurs as persons and communities *act*. Although both cultural ideas and material conditions influence social change, actions by institutions and individuals form the nexus of social change.

Fourth, relationships are crucial to social change. Actions take place among people—individuals and groups. Individuals do not create themselves or their worlds of meaning. Identities and meanings are constructed as people interact. The significance of an act is defined in a social setting, partly through the response to that act (Mead 1934; Smith 1982).

I learned this quickly as my own strangeness to Indonesian ways became evident when I arrived. Not only language but also cultural barriers set me apart. American philosopher Josiah Royce argued that relationships are triadic, with self, other, and a common loyalty among them forming a three-way relationship (1913, 41). In the encounter with a foreign culture, perhaps crucial dimensions of that common loyalty are missing.

The meaning of actions in relationships can also differ. I learned in Indonesia that a soft-spoken remark communicated not timidity but refinement. The meaning of an angry outburst was not a negotiation of content but a display of lack of emotional control. In this context I had to consider the cultural relativity of Beverly Harrison's work on the role of anger in the work of love, which is central to my thinking about women, freedom, and ethics in my own context (1985).

Fifth, social change is connected to values in a society. Different interpretations of a display of anger, for instance, reveal that valuing process. A society's character and convictions are shaped by what its members do. Their behavior is "valued" by social customs and mores. In the case of displaying anger, it is not enough for a Westerner to be clear and decisive to make an impact. Often such assertiveness backfires, for in Javanese society, the one with more power displays effortlessness in its use. If a person must be forceful, showing anger to make a point, it is evident to the Javanese that this person is not the stronger, but the weaker party in the interaction. In any society, one must emulate the attitudes of the powerful in order to influence others (Anderson 1990).

It is what is valued by society that, in turn, influences the direction of social change. The interpretive turn in sociology is matched by the narrative turn in ethics. Narrative ethics situates conceptions of the good as well as moral decision making in cultural narratives, communal interpretations of life in particular contexts.

Indonesian understandings of ethics are more related to actions and etiquette than to principles and convictions. Appropriate behavior in social situations is understood to be more determinative of character than words or statements of intent. For this reason, manners, polite interactions, and appropriate dress are seen, not as mere conventions of politeness, but as ethical concerns. Using a valuing theory dovetails very well, in this case, with the context of this study.

Engaging the Theory

Using this contextual-relational theory and the narrative methods that partner with it, my research showed:

1. A partial usefulness of the application of Western theories to the Indonesian context. Chapter 9 explores the usefulness of three moral development theories in identifying and analyzing moral agency, religion-identified resistance strategies, and everyday practices. Lawrence Kohlberg's hierarchy of moral decision making, Carol Gilligan's relational moral development theory, and Hubert and Stewart Dreyfus's skill acquisition model of moral development were used. There were some surprises and reversals from how I have appropriated those theories in Western contexts.

2. Some parallels between Indonesian and North American women's experiences of the pressure to conform to traditional gender roles emerged as the sociohistorical location of university life was examined. In Indonesia, as in North America, feminist evaluations of gender inequalities led women to resist from within their religious in-

stitutions. Their struggles for leadership in religious academic and denominational institutions parallel North American women's struggles for ordination, authority to preach, and leadership roles in the North American churches. Indonesian women developed practices that sustained them, even as North American women develop rituals and habits that nurture them in the sometimes lonely choices of independent and intellectual pursuits. Indonesian women found strength in women's groups, as do American women. Both groups find it helpful to talk about their struggles and to devise ways to support one another.

American and Indonesian women face similar obstacles because they value gender equality. The educated Indonesian women I worked with sought equality and understood it to be a basic human value. Chapter 10 explores the interaction between theory and advocacy in feminist scholarship, as women from different historical locations accept gender equality as a central value.

3. The usefulness of studying practices as agents of social change. By describing the interaction among religion-identified resistance, practices, resistance theologies, and social change, I am not proposing a universal theory but setting out a model of social change in one context that may be useful in other contexts. Although they avoid universal claims, contextualized theories can be tested in other contexts to find compatibilities among contexts and to increase applicability of theories. This study of women in Indonesia can be useful in that way to scholars working in other cultural contexts. A dialectic between concrete experience and observations with theories applied cross-culturally can reveal both limits and commonalities in theoretical approaches.

Janet L. Bauer suggests that the complexities researchers have found in researching women in fundamentalist groups should "direct our theoretical attention to the significance of negotiations and accommodations between individuals and their specific ideological and social circumstances which are essential to comprehending the complex patterns and processes of fundamentalisms" (1997, 246). A similar complexity and process of negotiation exists in the transition from traditional to egalitarian gender ideologies in Indonesia.

Because the method of this study is contextual and historically located, the use of theory sometimes seems to be limited, malleable, and uncertain. The next three chapters will show the importance of using theory in limited ways in contemporary social-scientific research and suggest some ways of doing that. Chapter 8 tells how the contextual-relational theory grew out of my own life and study. Chapter 9 explores the engagement of theories in a particular context by using theories of moral development in the current study as a test case. Chapter 10 questions how my feminist values influenced research in this study and outlines a hermeneutical method that can re-engage Western feminist theory and advocacy in research done in another society.

8

Social Theory as Practice
A North American Feminist in Indonesia

Combining ethnographic research with an analysis that uses theories contextually and consciously values gender equality gives this study a unique texture. I came to realize the importance of each of these facets of scholarly work through my own life's journey.

Questioning Gender Ideology

When I was about eight years old, I decided I was a tomboy. My older brother recalls my declaration: "I am a tomboy. I am *not* a girl."

Reasons for this momentous decision are clear to me now. Squeezed between two brothers, I learned to climb trees, make forts, have rock fights with the neighbor boys, and sneak through the culvert that ran under the highway to the forbidden land beyond. At school the boys teamed up to play "prisoners base," while the girls divided the places between the roots of a large tree into rooms and played "house." At recess, Margaret and Jane would pull me toward the tree. Wanting to be liked, I sometimes went with them. More often, I resisted, making my way toward the field. I was accepted there too, because I was good.

At home it was not that simple. My brothers made inclusion a tortured climb, and, like Sisyphus's journey up the mountain, one that I had to repeat endlessly.[1] I fought again and again against the litany: "Girls can't do that. Girls are too scared. No girls allowed." I did not like dolls or housework. Sewing was okay but could hardly compare with my brothers' misadventures. It was simple: I wanted desperately to be included—not to be the "other," the alien. And I wanted to do active things—physically challenging, fun, competitive, and exciting things. So I declared myself not a girl, but a tomboy.

To this love of active, spatial, competitive play was added an insatiable desire to know why things were the way they were and how they got that way. Such questions as "Why?" "How do you know?" and "Who says so?"—epistemological questions, as we adults like to call them—occupied my thoughts. It did not take me long to figure out that it was usually men who answered those questions. Things that seemed totally natural to me, such as singing loudly in church, voicing strong opinions, or winning the high school math prize my older brother expected to get, were declared unseemly or wrong. Or worse, sometimes my actions were thought to be funny—to others. They were never funny to me.

By age twelve I was going through the contortions that girls at puberty in our society go through. There were permanent waves to fluff out my silky hair, diets to tame my widening hips, and arguments with Mom about stockings and bras. By then I wanted desperately to be a girl. Even with all the ways that I had to curtail my natural instincts and to suppress my longings for space, competition, and answers to questions of meaning and social control, I did not want to become the "other."

By the 1970s I was living in Berkeley, California, a wife and the mother of two small girls. An older woman friend invited me to a demonstration at the university against Maribel Morgan's book *Total Woman*. I did not go, but I thought a lot about it. Reading *The Feminine Mystique*, *Ms. Magazine,* and Letha Scanzoni and Nancy Hard-

---

1. The Greek tale of Sisyphus tells of an ancient king of Corinth who displeased the gods and was punished with repeatedly having to roll a boulder up a steep mountain only to have it roll down again (D'Aulaire and Parin 1962, 126–27).

esty's book *All We're Meant to Be* changed the way I thought about myself as a woman.[2]

The emerging feminist thought of the 1970s sounded true. I had come to Berkeley with my husband because there was good work for *both* of us to do. Economic equity, equal rights, and freedom from restrictive notions of how a woman "should" look, dress, and "behave" were eminently reasonable to my mind. The "role question" was easy. The problem was that performing traditional roles was connected inextricably with social acceptance, which I still wanted badly. I did figure out that as long as I performed my mothering and homemaking duties well, I could manage to get that acceptance. And, I hoped, I could do other things as well.

With the encouragement of my feminist mentor, I wrote a chapter for *Our Struggle to Serve*, recounting my personal journey to Christian feminism (1979). My third child had just been born and I struggled to carve out time for writing from my hectic schedule. But I recalled being impressed by the words of Father Capon, an Episcopal priest, while I was in England in 1972. He said that among women there were ducks and swans. If a woman had talent she would be a swan, no matter what obstacles stood in her way. Determined to become a swan, I began a "superwoman" phase of life.[3]

In addition to my tasks as a co-pastor in my countercultural house church, a mentor to a young person living in my home, and the central caregiver for my three children, I began to work as a secretary for an organization that did research on new religious movements. I made a bargain with the director that I would work as his executive secretary for six weeks if I could then switch to research and writing. To my dismay, the man in charge of assigning research projects didn't

2. Friedan's book, now a classic, took Berkeley by storm in the late 1960s. *Ms. Magazine* came out in 1971 as a newspaper insert and began regular publication as a magazine in 1972. Scanzoni and Hardesty's work addressed issues of woman's equality from feminist Christian theological perspectives.

3. I realized how unrealistic this point of view was soon after when I read *The Cinderella Complex*, another early feminist book that outlined the unreasonable and contradictory expectations that characterized the socialization of women in the United States at that time (Dowling 1981).

assign one to me. Without a research project, I had to come to the research meetings with nothing to report. After three to four weeks of this embarrassing situation I was called into his office. "How would you like to do a movie review?" he asked. Then he immediately quelled my initial enthusiasm by suggesting that I assess the religious significance of *Superman II*. Hiding my distress as best I could, I took on the assignment, determined to find shreds of religious meaning, if there were any to be found, in the movie.

That experience taught me to pay attention to organizational power structures. I also became proactive, devising my own research projects. I began by bringing ideas and preliminary research findings to those research meetings. The first female researcher on an all-male team, I later became research director, directing the team of six male researchers. I organized and edited a journal on the human potential movement (Adeney 1980). I became a swan, but it cost a lot in psychic energy. Long work hours took me away from my children and caused tension with my husband. The battles of role expectations and "woman's place" were real.

Yet through that struggle with social roles, I learned that it was sometimes more important to do what my passions dictated than to fit in with social expectations. At the same time, I discovered ways to work *with* those in power, succeeding, even though the organization expected something different from me as a woman. I was learning to choose to become "other," to resist gender inequities in the religious institutions of my community, and to nurture myself in the process.

During these years I also struggled with the epistemological question. How did society "know" that women were more nurturing and men more assertive? How did we "know" that men should be leaders and women followers? I did not "know" these things in myself. They were contrary to the leadership urge and desire for knowledge that I felt. What was the basis for these beliefs? Authority, sources of nature, the Bible, social custom, and law somehow did not seem strong enough to support the idea that women were not as capable or as adult as men. Dorothy Sayers pointed out the strange dislocation of these ideas by titling her book *Are Women Human?* (1971).

Developing a Theory of Knowledge

I began doctoral work in religion and society at the Graduate Theological Union in 1983, bringing those questions with me. I looked at theories of the sources of knowledge from Plato through Michael Polanyi. I began to understand the influence of language, the tacit dimensions, and the role of community in human apprehensions of knowledge (Polanyi 1958).[4] I became fascinated with the notion of the social construction of knowledge—how society's self-creation devises social activities, assigns roles, and possibly even shapes consciousness itself.[5] Through discussions of Alasdair MacIntyre's reinterpretation of Aristotle, I discovered the importance of agency and practices in developing notions of the good.[6] The bifurcations of the Enlightenment (subject/object, fact/value, universal/particular), as well as its gifts (individual choice, equality, scientific method) also broadened my horizon.

These were not armchair studies for me but were integrally connected to how I viewed the world, what I valued, and how I believed knowledge was apprehended. Jürgen Habermas's work influenced my understanding of the diverging goals of the instrumental reason used in political and economic realms and the reason geared to understanding that operates in communities.[7] George Herbert Mead's

---

4. Professor Charles C. McCoy of the Pacific School of Religion at the Graduate Theological Union brought me into this wide-ranging discussion, nurturing my growing intellectual curiosity in creative ways.

5. The sociology of knowledge became a lens through which I began to see ideological dimensions of both religion and science (Mannheim 1929; Berger and Luckmann 1967; Berger 1969).

6. Through discussions of MacIntyre's book *After Virtue* (1981) at the Graduate Theological Union in Berkeley and sociology courses by Robert N. Bellah at the University of California, Berkeley, I also gained a sense for the importance of historically located traditions in ethics.

7. The first volume of Habermas's *A Theory of Communicative Action* (1984) was particularly helpful because he analyzed classic social theorists Marx, Weber, and Durkheim, using these traditions of social theory in new ways for contemporary society. Although Habermas justifies his creative dialogue with social theory as tradition

work on the social self (1934) and H. Richard Niebuhr's *The Responsible Self* (1963) showed me the integral part played by response in shaping social relations and creating meaning. Archie Smith's work on the social self in the context of the black church in the United States applied those understandings to the contemporary American milieu (1982). Charles McCoy helped me put together the significance of the rise of historical consciousness for apprehensions of knowledge and the development of human thought (1980). Through Hans Georg Gadamer's work, I learned the centrality of interpretation in that process.[8] Robert Bellah instructed me on the valuing aspects of sociology and led me to an exploration of the biblical and republican traditions that underlie American values while he was working on *Habits of the Heart* (Bellah et al. 1985).[9]

These studies convinced me of the historical situatedness of knowledge and the contextual embeddedness of ethics, which led me to search for resources for public ethics in limited historical traditions (Adeney 1989).

At the same time, I realized that our present communities have tremendous influence on the direction of our thinking and ethics. Thomas Kuhn's work *The Structure of Scientific Revolutions* (1970) convinced me of the crucial role that social approval of communities plays in what we believe to be accurate understandings of the world.[10]

---

set in narratives in a scientific methodology that I consider unsustainable, his approach influenced my own use of theory in Indonesia.

8. *Truth and Method* (1975) is Gadamer's major work on this topic. But I also learned much from his book *Reason in the Age of Science* and his articles and debates with Jürgen Habermas, found in numerous books and journals.

9. Interaction with Robert Bellah also convinced me of the importance of institutions in the process of social change, leading me to focus in Indonesia on the relationships of women in their institutional settings—families, churches, the university, women's groups, and academic affiliations. He, along with a team of scholars, explores this topic in *The Good Society* (1991).

10. Published in 1970, this work dovetailed with conclusions I was drawing about communal dimensions of knowledge, the role of emotions in configuring social roles and power dynamics, and the injustice of the power dynamics of many social constructions related to gender in the United States (Kuhn 1970).

Beverly Harrison's essential contribution to social ethics in the 1980s, *Making the Connections* (1985), showed me the injustice of current views of gender and ethics, something I had known deeply in my own experience since my tomboy days.[11] Through Elisabeth Schussler-Fiorenza's *In Memory of Her* (1983), I came to realize the neglect and bias religious communities displayed in recounting the narratives of women in Judeo-Christian sacred texts. Communities decided what was considered to be the truth about gender capabilities and appropriate roles. Traditions influenced communities in making those decisions.

Tradition needed to be changed. Tradition could be changed. Even to accurately reflect a tradition, it needed to be articulated differently. If new interpretation was necessary to reflect a tradition, new interpretation could be used to change a tradition. Feminist scholars were already changing the classical tradition with new interpretations and further insights into history, narrative, and traditions.[12]

These studies excited and challenged me. It dawned on me that although I believed that a reality governed by universal laws did exist, our understanding of that reality was, at the same time, always in flux—something Heraclitus argued centuries ago. Furthermore, understandings of universal principles varied, depending on the historical location and the tradition of the one attempting to understand that reality. Out of these new understandings, I developed an interpretive theory of knowledge. Rather than attempt to delineate formal universals, I assumed that the best any of us can ever do is to understand a situated truth, located in particular social and historical contexts.[13]

---

11. Harrison's essay in that volume, "The Role of Anger in the Work of Love" (1985), linked the emotions and actions to ethical comportment in a way that set the stage for further discussions of practices and ethics.

12. In *Nicomachean Ethics,* Aristotle argued that women were incapable of exercising practical reason, the kind of reason used to make moral decisions. Contemporary scholars reinterpret or reject this view (Nussbaum 1986).

13. John Coleman, S.J., refers to this stance as holding an "ontological faith with an epistemological humility" (Graduate Theological Union course, History of Social Ethics, 1985). That is, I believe that there are universal truths and values while at the

That interpretive understanding of knowledge that I bring to this work on women in Indonesia assumes:
1. The wholeness of knowledge. Knowledge cannot be divided up into separate disciplines or disparate parts. The wholeness of understanding, experience, and practice must be maintained. Although categories of analysis may be used, they are seen as heuristic devices.[14]
2. Knowledge is understood from a perspective: a location in time, culture, community, and a particular self.[15] Although not denying the possibility of universal truth, one knows truth only from a particular standpoint in a limited horizon.
3. Knowledge is developed in community. The self is social; both identity and knowledge are developed in connection with one's social group.[16] Cognitive and tacit dimensions of knowledge operate within paradigms of understanding arising in communities and sanctioned by them (Polanyi 1958, 321).
4. Knowledge arises through struggle. As one's view of truth, developed within a communally sanctioned paradigm, is exposed to other views of truth, conflict occurs. An openness to other points of view is necessary for the expansion of knowledge. Yet openness to the foreign tradition and the strange idea results in a clash of traditions.

It is through that clash of traditions that truth can be apprehended. Hans Georg Gadamer understood truth as a hermeneutic

---

same time I understand the limitedness of what can be known by an individual or a community.

14. Charles C. McCoy describes a primal wholeness that is later differentiated: "The wholeness of our fundamental experiences seems to be an inter-penetrative unity that we later differentiate, for various purposes, into inner and outer" (1980, 96).

15. Charles Taylor asserts that meaning is always "for a subject, of something, and in a field" (1985, 32–33).

16. Gadamer proposes that there is an excess of meaning in human artistic expressions. There is more meaning or truth embedded in the art than the artist realizes or intends. Once the artist releases a work, it becomes public. The artist relinquishes control over the meaning of the work, and others may understand it differently or see in it meanings other than those intended by the artist. This excess of meaning subsequently leads to new interpretations and understandings of what the work itself conveys (1975).

event. Confronting the "other" with openness, one is changed by it. The violence of the clash of two traditions can produce a "new" truth, one that has been and must continue to be restated in various ways throughout history.[17] For example, the truth spoken by Aristotle must now be stated differently in order to communicate the same truth to people today. That restatement can occur only as one is open to being changed by Aristotle's thought, although separated from him by time and culture. It is only through such struggle that new awareness can be achieved.

Identifying an Interpretive and Engaged Method

My challenge at that time was applying this interpretive theory of knowledge to the quest for public ethics in United States society. Developing an appropriate method became a central part of that task. Given my current understandings about the sources and apprehension of knowledge, I could not appeal to universal principles, whether theological, philosophical, or "scientific." Understandings are always interpreted and located in time and history. Conflict among appeals to universal principles led to irreconcilable differences about truth and goodness in the public realm, where a plurality of convictions reigned. Instead, I devised my task as one of "mining the traditions" in our past for future direction in public ethics. I believed that only a combination of historical resources and current notions of justice could yield a cogent public ethic in our democratic society today.

My interest in individual agency led me to focus not on the general contours of a public ethic, but on an ethic for citizens.[18] How, given the loss of a sense of secure universal values, established in the

---

17. Gadamer describes the "classical" as a kind of timeless present that is contemporaneous with every other age. To understand that idea, each generation must interpret history, embodying the timeless quality by articulating it in a temporal way. Only through that historical and interpretive process can the classical be understood (1975, 256).

18. I was not as concerned about the rise of individualism as my mentor, Robert Bellah. I argued that without the Enlightenment emphasis on equality and individual agency, I, a woman, would not be working on a Ph.D. at all.

past by religion or philosophical convictions, could citizens decide on good actions in the public realm? I explored this question in my dissertation, "Citizenship Ethics: Contributions of Classical Virtue Theory and Responsibility Ethics" (1989). The method I devised for this study brought ancient and contemporary figures into dialogue on the issue of the public good and citizen action toward that good. It focused on the context of thinkers, analyzed their perspectives, drew on the narrative of their lives as well as their writings, and recognized my own involvement in the process of seeking knowledge through this conversation.

At this time, 1987–88, I did not label this methodology "postmodern." It seemed to be a modest and realistic way to approach the subject of ethics in public life. Later I found in Zygmunt Bauman's *Post-Modern Ethics* (1993) the set of problems I was working with: failure of the Enlightenment project, loss of the possibility of a grand narrative, and realization of the contradictions inherent in modern Western public ethics. Public ethics in the West today champions both freedom of choice in ethics and a socially binding list of politically correct viewpoints, for example, freedom, democracy, and equality.[19] Those disparate claims caused tensions in Western ethics that led to a postmodern discourse (Stout 1990).

The situatedness of public ethics led me into comparative explorations, and in 1991 I went to Indonesia, intrigued by the civil religion of *Pancasila,* a religious declaration of national values.[20] I was convinced that all understanding was inextricably linked to context and to socially constructed values. The goal of the graduate program at Satya Wacana University suited this paradigm of knowledge. The program was designed to foster understandings peculiarly suited for and coming out of the historical and contextual situation of Indonesia.

I took to Indonesia ideas I had studied as universal theories of so-

---

19. For an analysis of this modern Western public ethic see my review of Charles Taylor's *Sources of the Self: The Making of the Modern Identity* (1991).

20. *Pancasila,* the national platform of public ethics in Indonesia, includes five principles: belief in one God, humanitarianism, national unity, leadership through wisdom and consensus, and civic cooperation (Wahana 1993, translation mine).

ciety, religion, and ethics. What would I *do* with those grand theories in a society so different from my own? How could I use them, realizing the social conditionedness of knowing? Yet that very idea was a "universal" theory that formed part of the backdrop of my understandings of the world. I looked at things through the lenses of perspectivalism and the social construction of reality. In his "Interpretation and the Sciences of Man" (Taylor 1985, 15–57), Charles Taylor taught me about my own connectedness as a researcher with anything I might study in Indonesia. He said that every research project is done in a field, for someone, and by someone (1985, 15f.). Nonetheless, I also knew that theory is indispensable to any study of society.

The realizations of perspectival knowledge, researcher "contamination," the presence of theories that underlie limited apprehensions, and the uniqueness of a strange context combined to make doing any research at all seem impossible. The complex ideas that constitute what we call the "postmodern turn" were cropping up everywhere.

Finding a Middle-Range Use of Theory

To move out of these dilemmas, I devised a theoretical framework that allowed for a use of theories that unavoidably claim universality within limited historical contexts. I envisioned the theories as "tools" that were more or less useful for interpreting meaning in specific situations. Marx, Weber, Durkheim, Habermas, Gadamer, Berger, Bellah, and Geertz were the social theorists. My students, I asserted, were the experts that could decide on the usefulness of those theories. They could apply part of all of them to the Indonesian contexts that, as church leaders and professors, they understood so well.

This "middle-range" use of theory allowed me to bring the conversation about meaning, values, and social change from my Western setting to Indonesian scholars who were looking for ways to analyze their complex social world. By using the theories in a light, even playful way, Indonesians could use, discard, break up, or create new interpretive tools for use in their society. I suggested that if a theory did not fit or suit the task at hand (or interpretation of a particular set of problems or social changes in Indonesia), it should be discarded, revised, or limited. Other theories should replace it. New theories could be developed from the social contexts in Indonesia. The theories themselves were merely heuristic devices to aid analysis, not ready-made knowledge to structure understandings of Indonesian society.

A highlight of those exciting years of teaching and dialogue with Indonesian students and scholars came one day when I read a front-page article in *Kompas,* a national newspaper. Written by one of my students, this article argued for a limited appropriation of Western social theory by Indonesian intellectuals—an appropriation that gave priority to Indonesian cultural ideas and social realities. The author, Pak Fritz, had revised and utilized social theory studied in my courses to make a contribution to intellectual life in Indonesia—an intellectual life that would foster positive social change. By empowering students to articulate, critique, and contextualize theories, we began to bridge the gap between Western "universal" ideas and Indonesian contexts and experience.

Religion and Gender Power: A Test Case

While teaching, I was also learning a great deal about both Indonesian cultures and women's traditional roles. I worked with women who were intellectual and social pioneers in a patriarchal society.

Despite certain liberating trends in Indonesian society, traditional roles and expectations for women were kept in place with strong social controls. Yes, the government argued, women could contribute to public life, but they did this mainly by nurturing children and taking care of their husbands so that *they* could be free to work in the public sector. If women wanted to take up public leadership, they needed to do so in time left after fulfilling their responsibilities with the home and extended families.[21]

---

21. During Suharto's years in office, this emphasis was very strong. It was reinforced by mandatory local meetings of wives of Golkar government workers. Golkar,

While in Indonesia, I saw many women choose to "become tomboys." They wanted acceptance in society, even as I had longed to be accepted by teachers, family members, and friends as a young girl. At the same time, they exhibited talents and strong-willed perseverance that drew them to study and to leadership roles in church and society. I marveled at their ability to resist limitations imposed by religious and social sanctions, *choosing* to become "other" by acts of individual agency and sustaining those choices by developing group solidarity. Impressed, I began to collect their stories.

The research that began with gathering those narratives was not a directed participant observation research project. Rather, I lived with the women as a guest, participating in their world. My presence at the university affected these women, and they attested to being changed by my work there. I was also changed by interacting with these women, both in their university context and through their complex and rich cultures.

During this time I had no "theory" about forms of resistance, choosing "otherness" and agency, or systematic understanding of how everyday practices sustained women in their endeavors. I did not associate everyday practices that mirrored ordinary routines of women with furthering women's advancement to positions of leadership or with providing material for new interpretations of their religion. But I observed. I asked questions. I participated in women's groups—academic, research, support, social, and theological discussion groups. Later, in a year of reflection on those experiences and on the lives of these women, I organized my thoughts about what I had observed. It was then that I developed connections between choosing "otherness," resistance strategies, practices, and women's leadership.

Holding theory at bay in this way is only partially possible. One must ward off premature theorizing. Yet one *needs* theory to figure out what is important, what questions to ask, what to observe. I had ideas about religion and resistance, human agency and "otherness,"

---

the major political party, included 75 percent of the populace and virtually all government workers. Consequently these groups, which studied women's roles and etiquette, were common.

moral development and practices, group solidarity and social change, determination instilled by a sense of calling and reinterpretations of religious beliefs. My work was also informed by a conviction that gender equality enhanced human flourishing. These ideas began to fit together in a more structured way as I came to realize that these women all had in common their decision to use religion as the center of resistance and creative change. It was those acts of choosing "otherness" within their communities of religious discourse that framed my contextual and particular study of women in Indonesia who aspired to leadership and equality.

Appropriating Theories

Operationalizing my method was simple. I kept looking at what I did not know. What motivated these women to choose to become Christian leaders? What did they do to solidify those choices? How did they interact with authoritative structures of church and university? How did they resist disempowering elements of religion and create gender-empowering ones? What gave them energy to continue making such choices, despite societal pressure to abandon their different path? What new interpretations of religion developed in their lives as they continued their struggle for equality?

In working with these questions I turned to a number of theories that I hoped could help me make sense of the behavior of these women. Theories of the social construction of reality, of "otherness" and relationality, of socialization, of legitimation, and of religion, action theories, gender role theories, theories about social change, the structure of moral development, and the causes of women's oppression of women were some of the sources I explored.

I appropriated those theories in a limited, contextual way, as I had taught my students to do. "Middle-range theory," as I began to call it, was my goal. I wanted to avoid an incommensurability of worlds, where Indonesian and American scholars could no longer discuss either social theory or ethics. Use of theories in a modest way seemed promising as a way to avoid that incommensurability and to continue conversation without either cultural imperialism from the West or rejection of Western theories as irrelevant to Indonesian societies. I utilized theories across cultural-historical differences, not as universal theories to be proved or disproved, as Lawrence Kohlberg's study of Filipino boys "supported" his universal theory of moral development.[22] Rather, I used Kohlberg's theory and others as tools to be tried out and adopted only if they "worked" to help interpret meaning and social change in the Indonesian context as I understood it.

Using theories from another setting—that is, the West—fosters a conversation about knowledge across lines of cultural difference. The conversation becomes one of analyzing and categorizing behaviors and understandings across cultural-societal lines without reifying the theories that aid that understanding or absolutizing the context itself. On the one hand, if theories are applied as thermometers of "truth," much will not be understood about the uniqueness of Indonesian society. If, on the other hand, the Indonesian context is seen as totally different from any other, the usefulness of theories for analysis within and among cultures will be lost.

For example, Clifford Geertz's theory of ideology as a cultural system was helpful in analyzing tradition gender roles in Indonesia (1973). But gender roles in the many cultures that make up Indonesian society cannot be subsumed under any particular gender ideology. Nor are the gender ideologies in Indonesian cultures exactly like gender ideologies in the West. Neither theory nor context can fully interpret meaning—each must yield to the other.

The next chapter will take up this subject in depth, using moral development theories to show how theories can be used to organize and analyze narratives in a context other than that in which those "universal" theories were developed.

---

22. To show the universality of his six-stage theory of moral development, Kohlberg did a study of fifty Filipino boys, concluding that their process of moral development was the same as that of the boys he studied in the West (Kohlberg 1984, 51).

9

Using Theories Across Cultures
Moral Development Theories as a Test Case

A central question of this study is what factors enhanced a woman's ability to resist social pressures and pursue her goal of leadership in religious institutions that did not fully support that goal? This chapter outlines three theories of moral development used to identify and analyze women's actions as they conformed to or resisted gender-based norms in religious institutions and in their social milieu.

By using Lawrence Kohlberg's hierarchy of moral development, Carol Gilligan's relational scheme of women's moral decision-making process, and Hubert and Stewart Dreyfus's model of ethical action as skill acquisition, a more nuanced understanding of the religion-identified resistance of these women came into focus. No theory worked as a definitive way to gauge moral maturity, but each was useful as middle-range theory, that is, as a tool used to identify and compare behaviors that fostered women's ability to develop and sustain religion-identified resistance to gender inequities. To show how those theories applied, a recapitulation of some salient features of Indonesian gender relations is presented. Narratives that illustrate the use of each theory in context are then analyzed.

A Cognitive Model

Lawrence Kohlberg, following Piaget, devised a cognitive scale of moral development that suggests that a person moves from blind obedience to rules and fear of punishment, through making moral choices on the basis of social conformity, to those based on relationships, and finally to reasoned decisions based on principles (Kohlberg 1984, 174–76) The rational, autonomous choice, made on the basis of ethical principles in this scheme, marks the highest level of development in this view.

Kohlberg asserts that "there are 'natural' culturally universal trends of age-development in moral judgment with a cognitive-formal base. Age trends, however, are not in themselves sufficient to define stages" (Kohlberg 1984, 43). He does claim that, developmentally, one can move through the stages to a point of independent moral agency. At that highest stage, moral decisions are made on the basis of the principle of justice. A freely choosing adult who makes moral decisions on the basis of what is considered rationally to be the most just choice marks, for Kohlberg, a universal level of moral maturity. This model directs attention to decisions and actions based on individual agency, moral reasoning, and principles of justice.

A Relational Model

Carol Gilligan argues that rational autonomous choice may not represent, for women, the highest level of moral development. Women, she argues, may be more oriented toward relationships in making ethical decisions. Gilligan suggests an alternative view: moral choices based on "connection, not hurting, care, and response" (Gilligan 1988a, 8).

Gilligan interviewed North American women facing unwanted pregnancies, discovering that most of them made their choice of whether to have an abortion on the basis of a sense of responsibility to relationships with their partner, families, and peers (1982). The women imposed a distinctive construction on moral problems, seeing moral dilemmas in terms of conflicting responsibilities. This construction proceeded from a concern with survival to a focus on goodness, and finally to a reflective understanding of care as the most adequate guide to the resolution of conflicts in human relationships (1982, 105).

Gilligan's work on a relational ethic of care is part of a conversation in ethics that suggests that everyday practices (Aristotle's "habits") may be more central in making mature ethical decisions than are principles.[1] That is, how we interact with others on a daily basis may be more influential in our ethical comportment than what we think about moral principles. This focus directs attention to the specific context, to negotiations of responsibilities toward others, and to daily practices oriented around relationships.

A Skill Acquisition Model

Hubert and Stewart Dreyfus suggest that developing ethical expertise can be likened to a skill acquisition, such as driving a car or learning to play chess (1992). One progresses from a rule-oriented novice status, through stages of grappling with moral ambiguities in specific situations, to reasoning out moral choices, to intuiting immediately the good response and acting on it. One becomes an ethical expert through practice (Dreyfus and Dreyfus 1986, 50).

If moral maturity can be learned through practice, everyday routines become significant in charting that development. Dreyfus and Dreyfus put intuitive action based on practice, rather than autonomous choice based on rational reflection, at the highest level of ethical expertise. Habits rather than rational acts or responsibility to relationships become pivotal in this view. The focus on learning ethical expertise as skill acquisition draws attention to the ways that everyday practices influence moral development.

Gender Relations in Indonesia

Utilizing those theories in the Indonesian context requires an understanding of how complex gender ideologies interact with ideas of moral maturity and agency in Indonesia during a period when these ideas are undergoing significant and rapid change.

---

1. The National Endowment for Humanities held an ethics institute at Stanford University in 1992 entitled Ethics: Principles or Practices. Lectures included papers by Annette Baier, Charles Taylor, Patricia Benner, Hubert Dreyfus, and Onora O'Neill.

We have seen that traditional and modern gender ideologies interact in complex ways in Indonesian society today. Ideas of gender equality have been part of many traditional ideologies, particularly those of matrifocal societies in Sumatra, Sulawesi, and Java. The contradictions and nuances of those ideologies have increased under the influence of both an Indonesian women's movement and the influence of an egalitarian gender ideology from the West. Models of women revolutionaries, political rights granted by the constitution, and government discussions of women as partners in development, as well as the formation of both conservative and feminist women's groups, all contribute to women's ability to act in the public realm. Yet the problem of social equality has not yet been solved.

We saw that women who act in ways that demonstrate gender equality embark on a life course that differs from that of their contemporaries. The religion-identified resistance that develops from their choice to pursue a career as a pastor or scholar results in a sense of separateness from their peers. That sense of "otherness" prods women to rely on their own judgments, to make independent decisions, and to develop practices that sustain them in pursuing their lives' directions.

The process of acting on one's convictions or sense of "calling" can serve as a motivation for further actions, which become routine ways to reflect gender equality. Reflection upon those practices leads to the reformulation of religious ideas, the development of resistance theologies. Continued action reinforces and deepens the commitment to a gender ideology of equality.

Despite conflicting gender ideologies in Indonesia, social expectations for women at every stage of life are well defined. A young, unmarried woman dresses and acts in certain acceptable ways. After marriage, her clothes and behavior reflect the change. Modest skirts replace colorful culottes; evening outings with her husband replace chats in the women's dormitory or evenings with the family. With the arrival of children, things change again. Many women remain at home while husbands sally forth in the evening. Relationships with mothers and mothers-in-law, cousins, aunts, and women friends with children begin to dominate a woman's social life.[2] Even if she works outside the home, a wife is still expected to care for children and family relationships.[3] As a woman grows older, she has more freedom to act independently, although she is always tied to her husband and is expected to defer to him.[4]

When a woman departs from these socially acceptable ways, she suddenly encounters a different world. Things do not work the way they used to; responses to her actions do not follow the usual pattern. An analogy in a Western cultural context can be seen in Lewis Carroll's *Alice's Adventures in Wonderland* (1935). When Alice slipped and slid down the long rabbit tunnel to arrive in Wonderland, she found that things did not work quite the way she thought they would. An obedient child, Alice saw a bottle that said, "Drink Me," and she did. In only a few seconds she had grown so big that her head was poking out the roof. Used to answering questions from authorities forthrightly, she found that answering the Queen's questions in that manner resulted in shouts of "Off with her head!"

When responses to Alice's "good" behavior—actions she was socialized to perform—became chaotic, Alice became confused. Her usual conforming behavior did not bring forth the good results she anticipated. In those strange surroundings, Alice soon began to disregard "the rules" she had learned, finding out by trial and error what

---

2. I am speaking here of educated, middle-class, urban women. Village women have strong societal expectations placed upon them as well, but they differ somewhat. A married woman who works in the market may arise at three or four o'clock in the morning to take her goods to market, for example.

3. *Peranakan* and Chinese Indonesians customarily contribute to the family's welfare through some kind of income-producing work. Among these groups, working outside the home is common and expected. The customary Indonesian expectation of women as primary caregivers is nonetheless upheld.

4. Although divorce is not uncommon, a divorced woman is looked upon with disfavor in Indonesian society. It is more usual for middle-class couples that are not happy together to establish separate households and maintain the formality of the marriage rather than to divorce. Each person leads a separate existence, *menikuti jalan hidunya masing-masing* (see Glossary).

behaviors brought forth a positive response from others. As a result, she became more attentive to the situation itself, more focused on seeking her own welfare, and more independent and bold in making decisions.[5]

In times of swift and radical social change, the world can seem as topsy-turvy as Alice's Wonderland. Meeting social expectations may not result in smooth interactions; forms of polite or ethical behavior may bring results quite different from what one expected. Going against social norms may bring good rather than disastrous results.

Gender relations are undergoing radical transformation today. Modern technologies, health care, and global communication systems present women with new opportunities, expectations, and ideas. Women today live longer, bear fewer children, and have more job and lifestyle options than their mothers did. As more and more women enter public life, social mores begin to shift.

In many societies, new expectations are added to traditional gender roles. The resulting "double burden" for women is challenged by egalitarian notions.[6] Following the old ways can result in women being criticized, as we saw in chapter 3, for not pulling their weight as "partners in development."[7] Leaving traditional roles behind can

---

5. This analogy reflects not only individual changes in behavior during societal transitions, but also the shift from applying universal theories that evaluate behaviors on the basis of invariable rules to a context-driven method that evaluates behaviors on the basis of multiple, often contradictory cues in the context itself.

6. The idea of a "double burden" for women characterizes discussions of women's situation, not only in Indonesia, but also in other places. Despite strict governmental sanctions on having more than one child per family, women's "double burden" became a theme at the International Conference on Women's Roles in Hangzhou, People's Republic of China, November 1993.

7. The term "partners in development" serves both as a reminder of responsibilities and as an interpretation of what those responsibilities entail, according to the Indonesian government. The Guidelines of State Policy declares that "overall development requires maximum participation of men and women in all fields. Therefore, women have the same rights, responsibilities, and opportunities as men to participate fully in all development activities" (Murdiati 1985, vii).

also result in women being criticized for not filling societal expectations of being good wives and mothers.[8]

In 1960, women in Indonesia still feared that repudiation by the powerful men in Indonesian society would result in social and economic instability (Vreede-de Stuers 1960, 165). Becoming "other" by defying social norms could lead to objectification as the not-real and the not-good, since those who follow norms created by existing authorities are defined as real and good (Massanari 1991, 5). Today, however, Christian women are successfully navigating that dualistic gap by claiming inclusion as part of their resistance to religious authorities. In the middle of societal transition, results of going against the norms are less predictable than they were in 1960.

How did Alice make her choices? Finding that her automatic socialized responses brought disastrous results, Alice had to forge her way through strange situations, relying on her own wits. Although she asked advice from creatures she met in the strange underworld, their words were so often contrary to common sense that Alice had no choice but to rely on her own logic and on values established in her other, everyday world.

How do Indonesian women make their choices? Is there a model that can make sense of their attempts at resistance and change?

Using Moral Development Theories in the Indonesian Context

Each of the models of moral development mentioned have merit in aiding understanding of moral agency in a particular setting. Even theories that purport to be noncontextual need a context in which to be understood.[9] Some may be more useful in one setting than an-

---

8. The Guidelines of State Policy states, "The role of women in development does not mitigate their role in fostering a happy family in general and guiding the young generation in particular, in the development of the Indonesian people in all aspects of life" (Murdiati 198, viif.).

9. Both Kohlberg and Dreyfus and Dreyfus attempt to build noncontextual models to be applied in any setting (Kohlberg 1984, 51; Dreyfus and Dreyfus 1986, 50).

other. But every model needs to be adapted to suit the actual dimensions of a real context, and no model of moral development can be universally applied without regard to social and historical context.[10]

Unlike Alice's dream world, the social world in transition in Indonesia has marks of the Old World order, as well as hints of a new one. Although there are chaotic elements, traditional mores and social institutions still influence one's understanding of ethical principles and the responses that come from the society when an individual makes choices that diverge from the norm. Theories of moral development can act as frameworks to identify and order these complex interlocking elements that affect moral agency in Indonesia.

Kohlberg's Hierarchy of Moral Development

Kohlberg's theory helped identify the cognitive choices of women who broke out of conformity to societal expectations and developed religion-identified resistance strategies. Since definitions of identity and morality are connected to conformity in Indonesia, choosing a different path required finding a reason to break out of the mold.

Dewi's story from chapter 5 illustrates this. As a Batak pastor, Dewi had found a reason to break with social convention in her sense of calling to church leadership. She studied theology as an undergraduate and received a post as pastor in a Batak church. She remained unmarried. Deciding to apply for graduate studies and to research the role of women in the Batak Church showed a strong sense of independent agency.

Gilligan's use of context has been understood in various ways. (See Kettay and Meyers 1987, 7; and articles by George Sher and Jonathan Adler in that volume.)

10. Kohlberg's a-contextual developmental stages are useful in understanding women's choices in the Indonesian setting because of the context itself. Carol Gilligan shows that in a different context, that is, Western women facing choices about abortion, his stages are less helpful, again, because of contextual features of a social milieu (1982).

Dewi's commitment to the principle of justice, specifically gender equality, continued to inform her decisions. Realizing that a "feminist" thesis might not further her cause, she framed her work on women in the church in terms of the traditional and well-accepted concept of the mother as central to family and community life. That religion-identified resistance strategy earned her inclusion in the academic world as she succeeded in earning her degree. She then received a part-time teaching appointment by co-teaching with a North American professor. Her goal of leadership was furthered by these reasonable choices geared to the justice principle of gender equality.

Continued actions as an independent moral agent working out of a principled justice orientation took Dewi into church politics. She resisted government intervention in the Batak Church. She took a strong public stand against that intervention, speaking in churches throughout Sumatra. Later, when the opposing church party gained power, Dewi was effectively barred from further advancement in the church institutional structures.

Her desire to do Ph.D. work was also based on a well-reasoned, independent choice. This was a move that would enhance her leadership potential and further her cause of gender equality in her church. This decision, however, failed to gain her an entrance into Ph.D. work. University authorities were too powerful to deflect in this case.

Throughout her time at the university, Dewi showed a strong, independent decision-making capability based on reason and principled decisions. Kohlberg's hierarchy of moral development was useful in identifying those behaviors and linking them to independent, reasoned choices that lead to religion-identified resistance. In the same way, Kohlberg's model showed that successful resistance requires an appreciation of the consequences of departing from the norm as well as the identification of an alternate good that makes those negative consequences bearable.

Traditional Indonesian values and the strong socialization that reifies those values in people's lives must be understood in order to see how radically different choices to resist actually were. For example, the idea of *kodrat,* which we explored earlier, carries with it connotations of both fate and God's will. It is considered an unalterable yet good fate for a woman to have children and supply devoted care to them, to her husband and aging parents, and to members of the extended family. Having a full and well-ordered home, good food, and disciplined and well-attired children is considered a primary ethical duty of women.

To resist those expectations requires an understanding of *kodrat* and an anticipation of the marginalization that results from not embracing that theology. Focusing on following a call to leadership as an alternate good that competes with the good of fulfilling one's *kodrat* motivated women to act decisively. The courage to act as subjects by remaining single in the face of this pressure showed the importance of autonomous moral decision making in religion-identified resistance.

Another example of the importance of a strong sense of moral autonomy is uncovered by viewing the powerful social sanctions that control individual behavior in Indonesia. Group social control through peer pressure can keep one from breaking the rules of propriety and can punish those who stray from social norms. People usually prefer to fit in rather than to stand out.[11] Intensely personal questions, such as "Where are you going?" "How much did that cost?" and "Why isn't your husband here with you?" are perfectly polite questions to ask in Indonesia. Vague answers are not inappropriate. But too much travel, too much spending, and too much time away from one's family are soon noticed and elicit gossip and more intense questioning from the group.

Those that consistently resisted the rejection that those social pressures exerted had developed along Kohlberg's scale, defining for themselves what moral agency entailed rather than acting in fear of or in conformity to social controls.

---

11. Indonesians enjoy dressing alike, for example. Uniforms are common in offices, clubs, schools, and other groups. Women often wear identical dresses. Students were intrigued when I told them that American women felt embarrassed if a duplicate of the dress they were wearing turned up at a party.

Gilligan's Relational Responsibility Model

Gilligan's model helped uncover the complexity of responsibilities to relationships that women felt in social situations and institutional religious contexts. A strong value in Indonesian society is relating properly to status hierarchies. What, specifically, does it mean to act upon a value of gender equality in a situation that asserts the greater value of the father figure and the responsibility of a daughter to remain tied to her family—to care for her elderly parents and to avoid confrontation with authority figures? In Dora's case, discussed in chapter 5, she seems caught between two worlds of social expectations: the achievement orientation of Western higher education and traditional Indonesian family values.

Analyzing this conflict of interests brought in Gilligan's relational views. Dora felt a responsibility to her family and, when pushed to choose, decided to return home to care for her sick mother. Rather than view this as a less mature choice, as Kohlberg's model suggests, Gilligan's theory allows us to see the strong evaluations that Dora made not only as viable, but as mature decisions in the context of the strong family orientations of Indonesian society.

Marianne Katoppo's narrative shows the importance of Gilligan's relational model in assessing religion-identified resistance strategies and the resistance theologies that can grow out of them.

Marianne's focus on her family fit in with traditional expectations for a single woman to relate to her nuclear family in a close-knit way. At the same time, the practices Marianne developed around honoring her family—displaying photos of them in her home, talking about her relationships with them, and spending time with them—nurtured her own life. Remaining close to her family gave Marianne the support network that she needed in her lonely path of resistance to church and university structures that ostracized her for her resistance to gender inequalities. Studies of resilience aid understanding of the ability of Marianne and other women to sustain rejection and develop flexibility in response to changing situations (Butler 1997).

That resilience, developed in Marianne's relational emphasis, can be traced in her resistance theologies. Arising from her study of indigenous myths, these reinterpretations of Christian theologies gave honor to Marianne's forebears. By conceptualizing God as mother, those interpretations elevated the figure of mother for Christian women.

Marianne's relational emphasis in her family interactions and in her theology shows a maturity on Gilligan's scale that can be seen not as conformity, but as a challenge to the status quo in religious institutions in Indonesia. Had I only used Kohlberg's hierarchy of moral development to analyze Marianne's narrative, I would have found an independent moral agency in her actions, but I might have missed the centrality of relational responsibility in her religion-identified path of resistance.

Another feature of Indonesian society that makes Gilligan's analysis useful in this context is that the definition and scope of ethics in Indonesia differs from Western understandings. Rather than a study of individual moral decision making,[12] ethics is understood as a system of interlocking social obligations that emphasizes the appearance of harmony, cooperation, and an unassuming attitude in all situations.[13] Using only a model of moral development based on an individual action in a context in which ethics is defined in terms of the harmonious workings of status-oriented social obligations ignores the sociality of ethics. Bringing in a relational model of moral behavior illuminates this aspect of Indonesian social life.

Dreyfus and Dreyfus's Skill Acquisition Model

Dreyfus and Dreyfus's model of skill acquisition in the development of ethical expertise also helped navigate the vagueness of this eti-

---

12. Vincent Ruggiero defines ethics as "the study of right and wrong." He goes on to explain: "The focus of ethics is moral situations, that is, those situations in which there is a choice of behavior involving human values (those qualities that are regarded as good and desirable)" (1984, 2f.).

13. Politeness and ethical behavior overlap nearly to the point of being synonymous. A good-mannered person is not only courteous but is also decent, respectful, and civilized. See the definition of *sopan* (polite) in the Indonesian dictionary (Echols and Shadily 1989).

quette-oriented notion of moral obligations.[14] Dreyfus and Dreyfus argue that ethical expertise is not dependent on articulation of rational, moral, abstract principles, but rather on the development of intuitive skills in understanding contextual features and appropriately applying maxims. Ethical expertise is developed through practice in specific situations rather than through detached deliberation of context-free principles (1992, 172). According to this scheme, a novice begins by applying the rules. When that ceases to work (remember Alice), the advanced beginner starts looking for contextual clues to guide her decision of whether to follow the rules. An orientation to justice in context develops with practice, as the competent ethical person rationally makes a plan for doing the right thing in an ambiguous situation. Finally, the ethical expert "sees" or perceives a situation and makes the intuitively perceived "proper" response, immediately bypassing the already internalized rational planning stage.

Indonesians seem to have a kind of radar that helps them determine the appropriate action in any given situation. While a Westerner listens for language cues to determine response, Indonesians rely on facial expressions, engagement or avoidance of eye contact, physical posturing, and other nonverbal cues to alert the other to their position and to request a fitting response. Thinking about moral maturity as an ability to read those cues and respond intuitively to them reveals another dimension of moral agency for Indonesian women who are resisting social structures and mores. Knowing when and how vigorously to resist, whether to resist in negative or positive ways, and how to remain poised through experiences of negative feedback and ostracism requires maturity of this kind.

Lucy, whom we met in chapter 6, resisted close family relationships in order to focus on her studies, which were frequently interrupted by pleas from family to re-engage in intense family delib-

---

14. The skill acquisition model itself is described in chapter 1 of *Mind over Machine: The Power of Human Intuition and Expertise in the Era of the Computer* and includes a chart illustrating this developmental model (Dreyfus and Dreyfus 1986, 50). I have summarized this model in the appendix.

erations or gatherings. Lucy's situation differed from Marianne Katoppo's and led to nearly opposite choices concerning family relationships, living situation, and ways of spending time. Yet both developed a mature sense of moral agency as they grappled with the tensions in their lives. Dreyfus and Dreyfus's scale is helpful in analyzing Lucy's development toward ethical maturity (see the appendix).

From the beginning of my relationship with Lucy as a student, I noted that she was not a rule-oriented person when it came to making ethical choices. Rather, she attempted to the best of her ability to meet every obligation that came along. Her thesis proposal, related to a women's position in an indigenous religion, was a contextually oriented project. When she came to the university, she evaluated situations on the basis of features or principles, but she also analyzed aspects of the situation, an advanced beginner level on Dreyfus and Dreyfus's scale. She did not have a hierarchical organizing scheme that helped her choose her issues and streamline her responses. Consequently, she often became overwhelmed by multiple obligations and had difficulty deleting any of them from her life. There was a pattern during her first two years, however, when Lucy consistently chose family obligations and social requests from the director of the program over her own academic responsibilities. Her acquiescence resulted in guilty feelings, late papers, and possibly stress-related illnesses.

After much encouragement, Lucy began organizing her ethical responses according to a hierarchy that gave a higher priority to her academic work, an activity that Dreyfus and Dreyfus put at level three. It is difficult to ascertain whether this was because of her desire to please her father and the strong ethical injunctions Indonesians place on loyalty to the *bapak* (father) or because of her own desire to reach her academic goals and a developing strength to choose herself. In any case, she operated consistently on what Dreyfus calls the level of competence for quite some time.

Dreyfus points out that at some time during the competence phase, features and aspects of a situation become overwhelming. This occurred in Lucy's life as demands from her family to perform obligations increased. It seemed that the more she succeeded academically, the more she was "needed" by her family. Lucy's response was not to move to stage four, the proficiency stage, intuitively assessing each situation as it arose. Rather, she chose to distance herself from her family, thus preventing family obligations from accruing. She knew that her family would disapprove, but she told them that she would not be returning home for visits for one year. That took a great deal of courage. What Lucy did here was to enforce a hierarchy upon her ethical obligations at the competence level. In doing that, she moved away from relationships, breaking up with a boyfriend, moving into a quiet and safe home with a family that befriended her, and cutting down on her social obligations at the university.

As Lucy organized her life in this manner, she developed an inner strength and a sense of obligation to herself and her work. When she was ready to return to her home island for her fieldwork, her project was well organized. She succeeded in gathering significant data and writing up a project that made a substantive contribution to the field of cultural anthropology.

After graduation, Lucy returned to Jakarta to care for her mother, who had fallen ill. But she delayed going home until after she defended her thesis. At the time I left Jakarta, Lucy was living in the family home and caring for her dying mother while seeking employment. I do not know if Lucy's ethical expertise reached another level, according to Dreyfus and Dreyfus's scale, during this time. I do know that during the five years I knew her as a student, Lucy developed inner strength, ability to focus and make ethical choices that affirmed her own goals, and resilience. By the time she graduated, Lucy possessed an impressive poise and competence in making ethical decisions in situations of conflict.

Understanding ethical choices on a scale of developing expertise can show how using a rational, abstract, universal principle in decision making can result in either a mature ethical response or a rigid, irrelevant one. The proficiency of the actor in apprehending, integrating, and responding to the context in all of its complexity becomes crucial. Dreyfus and Dreyfus argue that clinging to the demand for rational justification can actually block the development of expertise, preventing one from apprehending the appropriate intuitive response in a given situation (1992, 170).

These examples show that each of the models used revealed and helped evaluate different kinds of behaviors as women departed from automatically following social conventions.

Dangers of Using Moral Development Models Across Cultures

A danger arises in using such theories when levels of maturity are equated with a single set of standards. Even comparing theories in the Euro-American context revealed differences in standards gauging moral development. Gilligan's research showed the gender bias of Kohlberg's hierarchy of moral development. Women's maturity, when assessed on its own terms, was more relational and less oriented to individual cognitive assessment of situations (Gilligan 1982). To impose either Kohlberg or Gilligan or any other Western developmental model's standards of moral maturity on Indonesian women ignores the cultural relativity of any hierarchical model of moral behavior.

Understanding the complexity of Indonesian views on maturity in regard to cultural variations, differences in values, gender, class, and a myriad of other factors is beyond the scope of this study. Pointing out differences in the way maturity is evaluated in Indonesia can highlight this complexity.

For example, in using a skill acquisition model to chart moral development, one must recognize that not only the scope and meaning of ethics but also the process of skill acquisition in Indonesia does not mirror the skill acquisition process as Westerners know it.

For Dreyfus and Dreyfus, as for most of us, skill is acquired by learning the rules, figuring out the situation, and deciding how to fit the two together. Dreyfus and Dreyfus claim that the expert skips many of the rational steps because they have been internalized. The expert can immediately intuit the situation and act, applying maxims without thinking them through every time (1992, 160).

Skill acquisition in Indonesia looks different. The novice finds a teacher to imitate and from whom to learn. Trust, honor, and noncritical acceptance are the marks of a good apprentice.[15] Women students told me how glad they were that I was there to model for them the freedom, equality, and professional life they were striving toward. These remarks led to a growing awareness of the danger of cultural imperialism. I did not want the students to become like me, but to become equal, free, and powerful in their own ways.

The interaction of Western and Indonesian lifestyles and forms of education indicates that Dreyfus and Dreyfus's skill acquisition process may operate alongside the apprenticeship method. As they made choices against societal expectations, the women I worked with were thrown onto their own resources. Like Alice, they had to figure out new ways to respond to dilemmas in an unpredictable world. The more individualized skill acquisition model described by Dreyfus and Dreyfus offers insights into the process of developing moral agency among those women.

Although moral maturity cannot be evaluated across cultures, one can determine whether a woman achieved her stated goal of finishing graduate studies or becoming a pastor, or in another way reached her goal of becoming a Christian leader. Failure to achieve that goal, however, may not indicate a lack of moral development but rather a choice to excel in another realm of the intricate web of relationships in her context. Or, it might indicate that a different path of resistance was undertaken, replacing the resistance of working within religious institutions to achieve gender equality. Or, what seems like a lack of maturity may mask actions taken to reach another goal that Western researchers do not see.

For example, one student who failed to finish her program repeatedly complained that she was not heard and that women were continually curtailed in their efforts to achieve leadership in the

---

15. This approach is typical among Asians and can also be seen in the Indian respect for Hindu gurus, the Korean respect for the words of teachers, and the Chinese reverence of the elderly in their communities.

Sumatran Church.[16] Those complaints could be interpreted not as failure to achieve moral maturity but in one of the following ways. Perhaps she was succeeding in the domain of the familial relationships by taking care of her mother and giving up graduate studies. Or perhaps she was taking up a pattern of lament popular in ritual speech in Sumba and perhaps in other Indonesian cultures (Kuipers 1998). In that case, her complaints might be interpreted as a bold and mature way of highlighting the gender injustices that force women to give up careers to return home and care for aging parents.[17]

Gender studies across cultures can use moral development theory to identify actions and strong evaluations without imposing culturally conditioned evaluative standards of those theories on another culture. Scales of moral maturity must be developed from inside of the culture, based on attitudes and practices that reveal the values equated with maturity in that setting.

This contextualized study leads me to conclude that there is not one correct model. Although the models are not entirely compatible, not every model attempts to map out the same terrain. Kohlberg emphasizes individual growth and use of principles through rational analysis. Gilligan focuses on maturity in relationships. Dreyfus and Dreyfus link principles with perceptions of appropriate behavior in concrete situations. But only in specific contexts can the relative importance of each approach be assessed. The social context itself determines how relevant a particular developmental approach may be. No model can be assessed or applied universally; every model needs to be adapted for a specific social and cultural setting. This chapter provides a glimpse into that process of adapting models for understanding

---

16. These views were confirmed by Pdt. N. M. Hutahaean, another woman pastor from the Batak Church (HKBP). According to Hutahaean, the patriarchal structure of Batak society was brought directly into the church, thus denying a voice to women and youth. During the 1970s women were permitted to serve the church as elders and missionaries, but it was not until the 1980s that women were allowed to become pastors in the Godang Sinode of the HKBP Protestant Church (1994, 127).

17. Kohlberg relates a higher stage of moral development to an awareness of the emotions aroused by a moral situation, the formulation of alternative courses of action, and the taking of action on the basis of moral judgments (1984, 257).

moral development in a time of profound social change and shifting gender ideologies among middle-class Christian Indonesian women and men.

Feminist theorists from many cultures value independent agency as a mark of women asserting their status as subjects. But the form of that agency varies and can easily be misinterpreted or missed altogether by researchers doing cross-cultural work. Chapter 10 will discuss the interrelationship of broad feminist values and the expression of those values in particular cultural contexts.

10

Feminist Theory versus Advocacy
An Integrative Approach

Feminist theories arise out of intellectual movements found partly within the academy and partly within women's social and political efforts to end oppression" (Russell and Clarkson 1996, 116f.). The dual role that develops from these origins includes critical analysis of forces that produce gender inequality and advocacy to redress those inequalities. This agenda automatically produces a tension between the critical distance presumed necessary for "objective" study and the involved valuing stance of advocacy.

This tension is complicated by feminist methodologies that construct theory from experience, which also reduces critical distance. A focus on relationality further involves feminist researchers with their area of study. Add to this the problem of evaluating what constitutes gender equality when a researcher is studying gender oppression in another society, and the complexities of feminist theory and practice begin to come into focus.

The research necessary to analyze gender oppression usually spans a number of social science disciplines: sociology of religion, social psychology, cultural anthropology, and social theory, to name a few. Those disciplines are also theory and are value laden. Doing feminist studies across cultures necessitates critical evaluation of these crosscurrents among academic disciplines, advocacy, theories, and values.

Articulation of one's theoretical perspectives and values allows critical analysis to begin with awareness. If one is doing research across cultures, openness to the theories and values of those in that society is a next step. Understanding our own values as Western feminists and persons of a particular ethnic group, geographic location, socioeconomic class, and religious persuasion prepares us for encountering views of others with openness.

Western Feminist Values

That women and men are both endowed with abilities to think rationally, reason about values, and appreciate beauty is a premise of this study. The questions that are explored assume that men and women can, with equal facility, create ideas, develop leadership qualities, produce institutions and structures of society, and sustain systems of values and communal relationships. Feminist scholarship in religion works from this valuing position. Feminist critiques of history and social structures foster the critical process of reclaiming the biological and relational dimensions of women's experience without succumbing to an erroneous view of women as more "natural" and less "intellectual" than men.

The 1990s saw a proliferation of feminist writings on religion and reproductions of collections of historical writings: spiritual writings, prose and poetry.[1] Formal religions are being reexamined from women's perspectives. Numerous works on women in world religions have appeared, describing women's traditional "place" in the religion and outlining new theologies that challenge oppressive customs.[2] These works devise religion-identified resistance strategies and woman-affirming resistance theologies that remain true to the spirit of world religions.[3]

   1. A wide range of voices is heard in these writings, which include storytelling, Jungian psychology, Goddess worship, and monastic prayers.
   2. *Sacred Texts by and about Women*, edited by Serenity Young, introduces readers to views of women in historical traditions of major world religions (1995). Cooey Eakin, and McDaniel (1991) and Rita Gross (1993, 289) explore postpatriarchal feminist revisions of those traditions.
   3. For Indonesian views, see *Wanita dalam Percakapan Antar Agama: Aktualisasinya dalam Pembangunan* (Women in interreligious dialog: Actualization in devel-

Religion is not a prerequisite in the current explorations of identity and values by feminist scholars. Emily Culpepper, an atheist and "free thinker," relates her journey to a sense of the sacred (Cooey 1991, 146–65). African-American novelists Alice Walker and Toni Morrison describe their journeys in relation to spiritual roots that arose long ago in Africa. Jeanne Brooks Carritt speaks of the sacredness of women's bodies as they age in an era in the West when both sacredness and old age are denigrated (Gray 1988, 232–39).

Those feminist values are not shared by everyone in North America. They enjoy even less common assent in Indonesia. As a Westerner, working and teaching in Indonesia, can I assume that those values are applicable across cultures? Can I communicate them without doing harm to the cultural forms already in place in Indonesian society?[4] Can I practice them without inadvertently communicating that my way of resisting inequality or expressing equality is the right way, or even the only way? Can gender equality be practiced in ways that harmonize with Indonesian culture?

Valuing Gender Equality Across Cultures

The realization that modern Western understandings of knowledge arose in a specific historical-cultural setting influences our understanding of values in this century.[5]

If values are so tied to cultural milieu, how can we justify carrying

---

opment) (Mashruchan 1992) and *Spiritualitas Baru: Agama dan Aspirasi Rakyat* (New spiritualities: Religion and the aspirations of the people) (Sumartana 1993, 302).

    4. I use the term "cultural forms" to refer to symbols and customs that carry meanings for the society as a whole. Clifford Geertz defines culture as "an historically transmitted pattern of meanings embodied in symbols, a system of inherited conceptions expressed in symbolic forms by means of which men communicate, perpetuate, and develop their knowledge about and attitudes toward life" (1973, 89).

    5. Karl Mannheim's study *Ideology and Utopia* was intended to show that science was objective while other viewpoints were ideological. Instead, Mannheim's study convinced him of the ideological component of science itself ([1929] 1985). This discovery spawned the discussion in social theory known as the sociology of knowledge.

feminist values into other contexts? Michael Polanyi argues for a fiduciary element to knowledge (1958). All knowledge springs from unprovable assumptions. Scientific experiments, for example, are predicated on a belief in the uniformity of natural processes. Intellectual discourse in the West is predicated on notions of logic and consistency. Both assumptions spring from Western narratives of world construction.

Yet both are used to analyze and evaluate phenomena. When used in diagnosing illness, the scientific assumption of uniformity of natural processes is challenged by psychological and social complexities of human organisms (Benner 1984). When Western logic is applied to Eastern contexts, the certainty of either-or logic becomes strained. But neither science nor logic could yield knowledge unless those presuppositions were held consistently within a particular context.

Not only assumptions but also values are held with the conviction that they are applicable to other situations. Charles Taylor argues that people in the modern West hold to a set of "universal values" that includes ideals of freedom, equality, justice, and benevolence (1989). The moral sources used to define and outline those evaluations differ from culture to culture. But Taylor argues that moral evaluation is at the center of human identity. Persons gain a sense of their identity through the strong evaluations they make about what is good, and how that understanding directs their lives. Moral convictions cannot, then, be held lightly. Our perspective is situated, but we deem our values to be applicable to those in other contexts.

Using Theory while Honoring Values

Cultural anthropologists strive to study local understandings and values without imposing norms from their own society on their analysis.[6] No research study in any discipline operates without theories and

---

See *The Social Construction of Reality: A Treatise in the Sociology of Knowledge* (Berger and Luckmann 1967).

6. Clifford Geertz's notion of "local knowledge" is based on an assumption that knowledge in context is valid for a particular time and place. Through "thick descrip-

values that are contingent and culturally relative. The feminist scholar who presupposes experience and relationality as a basis for theory building is not more biased than the natural scientist who presupposes that knowledge is gained only through repeatable manipulation of physical objects.

Along with this "leveling" of views of truth in the postmodern era has come a new freedom for creative appropriation of indigenous values. Indonesian women, for instance, can embrace the validity of their own formulations of values and find affirmation for their points of view in the international scholarly community (Katoppo 1980; Murniati 1993; Kristnawati and Utrecht 1992).

Listening to other women and celebrating differences engenders both mutual respect and deeper creativity. In the pluralistic world of feminist theory and practice, women of various racial backgrounds and religious orientations meet together to find new meanings in their diversity. Cultural awareness replaces critical distance in this approach. Common values can be explored as a wider circle of discourse is created among feminists who value gender equality but express it in different ways.

The Mudflower Collective exemplifies this trend. A diverse group of North American women theologians met to discuss theological education. The interaction that occurred, however, went much deeper than developing curriculum. Discussions about meaning, racial oppression, and power arose. Heated letters were exchanged. Conflicts were worked through, and the resulting book, *God's Fierce Whimsy*, has been an asset to feminist educators (Cannon et al. 1985).

Valuing local knowledge has often presented problems for those working with people of other cultures whose values differ from their own. While respecting the normative structures of another culture, one cannot discard one's own values without risking a peculiarly

---

tion" he attempts to accurately record information from a culture without imposing value judgments or intellectual theories on that culture (1973, 6f.).

modern form of nihilism.[7] Tolerance for the values of another society needs to be balanced by an understanding and practicing of one's own convictions.

Interacting with another culture with differing values soon leads to a questioning of the generalizability of the values that one holds. Cultural forms of behavior and thinking are evaluated by one's own critical standard. The critical standard for this study is gender equality. On the face of it, this seems like a modern assumption: for us, as for all people at all times, and in all places, women and men are equal. The crucial difference lies in the understanding of our limited perspective, which pushes us to seek agreement on values rather than to impose our values on others.

Sharing a Value of Gender Equality with Indonesians

Many Indonesia women and men share the conviction of gender equality. Different sources for that conviction can be outlined, for example, human dignity, reason, biological similarity, and religious belief. Since Indonesians construct their social worlds in religious terms, many Indonesian Christian women find a source for the value of gender equality in theological warrant.[8] The sources for the value of gender equality need not be the same in order to hold agreement on the value itself.

For Westerners the tendency to universalize values can be seen as part of our way of knowing (Polanyi 1958). While we understand the cultural conditionedness of this value and the limitedness of our perceptions, we still hold the value of gender equality with conviction.

A Christian theological way of expressing this can be useful in

---

7. In "Humanism as Nihilism," Paul Rabinow argues that if cultural anthropologists attempt to make observations without value judgments, they cannot hold their own values and the values of the foreign culture without a loss of convictions (1983).

8. An example is Magdelena Tangkudung's thesis, "Mythos dan Kodrat" (Myth and fate), referred to in chapter 5 (1994). Tangkudung uses an interpretation of the biblical narratives of creation as a source for an ethic of gender equality.

connecting with Indonesian Christian theologians who also use theological warrant to uphold the value of gender equality: "Though we regard the universal, the image of the universal in our mind is not a universal image" is one Western way to state this idea (Niebuhr 1941, 10).

In this view, we apprehend our universally held values through our own historical narratives. Torajan women express gender equality through female leadership in religious ceremonies. Manado women carry their value of gender equality through strong assertions of equality in their family life and through active involvement in careers. Each sees the dignity and equality of all people from a particular perspective; each acts on it in unique ways. Realizing that we do not know all things, but understand values only from a limited perspective, we hold these beliefs confessionally. "We can proceed," Niebuhr states, "only by stating in simple, confessional form what has happened to us in our community, . . .how we reason about things and what we see from our point of view" (1941, 41). Although we see from a limited perspective, we believe that what we see is universal. The value of gender equality speaks of the worth and dignity of humans everywhere.

Whether Western feminists use this theological warrant for their belief in gender equality or whether they draw on other sources, by interacting with Indonesians who hold this value, we widen the circle of discourse that holds gender equality as a basic human value.

Creating Worth and Networks of Solidarity

Women from different cultures can benefit from working together around this shared value. This development allows women to critique views that are destructive to the interests of women. Carol Robb, for example, outlines what a "women-friendly" economy might look like.[9] Trusting women's perspectives on what is good leads to a cri-

---

9. Robb's critical standard for feminist ethics allows her to envision that women-friendly economy: "Feminist ethics is oriented toward the liberation of women and weighs the value of acts or policy in those terms" (1994, 16).

tique of what was formerly hidden—structures and practices that appear normal but actually hurt women.

Sharing ideas, working together, formulating strategies of resistance, and supporting one another's projects validates gender equality as a shared value. Recognizing that shared value then fosters solidarity and empowers women to carve out new space for work in the world. In the 1980s Nicaraguan women showed this kind of solidarity in action, forming support groups and networks during the Sandanista-Contra war (Adeney 1985). In the same decade in the United States women of color modeled this trend by joining forces to oppose gender-based oppression (Moraga and Anzuldua 1981).

Empowerment occurs as women affirm relationships within and across cultures, both as a spur to creativity and as a way of life. Women are realizing that many of their "monuments" to history are acts that sustain and nurture others. Connections based in gender equality can create a sense of worth, empowering women to value their contributions and to celebrate their life journeys.

The devaluing of women that necessitates the task of creating an awareness of worth is not a peculiarly North American phenomenon. Leila Ahmed reflects on her childhood experience in Egypt: "In childhood, I'd picked up this sense of contempt for women, and in particular the women around me—just from the air, from the books we read, the films we saw, the intangible attitudes at school and those in the world around me" (1999, 193).

Those attitudes can be reversed through religion-identified resistance, when women affirm one another in relationships and develop resistance theologies that reconstruct social realities. "To bring into being that which is only potential is an art form of living which binds women together," Elizabeth Dodson Gray remarks (1988).

Those bonds, often formed around ordinary practices, also create solidarity among women. For example, the mothers of National Basketball Association (NBA) players assembled in spring 2000 to play basketball together and to stitch a quilt made of old jerseys worn by their sons. The quilt was then auctioned off and the money given to charity. The event exemplifies the creative relationality of which

Gray speaks, which combines relating together as mothers and acting for the good of their communities.

Recent scholarship argues that a "we" can be constituted by everyday activities. This is a "feeling of solidarity that is usually passed over. It inspires us to a heightened activity precisely in the name of our ordinary ways of life" (Spinosa, Flores, and Dreyfus 1997, 137). This happens as women from different cultures develop conversations around the value of gender equality.

The Dilemma of Practice

There are many benefits of working on the basis of gender equality across cultures. The issue then becomes one of enacting that value appropriately in a given society. Sometimes the cultural forms that carry the shared conviction of gender equality in the West seem at variance with appropriate behavior in the Indonesian setting. Religion-identified resistance as well as practices that allow gender equality to flourish may differ. Let me illustrate this dilemma from my own experience.

As a American feminist professor I teach that all people are equal. I find sources for that value in reason, traditions of human rights and religion, feminist theory, and human dignity. Those sources result in claims that entitle every person to equal human rights and freedoms. Without gender qualifications, people can act upon their creative inclinations, fulfilling their potential. I teach gender equality and empowerment. I believe it is true.

Living and working in Indonesia presented difficulties as I attempted to embody and share this ethic of equality. I walked too fast, spoke too loudly, dressed in too-bright colors, and went out in the evenings and took overnight journeys unaccompanied by a male relative. Yet those actions displayed, for me, the values that I teach. Javanese standards of etiquette for married, middle-aged women seemed incompatible with the cultural forms through which I expressed my ethic of gender equality while in Indonesia. Sometimes I offended the sensibilities of my hosts. Sometimes in attempts to be sensitive to their standards, I hampered my ability to act.

Such cross-cultural dilemmas are increasingly common in our multicultural world. Overzealous accommodation to the norms of another culture can result in confusion about identity and values. In trying to honor all values, I actually honor none. However, confining the practices that spring from my valuing gender equality to my own Western context and not acting upon them in Indonesia, results in accepting oppressive structures in Javanese society without comment. I cannot simply practice gender equality at home in the United States. But if I offend local Javanese sensibilities too deeply by acting in culturally inappropriate ways, the value of gender equality itself will be obfuscated because my Indonesian hosts will lose respect for my actions.

Expressions of belief in human equality and dignity take on a cultural form. I walk fast because it is healthy for my body, because I value my limited time, and because I personally enjoy it. Walking fast is a resistance strategy of my own—an expression of my freedom to choose my own path in Indonesian society, which admires a womanly dignity that moves slowly and gracefully. It is a small example. But it can be multiplied a hundred times each week in various other situations. Small expressions of self-determination often veil larger issues.

If I accepted all of the Javanese cultural forms of etiquette for women, I believe I could not have fulfilled my task as a professor. I would have acted slowly, passively, and quietly. I would have stayed home unless accompanied by a man. I would have spoken too softly to be heard. I would have done little travel. Activities I participated in would have highlighted the importance of the men around me, and I would have attributed to them any credit for my own achievement. Taken together, those small actions amount to a self-imposed oppression of my dignity and value as a person. I could not passively accept what I considered to be oppression. Neither could I impose my uniquely Western ways of reducing gender inequalities upon those in Indonesia.

Feminists hold gender equality as a value that can benefit any society. Yet that value is mediated historically and narratively. Gender equality is, therefore, held differently in different contexts. Actions of resistance and creative practices and ideas that spring from the shared value of gender equality will be different for Indonesian women than for me, a North American. Feminists from any religious or cultural tradition may share their value of gender equality with women and men who share that value using sources from other traditions. But the expressions of gender equality will be particular and unique.

The Dilemma of Indonesian Professors

My own behavior as an American illustrates one side of the dilemma. But Indonesian professors confront the issue from another perspective. Women in Indonesia are increasingly gaining access to the education needed to become professors. Javanese politeness, however, demands that women be soft-spoken, reticent, and accommodating in their views. Those valued "feminine" qualities seem incompatible with the task of professors to communicate clearly in class, to express opinions boldly, to evaluate creatively, and to develop new lines of inquiry. A soft-spoken, polite, and intellectually malleable young woman will have a difficult time adequately fulfilling her role as professor.

This example is highlighted by an experience I had with an Indonesian professor from another university. I was asked to escort a Javanese woman professor of psychology to the library. Dressed in a traditional sarong (a very tight, full-length cloth wrapped as a skirt) and high-heeled slipper shoes with no back, *Ibu* Nona's walking style was extremely slow. She had a difficult time navigating the four long flights of stairs to reach the resources she needed. She asked only one or two cursory questions of the staff, not probing into the various options she might have used to find needed materials. The help she received from male staff at the library was minimal. The visit to the library took over one hour and proved fruitless. This professor cheerfully accepted her failure to find materials, thanked me politely for my time, and went on her way. As a Western colleague I was dismayed. But a Javanese cultural evaluation of her behavior would have deemed her actions fitting and her attitude admirable.

Moving Beyond the Dilemma: Recognizing the Problem

The first step in moving beyond this dilemma is to recognize it as a problem. There is value in preserving traditional practices. For *Ibu* Nona, Javanese dress and etiquette are an important expression of her identity as an Indonesian woman. The Indonesian professor should not have to leave behind her cultural style and become Westernized in her dress and attitudes. Yet I wonder why Professor Nona allows her work to be hampered by her adherence to cultural norms. A Western approach to library research would produce more results. It would look something like this: hurry up, seek staff help vigorously, leave no stone unturned in finding what you want. If *Ibu* Nona is aware that her style is hampering her work, I wonder why she does not change it.

This appraisal clearly shows my perspective as an achievement-oriented, career-conscious, Western woman. If changes in communication style, dress, or attitude enhance one's ability to accomplish a given task, it seems logical to my Western mind to take steps to make those changes (Adeney 1997). Career success is clearly a priority value from my point of view. Why does *Ibu* Nona not see it that way? No doubt the reasons are complex.

The Power of Not Understanding

I first need to recognize that I do not understand why following Indonesian norms of etiquette may be more important to *Ibu* Nona than doing those things that may, in my opinion, foster success in her chosen field. Recognizing that I do not have the knowledge necessary to understand her behavior is a first step toward mutual understanding. I become free to ask *Ibu* Nona about the practices that seem to inhibit her work, without taking a judgmental stance. That might foster a dialogue about the comparative value of Javanese etiquette and an ethic of efficient work.

That conversation could result in insightful suggestions by *Ibu* Nona about how the task might be done without sacrificing the cultural values of certain polite practices. Or, it might reveal that those cultural forms took priority, for *Ibu* Nona, over career advancement. Or, it might illumine the fact that those practices themselves constitute a subtle oppression. Perhaps a more direct approach would have even more disastrous effects on her career by alienating the staff at a university where she was a guest. In any case, insights, suggestions, and possible solutions would come from the Javanese professor herself, not from me, her Western guest. If the value of gender equality is clearly recognized as a shared value that cuts across the two cultures, then solutions coming out of the context itself would be culturally appropriate.

It is important to recognize, at the same time, that power is usually not given up freely. If men benefit from limitations placed on women through norms of politeness, probably the attempt to change those norms would be met with some resistance. Men could subtly ridicule the "fast-walking" professor. Ostracizing her politely would not be difficult in Javanese society. Indonesian women professors on our campus met this resistance by their own religion-identified resistance strategy—banding together to support one another and forming a gender studies research center. This approach to unconscious sexism arose from the cultural context, rich in self-understanding. The solutions that arose from within that milieu were culturally appropriate, resulting in the inclusion of the Gender Studies Center in the life of the university.

Inclusion may not come easily, however. Resistance to the Gender Studies Center caused tension on the campus. The leaders were described by some as "Westernized radicals." But the campus educational events sponsored by the Gender Studies Center are well attended. Undergraduates and professors are learning about gender oppression and how to change it.

Engaging in Cross-cultural Dialogue

As relationships and intellectual discourse develop among feminists across cultures, the value of equality can be recognized and implemented in culturally appropriate ways. I, as an outsider, must take care not to impose my patterns of behavior on a context in which people already feel badgered by Western imperialism. Conversely, I do practice my value of gender equality in cultural forms from my own context. For me to don a sarong and high-heeled slippers as professional attire would be culturally inappropriate. I can be accepted for who I am as a guest in Indonesia if I express my values in gentle, nonimposing ways. I even get tolerant smiles for walking fast.

Conversation across the two cultures becomes extremely important. As I periodically return to Indonesia, I continue to teach what I believe about the importance of gender equality. Yet, as time goes on, I do more and more listening. I try to understand if this value is accepted by my Indonesian students. Rather than attempt to interpret their experiences, I invite them to take center stage so that they may tell their own stories (Franzmann 2000, 109).

Usually, discussions on the topic of gender equality are met with delight by Indonesian women. It is an "aha" experience—"Yes" is their response. The men are, understandably, more cautious. But many men also respond positively when given the chance to express their hesitations, to explore their ambivalence, and to listen to women talk about their experiences of gender inequality.

Integrating Theory and Practice: A Hermeneutical Approach

Teaching feminist theory and practicing gender equality in another cultural setting involves a complex process of interaction (see Hermeneutic Circle).

1. *Present Experience.* I began that process as a person with a history, a culture, a community, and a set of strong evaluations. The sum of my experience was the starting place for interacting with another culture. Awareness of my cultural conditioning and limited perspective began the process of opening to the voice of the "other."

2. *Meeting the "Other."* When I went to Indonesia as a North American professor, I went to meet Indonesians and their society. I wanted to understand and accept them in their uniqueness and complexity. My goal was not to change their society but to understand it.

186 Theory and Method

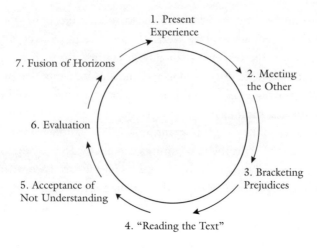

Hermeneutic Circle

Leaving moralistic agendas at home also prepared me to encounter the "other" with openness.

3. *Bracketing Prejudices.* In order to understand the values and thinking of another culture, I tried to put aside, temporarily, my own dearly held convictions. Rather than immediately evaluate every practice I encountered, I maintained an attitude of openness to foreign practices, differing understandings, and strange mores of another cultural world.[10] Laying aside my prejudices took practice and self-reminders that beneath what appeared to be strange was probably a rationale that I could understand if I allowed myself to listen.

4. *Reading the Text.*[11] Listening and learning about my new setting with an attitude of openness was the next step. I expected to learn and grow through the insights of Indonesian society. If my prejudices were bracketed, I need not evaluate practices on the basis of my own convictions, at least for a time. Even practices that seemed oppressive to women and contradicted my value of gender equality

---

10. Hans Georg Gadamer refers to "prejudices" as any valued conviction that may not be held by others (1975, 273).

11. Gadamer discusses this step as meeting the foreign text. Here I treat another society as the "text."

could be encountered with openness. Those practices could bring wisdom and depth to my understanding of Indonesian society and human values if I gave them a chance to speak on their own terms.[12]

5. *Acceptance of Not Understanding.* While I tried to remain open to Indonesian ways and mores, there were times when I could not accept them. The apparent contradictions with my own cherished values became too great. Believing in gender equality prevented me from accepting women's intellectual inferiority, for example.[13] After honestly struggling with the values of the "other," I concluded that there was no meeting ground on the issue of intellectual capacity related to gender. I simply did not understand. Accepting the totality of that difference became an important part of my own understanding.[14]

6. *Evaluation.* When I reached a point of not understanding, my openness to the foreign text gave way to evaluating the text from my own point of view. My acceptance of difference then formed a basis for evaluation and further interaction with the values of the "other." My own cultural values now came back into the conversation. Although I listened to the "other" with openness and a willingness to

12. An example from my experience is the practice of inviting my husband to lecture before I could be invited, even on a topic of my own expertise. This practice was frustrating and difficult to accept. Yet through listening and inquiring into reasons for this practice, I learned much about the dilemma of professional Indonesian men who are expected to honor traditional status hierarchies and at the same time need to utilize the achieved expertise of professors who may fall behind in traditional status hierarchies because they are women.

13. I encounter a similar problem in reading Aristotle's *Ethics.* As a foreign text, I attempt to be open to his ideas and have benefited greatly from his wisdom. However, I cannot understand his view that women do not possess practical reason. The incommensurability of my convictions with Aristotle's belief leads me to a point of nonunderstanding. I do not agree with Aristotle. Nor do I understand his reasons for his belief. And I cannot accept his conclusion about women.

14. Zaly Gurevitch at Hebrew University in Jerusalem taught me the "power of not understanding" through discussions and an unpublished paper of that name in 1989. In dialogue groups of Palestinians and Jews, he discovered that progress in understanding the "other" did not begin until an acceptance of an inability to understand the "other" was reached.

be changed, certain central convictions of my own clearly delineated points of difference with Indonesian values. I found myself at odds with certain aspects of traditional gender ideologies and certain practices that stemmed from those ideologies. I concluded that those ideas hampered women in their moral development and their ability to act in ways consistent with their full humanity. As that clarity arose, I could converse intelligently with those from the other culture.

7. *Fusion of Horizons*.[15] That dialogue resulted in my being changed by the values of Indonesian society. It also resulted in changes in Indonesian evaluations of gender issues. Those changes could be seen in the difference in my attitudes toward dress and politeness issues, and in new behaviors and thoughts related to gender issues on the part of my Indonesian students and colleagues.

8. *Experience*. At that point, I began to move around the circle again. The encounter with the "other" had changed my point of view, so the starting point of experience was a new starting point. As this learning and valuing process took place, understanding grew. Both my views and the understanding of Indonesians I worked with expanded.

Through this process, the interaction among feminist theorists and practitioners can create new cultural forms that express the value of gender equality across cultures. For the feminist scholar in another culture, becoming part of this process of change requires an attitude of openness toward people, a recognition of difference that sometimes results in irritation at strange cultural practices. It means realizing that, as a guest, there is much one does not comprehend about changing cultural understandings in the host culture. Understanding the move toward gender equality in Indonesia takes long conversations, striving together with others for new patterns of behavior that exhibit equality in culturally appropriate ways. These steps toward

---

15. Gadamer uses this term to refer to the new stance taken by one who has interacted with the foreign text with openness. The person has changed, and a new experience will be interpreted from a new perspective. He states, "The being of the interpreter pertains intrinsically to the being of what is to be interpreted" (1981, 136).

embodying the value of gender equality in a particular context take time and require effort and mutual acceptance.

I believe that those efforts are worthwhile. In 1998 I returned to Indonesia to teach at the university in Tomohon, north Sulawesi. There were twenty-four students in my class in feminist theology. Besides women there were six men, four of whom were Muslims. The openness of these students, who were from many cultures in Indonesia, to intercultural exchange on topics of gender and ethics was impressive. Their projects covered topics from oppression of women through cultural images to the rights of second wives. Despite differences, we shared a conversation, explored new possibilities, and envisioned more just social structures on both sides of the Pacific.

This experience confirmed to me the importance of research projects that are descriptive, narrative, and contextual. Those projects recognize the involvement of the researcher and take a stance on values. Such research is crucial for scholars who are seeking to continue a global conversation about meaning and values in a postmodern and multicultural world.

Appendix

Glossary

References

Index

Appendix
Dreyfus Skill Acquisition Model

According to Dreyfus, moral development can be understood as a kind of skill acquisition, similar to learning to drive or to play chess.[1] Development proceeds through five stages:

1. *Novice.* Applying rules. Decomposing the task, identifying features, and following a program of action. Application of nonsituated principles.

2. *Advanced Beginner.* Coping with a real situation. Observing examples of similar situations. Identifying salient aspects of the situation and maxims that may apply. Fitting maxims into the situation. This stage assumes some experience of applying rules.

3. *Competence.* A situation is observed and salient principles identified. An overwhelming number of features (of principles) and aspects (of the situation) present themselves. Therefore, a hierarchical view of decision making is adopted. This includes the following steps:

   a. *Detached planning.* Making a plan by choosing a goal and a perspective that organizes the situation.

   b. *Assessment of the relevant elements of the situation.* Paying attention only to features and aspects relevant to the goal.

   c. *Making a rule-guided choice.* Choosing the hierarchical model and assessing the relevant aspects of the situation simplifies decision making and improves performance.

   d. *An emotionally involved experience of the outcome.* Observing the out-

---

1. Model summarized from Hubert L. Dreyfus and Stuart E. Dreyfus, "What Is Moral Maturity? Towards a Phenomenology of Ethical Expertise," a paper given at the conference Ethics: Principles or Practices? sponsored by the National Endowment for the Humanities Ethics Institute, Stanford University, Calif., 1992. See chart in Dreyfus and Dreyfus (1986, 50).

come and reflecting on it: did it accomplish the goal? How were people affected?

4. *Proficiency.* When presented with a situation, one is "struck by" a plan or goal and takes a perspective immediately. The spell of involvement is not broken by detached, conscious planning. After perceiving what is going on, one thinks about what to do. As elements present themselves, they are assessed if salient and ignored if not. Engaged action is followed by emotional involvement with the outcome.

5. *Ethical Expertise.* After repeated applications at the proficiency level, ethical decisions become intuitive, almost automatic, without the need to invoke detached thinking about abstract principles.

Dreyfus and Dreyfus sum up their skill acquisition model for developing ethical expertise in this way: "It seems that beginners make judgments using strict rules and features, but that with talent and a great deal of involved experience the beginner develops into an expert who sees intuitively what to do without applying rules and making judgments at all."[2]

---

2. Dreyfus and Dreyfus 1992, 5.

Glossary

adat: Systems of informal, traditional religious laws of indigenous Indonesian culture groups. The laws cover family relationships, etiquette, social customs, and religious rites.

akal: Reason, the ability to think cognitively.

Bahasa Indonesia: A form of Malay, a common trade language in Southeast Asia, that was adopted in 1945 as the national language of Indonesia.

bapak: The literal meaning of this Indonesian word is "father." A shortened form, *Pak*, is used as a title for all older men, as "Mr." is used in English.

bapakism: The custom of referring all decisions to male figures in authority, seeing them as fathers. The common decision-making process in this system consists of the father figure sensing a consensus and stating it for the group. It is believed that his inner power enables him to do this.

Batik: Cloth dyed using a wax-resistant process. Repeated dyeing with wax applied to different sections of the cloth creates intricate colored patterns. Traditional batik patterns used for sarongs for court officials in Javanese palaces are done in brown and black tones. Other regions feature different color combinations in their traditional batik cloths.

becas: Bicycle-powered cabs that serve as taxis.

bejeis: Motorcycle-powered cabs that serve as taxis.

dalang: The storyteller who performs the *Wayang Kulit*, traditional puppet performances of ancient tales.

double burden: An expression used to refer to women's responsibilities at home and in the workplace.

embeddedness: The inextricable involvement with and influence of a researcher on a project.

gamelan: A set of traditional Javanese instruments consisting of brass gongs and xylophones, which are used to play traditional music on a twelve-tone scale.

hijab: Islamic head covering that covers the hair but leaves the face open.

horse dance: A traditional Javanese trance dance, done with stick horses, usually by young men.

ibu: The literal meaning of this Indonesian word is "mother." It is used as a polite title for all older women.

kebatinan: A Javanese discipline of meditation that strengthens one's life force and inner power.

kabaya: Form-fitting lace blouse open in the front. It was introduced by the European colonialists to be worn with the traditional Indonesian sarong, which was worn without a top in traditional societies.

kafir: A derogatory adjective referring to irreligious people who lack the refinement and morals expected by society.

kampung: A village or neighborhood in a large city, usually fairly uniform in socioeconomic and cultural-religious characteristics.

karawan: Cloth made in Manado, north Sulawesi, by an embroidery method that consists of pulling out threads of a piece of material and weaving back into the cloth threads of other colors.

kodrat: The destiny or fate of a woman to bear and care for children as the God-given task of her life. It is an Arabic word that has become part of Bahasa Indonesian, probably through Islamic influence.

Mahabharata: Traditional Hindu tales that tell epic stories of Javanese ancient gods and heroes. Contemporary motifs of a political, moral, or humorous nature are interwoven with these stories as they are performed today in villages throughout Indonesia.

makanan khas: Special regional foods that are typical of an area and brought back to friends and family when one visits that region, for example, peanut candy from Salatiga, Mikasa drink from south Sulawesi.

Manado: Major city and center of Minahasan culture in north Sulawesi.

matrifocal: Family arrangements that trace hereditary lineage through the mother's side of the family.

menikuti jalan hidupnya masing-masing: Literally, "following various roads in life." An expression that refers to a married couple who may live in the same dwelling but do not share life together.

Minahasa: A culture group in north Sulawesi that practices Christianity.

musafahat: Consensus-seeking group discussion of an issue of disagreement.

musyawarat: Consensus reached through group discussion.

omong-omong: Informal chatting or conversation.

Orang Jawa: Literally, "Java person." This phrase is used in Java to refer to a cultured person; to be civilized is to be Javanese.

other: The outsider, the stranger—one who is not understood or included.

Pancasila: The five-fold platform of Indonesian public ethics developed by Indonesia's liberator and first president, Sukarno. The five tenets of *Pancasila* are (1) belief in one God, (2) guided democracy, (3) nationalism, (4) humanitarianism, and (5) mutual cooperation.

Peranakan: People of Chinese and Indonesian racial heritage.

perspectivalism: An approach to information that stresses the limited point of view of the interpreter.

practice: An ordinary or ritual act, done intentionally and routinely, that with repetition becomes habitual.

Qur'an: The holy book of Islam, which is believed to be a literal Arabic dictation from God through the angel Gabriel to Muhammad in the seventh century C.E.

Ramayana: Traditional Hindu tales from India that tell epic stories of ancient gods and heroes.

Samangat: The spirit of life in a person that can be nurtured through meditation and clean living, fasting, prayer, and other forms of ascetic practice.

sarong: Cloth wrap used to cover the lower half of the body. Regionally defined traditional weaving or batik motifs are used. A man's sarong is sewed together to form a wide tube that is wrapped around the body. This cloth may be wrapped in a shortened or full-length manner and may also be used as a wrap to sleep under. A woman's sarong is an approximately two-yard length of cloth that is wrapped and folded around the waist.

Selamatan: Celebrations of welcome, given by family and neighbors, to honor and bless life passage events such as births, graduations, and marriages.

situatedness: The unavoidable contextual location of institutions in time and history.

Sopo Tresno: The first Indonesian women's movement working for the rights and welfare of women, 1914–23.

terus terang: Having an open and frank attitude toward others, shown by clear verbal communication of thoughts and feelings.

theologies: Systems of meaning-construction, related to understandings of the divine.

Toraja: A cultural region in mid-Sulawesi that practices elaborate funeral rites, which include gift exchange and the slaughter of water buffalo.

Wayang Kulit: Shadow puppet plays of ancient tales, played in all-night performances in villages. These plays feature Indonesian versions of the Hindu *Ramayana* tales and the five major gods of the Hindu *Mahabharata* stories.

References

Adeney, Frances S. 1979. "Frances Adeney." Chap. 6 in *Our Struggle to Serve*, edited by Virginia Hearn. Waco, Texas: Word Books.

———. 1980. *Empowering the Self: The Flowering of the Human Potential Movement*. Berkeley, Calif.: Berkeley Christian Coalition.

———. 1985. "Desert Blooms: Nicaraguan Women in the '80s." *Radix Magazine* 16, no. 5.

———. 1989. "Citizenship Ethics: Contributions of Classical Virtue Theory and Responsibility Ethics." Ph.D. diss., Graduate Theological Union.

———. 1991. Review of *Sources of the Self: The Making of the Modern Identity*, by Charles Taylor. *Theology Today* 48, no. 2:204–10.

———. 1993. "Spiritualitas Perempuan pada Era Post-Modern: Suatu Perspektif Internasional" (Women's spirituality in a post-modern era: An international perspective). In *Spiritualitas Baru: Agama dan Aspirasi Rakyat* (New spiritualities: Religion and the aspirations of the people), edited by P. Sumartana. Yogyakarta: Interfides Press.

———. 1994. "Political Ideologies." Chap. 6 in *The Unique Christ in a Pluralistic World*, edited by J. Nicholls. Carlisle, U.K.: Paternoster Press.

———. 1995a. "Kemitraan Gender Dalam Gereja Kristen di Indonesia Ini: Akibat Dua Faktor Sosiologis, Yaitu Ideologi Gender dan Sosialisasi Anak-anak" (Gender partnership in the Christian church in Indonesia: The effects of two sociological factors—Gender ideology and socialization of children). *Buletin Mahasiswa Sekolah Tinggi Teologi Jakarta* 1, no. 6:2–4.

———. 1995b. "Universal Values and Cultural Forms: A Study in Women's Equality Across Cultures." *Dialog* 34, no. 4.

———. 1997. "Bentuk Komunikasi dalam Pendidikan Teologi" (Forms of communication in theological education). In *Berikanlah Aku Air Hidup Itu: Bahan Sumber Studi Gender* (Give me living water: Source materials for gender studies), edited by Stephen Suleeman and Bendalina Souk. Jakarta: Terbitan Perhimpunan Sekolah-sekolah Theologia di Indonesia.

———. 1999. "A Matter of Veils." In *Ethics and World Religion: Cross-cultural Case Studies*, edited by Regina W. Wolfe and Christine C. Gudorf. Maryknoll, N.Y.: Orbis Books.

———. 2001. "Jean Bethke Elshtain: Political Theorist or Post Modern Prophet?" *Religious Studies Review* 27, no. 3 (July):13–16.

Adeney, Frances S., and Stephen Suleeman, eds. In Press. *Perempuan Indonesia Menerungkandiri atas Isu Kontemporer* (Indonesian Women Reflect on Contemporary Issues). Jakarta: G. K. Mulia.

Adler, Rachel. 1999. *Engendering Judaism: An Inclusive Theology and Ethics.* Boston: Beacon Press.

Ahmed, Leila. 1999. *A Border Passage: From Cairo to America—A Woman's Journey.* New York: Farrar, Straus and Giroux.

Allen, Linda. 2001. "Participation as Resistance: The Role of Pentecostal Christianity in Maintaining Identity for Marshallese Migrants Living in the Midwestern United States." *Journal of Ritual Studies* 15, no. 2:55–61.

Aminy, Aisyah. 1993. "Women and National Development." Interview in *Kompas* (August 29):2.

Anderson, Benedict R. O'G. 1990. *Language and Power: Exploring Political Cultures in Indonesia.* Ithaca, N.Y.: Cornell Univ. Press.

Andrews, William L., ed. 1986. *Sisters of the Spirit: Three Black Women's Autobiographies of the Nineteenth Century.* Bloomington, Ind.: Indiana Univ. Press.

Aristotle. 1952. *Nicomachean Ethics.* Translated by W. D. Ross. In Vol. 9 of *Great Books of the Western World*, edited by Robert Maynard Hutchins, 9:333–446. Chicago: Encyclopedia Britannica.

Atkinson, Jane Monnig, and Shelly Errington. 1990. *Power and Difference: Gender in Island Southeast Asia.* Stanford, Calif.: Stanford Univ. Press.

"Battle of the Sexes: Paternalistic Societies Are Challenged to Give Women a Break." 1993. *AsiaWeek* 19, no. 34 (August 25):22–23.

Bauer, Janet L. 1997. "The Mixed Blessings of Women's Fundamentalism: Democratic Impulses in a Patriarchal World." In *Mixed Blessings: Gender and Religious Fundamentalism Cross Culturally*, edited by Judy Brink and Joan Mencher. New York: Routledge.

Bauman, Zygmunt. 1993. *Postmodern Ethics.* Oxford: Blackwell Publishers.

Bednarowski, Mary Farrell. 1999. *The Religious Imagination of American Women.* Bloomington, Ind.: Indiana Univ. Press.

Belenky, Mary Field, Blythe McVicker Clinchy, Nancy Rue Goldberger, and Jill Mattuck Tarule, eds. 1986. *Women's Ways of Knowing: The Development of Self, Voice, and Mind.* New York: Basic Books.

Bellah, Robert N. 1970. "Religious Evolution." In *Beyond Belief: Essays on Religion in a Post-traditional World,* by Robert N. Bellah. San Francisco: Harper and Row.

Bellah, Robert N., Richard Madsen, William M. Sullivan, Ann Swidler, and Steven M. Tipton. 1985. *Habits of the Heart: Individualism and Commitment in American Life.* Berkeley and Los Angeles: Univ. of California Press.

———. 1991. *The Good Society.* New York: Random House.

Benner, Patricia. 1984. *From Novice to Expert: Excellence and Power in Clinical Nursing Practice.* Menlo Park, CA: Addison-Wesley.

Berger, Peter L. 1963. *Invitation to Sociology: A Humanistic Perspecitve.* Garden City, N.Y.: Anchor Books, Doubleday.

———. 1969. *The Sacred Canopy: Elements of a Sociological Theory of Religion.* Garden City, N.Y.: Anchor Books, Doubleday.

Berger, Peter L., and Thomas Luckmann. 1967. *The Social Construction of Reality: A Treatise in the Sociology of Knowledge.* Garden City, N.Y.: Anchor Books, Doubleday.

Bernstein, Richard. 1983. *Beyond Objectivism and Relativism: Science, Hermeneutics, and Praxis.* Philadelphia: Univ. of Pennsylvania Press.

Blackwood, Evelyn. 1995. "Senior Women, Model Mothers, and Dutiful Wives: Managing Gender Contradictions in a Minangkabau Village." In *Bewitching Women, Pious Men: Gender and Body Politics in Southeast Asia,* edited by Aihwa Ong and Michael G. Peletz. Berkeley and Los Angeles: Univ. of California Press.

———. 2001. "Representing Women: The Politics of Minangkabau *Adat* Writings." *The Journal of Asian Studies* 60, no. 1 (February):125–49.

Booth, Wayne C., Gregory G. Colomb, and Joseph M. Williams. 1995. *The Craft of Research.* Chicago: Univ. of Chicago Press.

Bos, Johanna. 1997. *Reformed and Feminist.* Louisville, Ky.: Westminster John Knox Press.

Bourdieu, Pierre. 1991. *Language and Symbolic Power.* Translated by Gino Raymond and Matthew Adamson. Cambridge: Harvard Univ. Press.

Brenner, Suzanne A. 1995. "Why Women Rule the Roost: Rethinking Javanese Ideologies of Gender and Self-Control." In *Bewitching Women, Pious Men: Gender and Body Politics in Southeast Asia,* edited by

Aihwa Ong and Michael G. Peletz. Berkeley and Los Angeles: Univ. of California Press.

Brink, Judy, and Joan Mencher, eds. 1997. *Mixed Blessings: Gender and Religious Fundamentalism Cross Culturally.* New York: Routledge.

Butler, Katy. 1997. "The Anatomy of Resilience." In *Family Therapy Networker* (March-April):22–31.

Cannon, Katie G., et al. (Mud Flower Collective). 1985. *God's Fierce Whimsy: Christian Feminism and Theological Education.* New York: Pilgrim Press.

Carey, Peter, and Vincent Houben. 1987. "Spirited Srikandhis and Sly Sumbadras: The Social, Political and Economic Role of Women at the Central Javanese Courts in the Eighteenth and Early Nineteenth Centuries." In *Indonesian Women in Focus: Past and Present Notions,* edited by Elsbeth Locher-Scholten and Anke Niehof. Dordrecht, Holland: Foris.

Carmody, Denise. 1995. *Christian Feminist Theology.* Oxford: Blackwell.

Carroll, Lewis. 1935. *Alice's Adventures in Wonderland.* New York: Dial Press.

Casey, Ethan. "A Nation Out of Control?" *Christianity Today* 41, no.3 (March 3):50.

Christ, Carol P. 1998. *Rebirth of the Goddess: Finding Meaning in Feminist Spirituality.* New York: Routledge.

Chung, Hyun Kyung. 1990. *Struggle to Be the Sun Again: Introducing Asian Women's Theology.* Maryknoll, N.Y.: Orbis Books.

——. 1991. "Welcome the Spirit; Hear Her Cries: The Holy Spirit, Creation, and the Culture of Life." *CrossCurrents* 51 (July 15):220–23.

Cohen, Margot. 1997. "Indonesia: Religion, Climate of Distrust." *Index on Censorship* 26, no. 2 (February).

Collins, Elizabeth. 1998. "Reflections on Ritual and on Theorizing about Ritual." *Journal of Ritual Studies* 12, no. 1 (summer):1–7.

Cooey, Paula M., William R. Eakin, and Jay B. McDaniel, eds. 1991. *After Patriarchy: Feminist Transformations of the World Religions.* Maryknoll, N.Y.: Orbis Books.

Daly, Lois K., ed. 1994. *Feminist Theological Ethics: A Reader.* Louisville, Ky.: Westminster John Knox Press.

D'Aulaire, Ingri, and Edgar Parin, eds. 1962. *Book of Greek Myths.* New York: Doubleday.

Dawood, N. J., trans. 1997. *The Koran.* 5th ed. New York: Penguin Books.

Day, Dorothy. 1952. *The Long Loneliness: An Autobiography*. San Francisco: Harper and Row.

Dowling, Collette. 1981. *The Cinderella Complex: Women's Hidden Fear of Independence*. New York: Pocket Books.

Dreyfus, Hubert L., and Stuart E. Dreyfus. 1986. *Mind over Machine: The Power of Human Intuition and Expertise in the Era of the Computer*. New York: Free Press.

———. 1992. "What Is Moral Maturity? Towards a Phenomenology of Ethical Expertise." Paper included in the National Endowment for the Humanities Ethics Institute advanced readings for the conference Ethics: Principles or Practices, Stanford Univ., Calif. Published in *Revisioning Philosophy*, edited by James Ogilvy. Albany: State Univ. of New York Press.

Echols, John M., and Hassan Shadily. 1989. *Kamus Indonesia Inggris: An Indonesian-English Dictionary*. 3d ed. Jakarta: Gramedia Press.

Eisland, Nancy. 1997. "A Strange Road Home: Adult Female Converts to Classical Pentecostalism." In *Mixed Blessings: Gender and Religious Fundamentalism Cross Culturally*, edited by Judy Brink and Joan Mencher. New York: Routledge.

Engineer, Ali Asghar. 1992. "Islam and Social Liberation." *Islam Iman* (November-December).

Estes, Clarissa Pinkola. 1992. *Women Who Run with the Wolves: Myths and Stories of the Wild Woman Archetype*. New York: Ballantine Books.

Falk, Nancy Auer, and Rita M. Gross. 1989. *Unspoken Worlds: Women's Religious Lives*. Belmont, Calif.: Wadsworth Publishing.

Famighelli, Robert, ed. 1996. *World Almanac and Book of Facts 1997*. Mahwah, N.J.: World Almanac Books.

Fautre, Willy, ed. 2000. Press and Information Service Section: "Religious Intolerance and Discrimination. *International Secretariat*. 2000. *Human Rights Without Frontiers*. Http:.www.hrwf.net.

Fischer, Clare. 1994. "Ratu Kadul: Queen of the South Seas." In *The Folk Art of Java*, by Joseph Fischer. New York: Oxford Univ. Press.

Fischer, Clare, with Luh Estiti Andarawati. 1998. "Tooth-Filing in Bali: One Woman's Experience." *Journal of Ritual Studies* 12, no. 1 (summer):39–46.

Fischer, Joseph. 1994. *The Folk Art of Java*. New York : Oxford Univ. Press.

Franzmann, Majella. 2000. *Women and Religion*. New York : Oxford Univ. Press.

Friedan, Betty. 1963. *The Feminine Mystique.* New York: W. W. Norton.

Fulkerson, Mary McClintock. Quoted in Mary Farrell Bednarowski, *The Religious Imagination of American Women.* (Bloomington, Ind.: Indiana Univ. Press, 1999), 146.

Gadamer, Hans Georg. 1975. *Truth and Method.* New York: Seabury Press.

———. 1981. *Reason in the Age of Science.* Translated by Frederick G. Lawrence. Cambridge, Mass.: MIT Press.

Geertz, Clifford. 1960. *The Religion of Java.* Glencoe, Ill.: Free Press.

———. 1973. *The Interpretation of Cultures.* New York: Basic Books.

Gilligan, Carol. 1982. *In a Different Voice: Psychological Theory and Women's Development.* Cambridge: Harvard Univ. Press.

Gilligan, Carol. 1988a. "Introduction." In *Mapping the Moral Domain: A Contribution of Women's Thinking to Psychological Theory and Education,* edited by Carol Gilligan, Janie Victoria Ward, and Jill McLean Taylor. Cambridge: Center for the Study of Gender, Education, and Human Development, Harvard Univ.

Gilligan, Carol, Janie Victoria Ward, and Jill McLean Taylor, eds. 1988b. *Mapping the Moral Domain: A Contribution of Women's Thinking to Psychological Theory and Education.* Cambridge: Center for the Study of Gender, Education, and Human Development, Harvard Univ.

Gittons, Anthony J. 1989. *Gifts and Stangers: Meeting the Challenge of Inculturation.* New York: Paulist Press.

Gray, Elizabeth Dodson, ed. 1988. *Sacred Dimensions of Women's Experience.* Wellesley, Mass.: Roundtable Press.

Grob, Leonard, Riffat Hassan, and Haim Gordon, eds. 1991. *Women's and Men's Liberation: Testimonies of Spirit.* New York: Greenwood Press.

Gross, Rita. 1993. *Buddhism after Patriarchy: A Feminist History, Analysis, and Reconstruction of Buddhism.* Albany, N.Y.: State Univ. of New York Press.

———. 1996. *Feminism and Religion: An Introduction.* Boston: Beacon Press.

Gurevitch, Zaly. 1989. "The Power of Not Understanding." Unpublished paper.

Habermas, Jürgen. 1979. *Communication and the Evolution of Societies.* Translated by Thomas McCarthy. Boston: Beacon Press.

———. 1984. *A Theory of Communicative Action: Reasons and the Rationalization of Society.* Vol. 1. Translated by Thomas McCarthy. New York: Beacon Press.

Hardesty, Nancy A. 1984. *Women Called to Witness: Evangelical Feminism in the Nineteenth Century.* Nashville: Abingdon Press.

Harris, Solomon. 1997. "Ritual: Communication and Meaning." *Journal of Ritual Studies* 11, no. 1 (spring):35–44.

Harrison, Beverly. 1985. "The Role of Anger in the Work of Love." Chap. 1 in *Making the Connections: Essays in Feminist Social Ethics*, edited by Beverly Harrison and Carol Robb. Boston: Beacon Press.

Harrison, Beverly, and Carol Robb, eds. 1985. *Making the Connections: Essays in Feminist Social Ethics.* Boston: Beacon Press.

Haryati, Soebadio Saparinah Sadli. 1990. *Kartini Pribadi Mandiri* (Kartini stands alone). Jakarta: Gramedia.

Hellwig, Liesbeth. 1987. "Prostitution: A Necessary Evil, Particularly in the Colonies; Views on Prostitution in The Netherlands Indies." In *Indonesian Women in Focus: Past and Present Notions*, edited by Elsbeth Locher-Scholten and Anke Niehof. Dordrecht, Holland: Foris Publications.

Hoskins, Janet. 1993. *The Play of Time: Kodi Perspectives on Calendars, History, and Exchange.* Berkeley and Los Angeles: Univ. of California Press.

Howell, Signe. 1997. *The Ethnography of Moralities.* New York: Routledge.

Hutahaean, Nelly M. 1994. "Keluarga Kristen Dalam Pekembangan Gereja" (The Christian family in the growth of the church). Master's thesis, Satya Wacana Christian Univ.

Index on Censorship. 1997. Vol. 26, no. 3 (March-April):25.

Kanyoro, Musimbi, and Mercy Oduyoye, eds. 1994. *The Will to Arise: Woman, Tradition, and the Church in Africa.* Maryknoll, N.Y.: Orbis Books.

Kartowijono, N. Y. Sujatin. 1982. *Perkembangan Pergerakan Wanita Indonesia.* Jakarta: PT Inti Idayu Press.

Katoppo, Marianne. 1980. *Compassionate and Free: An Asian Woman's Theology.* Maryknoll, N.Y.: Orbis Books.

Keane, Webb. 1997. *Signs of Recognition: Powers and Hazards of Representation in an Indonesian Society.* Berkeley and Los Angeles: Univ. of California Press.

Kettay, Eva Feder, and Kiana T. Meyers. 1987. *Women and Moral Theory.* Totowa, N.J.: Rowman and Littlefield.

King, Ursula, ed. 1994. *Feminist Theologies from the Third World.* Maryknoll, N.Y.: Orbis Books.

Kobong, Bunga. 1995. "Aluk Tedoro: Agama Torajah dalam Perasaan Perempuan" (Aluk Tedoro: The role of women in Torajan religion). Master's thesis, Satya Wacana Christian Univ.

Koentjaraningrat. 1985. *Javanese Culture.* Singapore: Oxford Univ. Press, Institute of Southeast Asian Studies.

Kohlberg, Lawrence. 1984. *Essays on Moral Development.* Vol. 2 of *The Psychology of Moral Development: The Nature and Validity of Moral States.* San Francisco: Harper and Row.

Krier, Jennifer. 1995a. "Disruptive Discourses." In *Bewitching Women, Pious Men: Gender and Body Politics in Southeast Asia,* edited by Aihwa Ong and Michael G. Peletz. Berkeley and Los Angeles: Univ. of California Press.

———. 1995b. "Narrating Herself: Power and Gender in a Minangkabau Woman's Tale of Conflict." In *Bewitching Women, Pious Men: Gender and Body Politics in Southeast Asia,* edited by Aihwa Ong and Michael G. Peletz. Berkeley and Los Angeles: Univ. of California Press.

Krisnawati, Tati, and Artien Utrecht. 1992. "Women's Economic Mediation: The Case of Female Petty Traders in Northwest Lombok." In *Women and Mediation in Indonesia,* edited by Sita van Bemmelen, Madelon Djajadiningrat-Nieuwenhuis, Elsbeth Locher-Scholten, and Elly Touwen-Bouwsma. Leiden: KITLV Press.

Kuhn, Thomas. 1970. *The Structure of Scientific Revolutions.* 2d ed. Chicago: Univ. of Chicago Press.

Kuipers, Joel C. 1998. *Language, Identity, and Marginality in Indonesia: The Changing Nature of Ritual Speech on the Island of Sumba.* Cambridge: Cambridge Univ. Press.

Layanan Kliping. 1992. *Kajian Keperempuanan: Dari Kodrat Hingga Iptek.* Edisi no. 1. Salatiga, Indonesia: Yayasan Bina Darma.

Lincoln, Bruce. 1999. "Theses on Method." In *The Insider/Outsider Problem in the Study of Religion: A Reader,* edited by Russell T. McCutcheon. New York: Cassell.

Locher-Scholten, Elsbeth, and Anke Niehof, eds. 1987. *Indonesian Women in Focus: Past and Present Notions.* Dordrecht, Holland: Foris Publications.

MacIntyre, Alasdair. 1981. *After Virtue: A Study in Moral Theory.* Notre Dame, Ind.: Univ. of Notre Dame Press.

Manderson, Lenore, ed. 1983. *Women's Work and Women's Roles: Economics and Everyday Life in Indonesia, Malaysia, and Singapore.* Canberra, Australia: Australian National Univ. Press.

Mannheim, Karl. [1929] 1985. *Ideology and Utopia: An Introduction to the Sociology of Knowledge.* Translated by Louis Wirth and Edward Shils. Reprint, New York: Harcourt, Brace.

Marwah, Daud Ibrahim. 1993. "Muslimah dan Modernisasi" (Islam and modernization). In *Femina* 11 (March):8–9.

Mashruchan, M. Mayhur Amin, ed. 1992. *Wanita dalam Percakapan Antar Agama: Aktualisasinya dalam Pembangunan* (Women in interreligious dialogue: Actualization in development). Yogyakarta: LKPSM NU DIY.

Massanari, Ronald L. 1991. "Sexual Imagery and Religion: An Intercultural Exploration of the Linga-Yoni and Temples at Khajuraho." *Journal of Gender in World Religions* 2:1–13.

Matuli-Waland, A. P., and Jan V. Matuli. 1989. *Women's Emancipation in North Sulawesi: The Story of Maria Walanda-Maramis.* Jakarta: Pustaka Sinar Harapan.

Mazumdar, Shampa, and Sanjoy Mazumdar. 1999. "Ritual Lives of Muslim Women: Agency in Everyday Life." *Journal of Ritual Studies* 13, no. 2:58–70.

McCoy, Charles C. 1980. *When Gods Change: Hope for Theology.* Nashville: Abingdon Press.

McCutcheon, Russell T., ed. 1999. *The Insider/Outsider Problem in the Study of Religion: A Reader.* New York: Cassell.

Mead, George Herbert. 1934. *Mind, Self, and Society.* Chicago: Univ. of Chicago Press.

Meehan, Bridget May. 1995. *Praying with Passionate Women: Mystics, Martyrs, and Mentors.* New York: Crossroad Books.

Moraga, Cherrie, and Gloria Anzuldua, eds. 1981. *This Bridge Called My Back: Writings by Radical Women of Color.* New York: Kitchen Table, Women of Color Press.

Morgan, Marabel. 1973. *The Total Woman.* Old Tappan, N.J.: Fleming H. Revell.

Murdiati, Diati Ganis, Kartini Sabekti, and Sabarish, eds. 1985. *The Women of Indonesia.* Rev. ed. Jakarta: Department of Information, Republic of Indonesia, in cooperation with the Office of the Minister of State for the Role of Women.

Murniati, Nunuk Prasetyo. 1993. "Dari Belis Menuju Kemerdekaan" (From slavery to freedom). *Hidup* 47, no.3 (August 8):8–10.

Muskens, M. P. M. 1970. *Indonesie Een Strijd om Nationale Identiteit: Nationalisten/Islamieten/Katholieken* (Indonesia constructs a national identity: Nationalization, immigration, and unity). Uitgeverij Paul Brand, Tweede druk Bussum.

Niebuhr, H. Richard. 1941. *The Meaning of Revelation*. New York: Macmillan.

———. 1963. *The Responsible Self*. New York: Harper and Row.

Nussbaum, Martha. 1986. *The Fragility of Goodness*. Cambridge: Cambridge Univ. Press.

Oduyoye, Mercy Amba, and Musimbi R. A. Kanyoro, eds. 1994. *The Will to Arise: Women, Tradition and the Church in Africa*. Maryknoll, N.Y.: Orbis Books.

Oey, Eric, ed. 1989. *Indonesia*. Singapore: APA Publications.

Ong, Aihwa, and Michael G. Peletz, eds. 1995. *Bewitching Women, Pious Men: Gender and Body Politics in Southeast Asia*. Berkeley and Los Angeles: Univ. of California Press.

Parks, Sharon. 1988. "Eating and Home as Ritual Space." In *Sacred Dimensions of Women's Experience*, edited by Elizabeth Dodson Gray. Wellesley, Mass.: Roundtable Press.

Parsons, Talcott. 1977. *The Evolution of Societies*. Englewood Cliffs, N.J.: Prentice-Hall.

Pembaruan Minggu. 1988. (April 4):5–6.

Plaskow, Judith. 1979. *Womenspirit Rising: A Feminist Reader in Religion*. San Francisco: Harper and Row.

Plaskow, Judith, and Carol Christ. 1989. *Weaving the Visions: New Patterns in Feminist Spirituality*. San Francisco: Harper and Row.

Polanyi, Michael. 1958. *Personal Knowledge: Towards a Post-Critical Philosophy*. Chicago: Univ. of Chicago Press.

Porterfield, Amanda. 1998. *The Power of Religion: A Comparative Introduction*. Oxford: Oxford Univ. Press.

———. 2001. *The Transformation of American Religion: The Story of a Late-Twentieth-Century Awakening*. Oxford: Oxford Univ. Press.

Postel-Coster, Els. 1987. "The Image of Women in Minankabau Fiction." In *Indonesian Women in Focus: Past and Present Notions*, edited by Elsbeth Locher-Scholten and Anke Niehof. Dordrecht: Foris Publications.

Pucci, Idanna. 1992. *Bhima Swarga: The Balinese Journey of the Soul*. Boston: Little, Brown.

Rabinow, Paul. 1983. "Humanism as Nihilism: The Bracketing of Truth and Seriousness in American Cultural Anthropology." In *Social Science as Moral Inquiry*, edited by Norma Haan, Robert N. Bellah, Paul Rabinow, and William M. Sullivan. New York: Columbia Univ. Press.

Ramage, Douglas E. 1995. *Politics in Indonesia: Democracy, Islam and the Ideology of Tolerance.* New York: Routledge.

Rappaport, Roy A. 1999. *Ritual and Religion in the Making of Humanity.* Cambridge: Cambridge Univ. Press.

"Restive Indonesians Find Little Hope in Vote." 1997. *New York Times,* May 29.

Riceour, Paul. 1981. "Science and Ideology." In *Hermeneutics and the Human Sciences,* edited by John B. Thompson. Cambridge: Cambridge Univ. Press.

Robb, Carol. 1994. "A Framework for Feminist Ethics." In *Feminist Theological Ethics: A Reader,* edited by Lois K. Daly. Louisville: Westminster John Knox Press.

Roth, John K., ed. 2000. *World Philosophers and Their Works.* Vol. 1. Pasadena: Salem.

Royce, Josiah. 1913. *The Problem of Christianity.* 2 vols. New York: Macmillan.

Ruether, Rosemary Radford. 2000. *In Our Own Voices.* Louisville: Westminster John Knox Press.

Ruggiero, Vincent. 1984. *The Moral Imperative.* 2d ed. Mountain View, Calif.: Mayfield Publishing.

Russell, Letty M., and J. Shannon Clarkson, eds. 1996. *Dictionary of Feminist Theologies.* Louisville, Ky.: Westminster John Knox Press.

Sayers, Dorothy L. 1971. *Are Women Human?* Downers Grove, Il.: Intervarsity Press.

Scanzoni, Letha, and Nancy Hardesty. 1974. *All We're Meant to Be.* Waco, Tex.: Word Books.

Schussler-Fiorenza, Elizabeth. 1983. *In Memory of Her: A Feminist Reconstruction of Christian Origins.* New York: Crossroads.

Sears, Laurie, ed. 1996. *Fantasizing the Feminine in Indonesia.* Durham, N.C.: Duke Univ. Press.

Shaw, Rosalind. 1999. "Feminist Anthropology and the Gendering of Religious Studies." In *The Insider/Outsider Problem in the Study of Religion: A Reader,* edited by Russell T. McCutcheon, 104–23. London: Cassell.

Sher, George. 1987. "Other Voices, Other Rooms? Women's Psychology and Moral Theory." In *Women and Moral Theory,* edited by Eva Feder Kettay and Kiana T. Meyers. Totowa, N.J.: Rowman and Littlefield.

Shiva, Vananda. 1989. *Staying Alive: Women, Ecology and Development.* London: Zed Books.

Sidharta, Myra. 1987. "The Making of the Indonesian Chinese Woman." In *Indonesian Women in Focus: Past and Present Notions,* edited by Elsbeth Locher-Scholten and Anke Niehof. Dordrecht, Holland: Foris Publications.

Smith, Archie. 1982. *The Relational Self: Ethics and Theology from a Black Church Perspective.* Nashville: Abingdon Press.

Smyth, Ines. 1992. "Indonesian Women as (Economic) Mediators." In *Women and Mediation in Indonesia: Some Comments on Concepts,* edited by Sita van Bemmelen, Madelon Djajadiningrat-Nieuwenhuis, Elsbeth Locher-Scholten, and Elly Touwen-Bouwsma. Leiden, The Netherlands: KITLV Press.

Spinosa, Charles, Fernando Flores, and Hubert L. Dreyfus. 1997. *Disclosing New Worlds: Entrepreneurship, Democratic Action, and the Cultivation of Solidarity.* Cambridge, Mass.: MIT Press.

Stoler, Ann Laura. 1996. "A Sentimental Education: Native Servants and the Cultivation of European Children in The Netherlands Indies." In *Fantasizing the Feminine in Indonesia,* edited by Laurie Sears. Durham, N.C.: Duke Univ. Press.

Stout, Jeffrey. 1990. *Ethics after Babel: The Language of Morals and Their Discontents.* Boston: Beacon Press.

Suleeman, Stephen. 2001. "Indonesian Women in Media: A Portrait of Patriarchy." Unpublished paper.

Suleeman, Stephen, and Bendalina Souk, eds. 1997. *Berikanlah Aku Air Hidup Itu: Bahan Sumber Studi Gender* (Give me living water: Source materials for gender studies). Jakarta: Terbitan Perhimpunan Sekolah-sekolah Theologia di Indonesia.

Sullivan, Norma. 1983. "Indonesian Women in Development: State Theory and Urban Kampung Practice." In *Women's Work and Women's Roles: Economics and Everyday Life in Indonesia,* edited by Lenore Manderson. Canberra: Australian National Univ.

———. 1994. *Masters and Managers: A Study of Gender Relations in Urban Java.* St. Leonards, Australia: Allen and Unwin.

Sumartana, P., ed. 1993. *Spiritualitas Baru: Agama dan Aspirasi Rakyat* (New spiritualities: Religion and the aspirations of the people). Yogyakarta: Interfides Press.

Tan, Mely, ed. 1991. *Perempuan Indonesia: Pemimpin Masa Depan?* (Indonesian women: Leaders of the future?). Jakarta: Pustaka Sinar Harapan.

Tangkudung, Magdelena H. 1994. "Mitos dan Kodrat: Suatu Kajian Mengenai Kedudukan dan Peranan Wanita Kristen di Minahasa" (Myth and fate: One view of the status and roles of Christian women in Minahasa). Master's thesis, Satya Wacana Christian Univ.

Tannen, Deborah. 1990. *You Just Don't Understand: Women and Men in Conversation*. New York: Ballantine Books.

Taylor, Charles. 1985. *Philosophical Papers*. Vol. 2. Cambridge: Cambridge Univ. Press.

———. 1989. *Sources of the Self: The Making of the Modern Identity*. Cambridge: Harvard Univ. Press.

Tilaar, Martha. 1991. "Citra Wanita Indonesia Tahun 2000: Kemandirian Dalam Menjawab Tantangan Pembangunan" (Vision for Indonesian women in the year 2000: Independence in responding to the challenge of development). In *Perempuan Indonesia: Pemimpin Masa Depan?* edited by Mely Tan, 64–73. Jakarta: Pustaka Sinar Harapan.

van Bemmelen, Sita. 1992. *Women and Mediation in Indonesia*. Leiden, The Netherlands: KITLV Press.

Vreede-de Stuers, Cora. 1960. *The Indonesian Woman: Struggles and Achievements*. The Hague: Mouton.

Wahana, Paulus. 1993. *Filsafat Pancasila* (The philosophy of Pancasila). Yogyakarta: Penerbit Kanisius.

Wahid, Abdurrahman. 1987. "Religion and Women's Status in Development." *Suara Pembaruan* (Dec. 12):1.

Walsh, Froma. 1996. "The Concept of Family Resilience: Crisis and Challenge." *Family Process* 35, no. 3:262ff.

Weber, Max. 1958. Author's Introduction to *Sociology of Religion*. In *The Protestant Ethic and the Spirit of Capitalism*, translated by Max Weber. New York: Charles Scribner's Sons.

Weber, Max. 1990a. "The Meaning of Discipline." In *Max Weber: Essays in Sociology*, edited by H. H. Gerth and C. Wright Mills. New York: Oxford Univ. Press.

———. 1990b. "Science as a Vocation." In *Max Weber: Essays in Sociology*, edited by H. H. Gerth and C. Wright Mills. New York: Oxford Univ. Press.

———. 1990c. "The Sociology of Charismatic Authority." In *Max Weber: Essays in Sociology*, edited by H. H. Gerth and C. Wright Mills. New York: Oxford Univ. Press.

Welch, Sharon. 1999. *A Feminist Ethic of Risk*. Minneapolis: Fortress.

"Why Indonesia?" 1977. *Pro Mundi Vita Bulletin: Meeting Place of World Religions* 64 (January-February):8–16.

William, Walter H. 1991. *Javanese Lives: Women and Men in Modern Indonesian Society.* New Brunswick, N.J.: Rutgers Univ. Press.

Williams, Delores. 1995. *Sisters in the Wilderness: The Challenge of Womanist God-Talk.* Maryknoll, N.Y.: Orbis Books.

Woolf, Virginia. 1990. "Professions for Women." In *Current Issues and Enduring Questions,* edited by Sylvan Barnet and Hugo Bedau. 2d ed. Boston: Bedford Books of St. Martin's Press.

Young, Pamela Dickey. 1995. "Feminist Theology: From Past to Future." In *Gender, Genre and Religion: Feminist Reflections,* edited by Morny Joy and Eva K. Neumaier-Dargyay. Waterloo, Ontario, Canada: Wilfred Laurier Univ. Press.

Young, Serenity, ed. 1995. *Sacred Texts by and about Women.* New York: Crossroad.

Index

actions of social change, 134
adat: basis of, 16–17; historical accounts of women's rights in, 46; influence of, 22; rituals of, 20n. 9; roles of women in, 30, 44–45
Adeney, Frances S.: afternoon with Marianne Katoppo, 117–20; approach of, 133–35, 149–51; background of, 138–42; conflict of ideologies and, 48–49; development of theory of knowledge, 142–46, as faculty sponsor of women's support group, 72; identification of methodology, 146–48; integration of theories and practice by, 184–89; neighbor's disapproval of, 32; prestige structures and, 62–63; return to Indonesia, 189; teaching experience in Indonesia, 16–17, 149–50
Agoeng, Endry, 37–38, 40n. 14
Ahmed, Leila, 179
akal (reason), 53–54
Alice in Wonderland (Carroll), 157–58, 159, 169
Alicia (pseud.), 29–30
All We're Meant to Be (Scanzoni, Hardesty), 139–40
Ambon: Dutch Reformed Church of, 18–19; Islamization of, 21, 25–26; paternalism in, 95; Protestant predominance in, 25; protocol for women in, 64
Aminy, Aisyah, 37
anthropological research, 13–14, 131–32, 175–76, 177n. 7
appearances: attention to in Indonesia, 21, 32–33, 118–19; gender roles and, 28–29, 65–67. *See also* dress
Are Women Human? (Sayers), 141
Aristotle, 144n. 12, 187n. 13
atheism, 23
Atkinson, Jane Monnig, 10n. 5

Bali: Hindu predominance in, 19, 25; Islamization of, 21, 25–26; women creating beauty in, 110–11
bapakism, 94
Batak Church, 19, 89–90, 92, 170n. 16
Batak society, 55, 64
Bauer, Janet L., 136
Bauman, Zygmunt, 147
Bednarowski, Mary Farrell, 3, 79
behaviors, 104–5
Belenky, Mary Field, 3, 79
Bellah, Robert N., 20nn. 5–6, 141n. 6, 143, 148
Bemmelen, Sita van, 55
Berger, Peter, 33n. 3, 148

214   Index

birth control, 8, 30
Bourdieu, Pierre, 121n. 11
Brenner, Suzanne, 73n. 17
bride price, 44
Buddhism: influence in Indonesian society, 21; influence on indigenous cultures, 8; practice of in Indonesia, 17, 19, 20; predominance among Chinese, 25n. 22. *See also* religion

Capon, Father, 140
Carritt, Jeanne Brooks, 174
Catholicism, 19, 25, 78, 83. *See also* Christianity; religion
Centrist Archipelago, 9, 42, 43, 76–77n. 1
Chinese Indonesians, 25n. 22, 58, 87n. 8
Christianity: acceptable models of leadership in, 97–103; basis of hospitality in, 108; education for in Indonesia, 9; effects on gender equality, 5, 17; governmental biases and, 25–27; influence on indigenous cultures, 8, 19; view of women's role, 67–69, 78–79; women in leadership and, 89–90; women's groups within, 74. *See also* Catholicism; Protestantism
Christian theology: basis for submission doctrine, 78; expression of gender equality and, 4–5, 177–78; impact of practices, 106; new direction of, 116; reflecting on practices and, 105; role of women and, 19; Western views of reason/emotion and, 54; women's role in development of, 70–71

Chung, Hyun Kyung, 3, 105, 116
Cinderella Complex, 140n. 3
"Citizenship Ethics" (Adeney), 147
Clinchy, Blythe, 3, 79
cognitive model of moral development, 153–54, 160–62, 163–64
Coleman, John, S. J., 144–45n. 13
college students, 54n. 2
colonialism: cultural/religious changes and, 18–19; freedom from and women's rights, 8; impact on gender ideology, 27, 54; religion and, 67; women in struggle against, 39
communication: across cultures, 184–85; among feminists globally, 3–4; as basis of understanding/problem resolution, 183–84; impact on gender ideology, 46; Javanese etiquette and, 64; styles of, 59n. 7
Communism, 25
communities: conflict of ideologies and, 49; decisions on gender roles and, 143–44; influence on ethics/thinking, 143; knowledge development and, 145; reinterpretation of practices and, 104, 106, 108, 110; women's leadership and, 7, 14
Compassionate and Free (Katoppo), 86, 116
conduct: attention to in Indonesia, 21, 32–33, 118–19; gender roles and, 28–29, 162
confinement of girls, 43
conflict: knowledge from, 145–46; prestige structures and, 62–63; resolution methods, 69n. 14, 71; results of, 49–50; Satya Wacana

Christian University and, 57;
transitions in gender ideology and,
34–35, 40–41, 47–50
Confucianism, 25n. 22
Connie (pseud.), 17, 18
conscious valuing, 132
Constitution of Indonesia, 34n. 7,
35–36, 39, 156
context issues: development of theories
and, 133, 168–71; feminist
practices and, 180–82; feminist
theory and, 172–73; gender
equality and, 174–75; in Indonesia,
8–11, 130–32; of research projects,
148; sense of freedom to act
and, 84; valuing knowledge and,
176
contextual-relationship theory of social
change: approach of, 11, 132,
133–35; conclusions of, 170;
development of, 148–49;
engagement of, 135–37;
integration of theory/advocacy
and, 5–6; operationalization of,
151–52; Western theories in
Indonesian context and, 12
creation of beauty: as deterrent to
leadership, 112; by Marianne
Katoppo, 120, 125; as link to
service, 14, 110–12; Lucy and,
123, 125; potential of, 7; as
resistance strategy, 11
creation story, 67–68, 69, 78, 114
cross-cultural families, 86–87
cross-cultural studies, 3–4, 172–73,
175–78, 180–82
Culpepper, Emily, 174
cultural groups, 16n. 1, 17–18
cultural imperialism, 151–52, 169,
184–85
culture, 20n. 5, 42, 152, 174n. 4

Dahlan, Nyai Achmad, 35–36,
45–46
Dani society, 55
David (husband of Diati), 65–67
decision making: based on
reason/principle, 160–61, 167–68;
cognitive model of moral
development and, 154; of graduate
students, 85; growth from,
124–25; Lucy's path to, 165–67;
moral agency and, 119; otherness
and, 89, 156; relational model of
moral development and, 154; skills
acquisition model and, 155,
193–94
development theories: cognitive
model, 153–54, 160–62, 163–64;
cross-cultural application of, 12,
168–71; examination of test cases
with, 84–85; as framework of
understanding, 160; gender
relations in Indonesia and, 155–59;
need for context, 159–60;
relational model, 154–55, 163–64;
skills acquisition model, 155,
164–69, 193–94; used in this
research, 135
Dewi (pseud.), 92–94, 160–62
Diati (pseud.), 57–58, 65–67
dispute narratives, 60
divorce, 157n. 4
domestic violence, 45, 74
domestic workers, 49
Donna (pseud.), 58
Dora (pseud.), 89–91, 163
double burden: Frances Adeney and,
140–41; effects of, 35, 49;
expectations for women, 27–31;
implementation of new ideologies
and, 41–42, 158; for Kartini,
102–3; Lucy and, 123; women in

double burden (*cont.*)
    leadership and, 47–49, 81–82, 83;
    for working women, 157
double standard, 89–91
dress: changes in author's view of, 188;
    Islamic influence on, 22–23;
    Manado style, 100n. 26; as
    reflection of life stage, 156;
    traditional forms of, 33; of women
    in Bali, 110–11; of women in Java,
    111
Dreyfus, Hubert: emphasis of, 170; on
    expert ethicists, 168; moral
    development theory of, 12, 85,
    135, 155–59, 164–68, 193–94;
    noncontextual aspect of model,
    159
Dreyfus, Stewart: emphasis of, 170; on
    expert ethicists, 168; moral
    development theory of, 12, 85,
    135, 155–59, 164–68, 193–94;
    noncontextual aspect of model,
    159
Dutch colonizers, 19, 54, 67
Dutch Reformed Calvinism, 17, 19,
    67, 78

economy: of eastern islands, 25;
    family-focused roles and, 30;
    feminism and, 8; hardships with
    devaluation, 22n. 14; impact on
    gender ideology, 27; international
    recognition and, 101; of Irian Jaya,
    24n. 21; reforms in, 25; women's
    advancement and, 51
education: impact on women in
    leadership, 9, 13; part religion
    plays in, 130; for women, 38, 46,
    54–55
egalitarianism: challenges to, 119; as
    challenge to double burden, 158;
    in Christian churches, 96;
    development of women's role and,
    51–52; implementation of, 40n.
    14, 46; Indonesian gender
    ideologies and, 156; thesis of
    Magdalena and, 71; transition to,
    34–35
Eisland, Nancy L., 97
Eliade, Mircea, 132
empowerment, 4, 8, 179
Engineer, Asghar Ali, 43n. 19
epistemological questions, 139, 141
Errington, Shelley, 10n. 5
ethics: construction of, 146–47;
    Indonesian view of, 135, 164;
    theories of acquiring expertise in,
    153–55, 164–68, 193–94; of West,
    164n. 12
ethnographic research: approach of,
    131–32, 138; central question of,
    153; challenges of, 11; goals of,
    11–12; issues raised, 129–31; on
    religion-identified resistance, 6–7;
    test case of, 149–51
etiquette: as ethical concerns, 16n. 1,
    135, 164–65; relational model and,
    164; skills acquisition model and,
    164–68; for visitations, 117; for
    women's speech, 64. *See also*
    traditions
everyday practices. *See* practices
Exchange Archipelago, 9, 42, 85
experience, as source of authority,
    79–80

family relations: *adat* and, 16n. 2; in
    cross-cultural marriages, 86–87;
    financial responsibilities and, 96; as
    modeled by *Ibu* Kartini, 99–100;
    need for restructuring of, 51;
    position of women in, 43–45;

Index 217

university women and, 65–67; women pastors and, 106
Fatima (pseud.), 17, 57–58, 111–12
Femina, 10n. 6
feminism: author's introduction to, 139–40; contextual issues for, 180–81; Indonesian view of, 92n. 18; Western values of, 173–74
feminist advocacy: feminist theory vs., 12, 172–89; Indonesian study and, 6; limitations of, 4, 5
Feminist Mystique, The (Friedan), 139, 140n. 2
feminist theologians: Indonesian study and, 5–6; Marianne Katoppo as, 116, 119–20, 121, 125; tenets of methodology of, 79; work of, 3
feminist theology, 57
feminist theories: complexity of, 172; construction of, 172–74; cultural awareness of, 176; feminist advocacy vs., 12, 172–89; limitations of, 4
feminist theorists: approach of, 176; independent agency and, 171; Indonesian study and, 5–6; interaction with practitioners, 188; recent work of, 3; struggle of, 12
Fischer, Clare, 3, 46n. 24
Flores, 19, 25
Pak Fritz (pseud.), 149
fusion of horizons, 188

Gadamer, Hans Georg, 143, 145–46, 148, 186n. 10, 188n. 15
gamelan music, 20
Geertz, Clifford: definition of culture, 174n. 4; on gender equality in Indonesia, 10n. 5; on ideologies, 38–39; on local knowledge, 175–76n. 6; as theorist, 148;

theory of ideology as cultural system, 152
gender equality: author's convictions on, 151; Christian religions and, 19; conflict with tradition, 41; cross-cultural applications of, 12; cross-cultural dialogue on, 185; customs/social structures and, 94; dispute narratives and, 60; evaluation of, 131, 172, 174–75, 181–82; honoring relationships and, 112–16; in Indonesia, 9, 156; in Javanese homes, 29; within kinship systems, 8; modeling of in churches, 97; networks of solidarity and, 178–80; patriarchy and, 163–64; process of cross-cultural understanding of, 185–88; reality vs. legality, 37–38; reflecting on everyday practices and, 14; reflections of, 156; religion-identified resistance and, 14–15; thesis test case, 67–71; value sharing with Indonesia, 177–78; women's pursuit of, 12–13, 64–67, 136
gender ideologies: Suzanne Brenner on, 73n. 17; common practices and, 14; complexity of in Indonesia, 9–10, 152, 156; conflicts of transition, 33–34, 47–50, 158; as core of traditions, 42–45; decision making and, 7; dominant form in Indonesia, 9, 13n. 7, 27–31, 42–43, 53; double burden of, 41–42; effect on women's moral development, 188; formulation of new concepts, 35–36; Magdalena's challenge to, 67–71; as modeled by *Ibu* Kartini,/*Ibu* Lena, 98–102; motivations of, 5; practices

gender ideologies (*cont.*)
  showing continuity with, 106;
  questioning of, 137–41; religious
  calling and, 83–84, 102–3;
  revision of, 32–34, 50–52; role
  conflicts and, 34–35; Satya Wacana
  Christian University and, 57; social
  change and, 12–13; transitional
  difficulties, 38–41, 45–47, 119;
  university men's struggle with,
  59–64; university women's
  struggle with, 64–67; women as
  partners in development and,
  37–38
gender stereotypes: avoidance of,
  95–97; contradictions to, 73;
  influence on female graduate
  students, 57–58; male struggles
  with, 60–61; of men, 73n. 17;
  results of, 59–60; traditional forms
  of, 53–54, 55; women's support
  groups and, 71–73
Gender Studies Center, 184
Gilligan, Carol: emphasis of, 170; on
  Kohlberg's noncontextual model,
  160n. 10, 168; moral development
  theory of, 12, 85, 135, 154–55,
  163–64; use of context, 160n. 9
Gitton, Anthony, 34n. 5
globalization, 9, 46, 102n. 29
God's Fierce Whimsy, 176
Goldberger, Nancy Rue, 3, 79
government: demise of Suharto
  regime, 9; impact on gender
  ideology, 27; implementation of
  new ideology, 45–46;
  implementation of women's role
  and, 28n. 32, 36–38; intervention
  in religious affairs, 25–27, 92; need
  for women's programs, 51; power
  games in, 49–50; prestige
  structures and, 62; religious

affiliation and, 25; relocation
  programs of, 21; under Sukarno,
  24; Sukarnoputri and, 94; women
  in leadership roles, 47n. 25, 94;
  women's role and, 28, 30, 45–46;
  women's status in, 34–38, 156
graduate programs, 55–56
Graduate Students' Women's
  Association, 4–5, 6n. 1, 71–73,
  112–13, 115
Graduate Theological Union, 142
Gray, Elizabeth Dodson, 106n. 2,
  179
Gross, Rita, 3, 31n. 37
Guidelines of State Policy, 36, 158n. 7,
  159n. 8
Gurevitch, Zaly, 187n. 14

Habermas, Jürgen, 142, 148
habitus, 121n. 11
Hardesty, Nancy, 139–40
harmony, 21, 22, 71
Harrison, Beverly, 134, 144
head coverings, 26, 110
Heraclitus, 144
hermeneutic approach, 145–46,
  185–89
hermeneutic of suspicion, 96
hierarchical social structures, 43,
  50–51
Hinduism: influence on indigenous
  cultures, 8; integration with
  indigenous religion, 21; in Java,
  19–20; predominance in Bali, 25;
  women creating beauty in, 110–11.
  See also religion
historical location, 84, 130, 144,
  145
horse dance, 21
hospitality: as deterrent to leadership,
  108–10; of Marianne Katoppo,

117–18; as link to new theologies, 107–8; Lucy and, 122–23; as resistance strategy, 7, 11, 14
human rights, 51
Hutahaean, N. M., 90n. 14, 170n. 16

Ibrahim, Marwah Daud, 44n. 19
Ida (pseud.), 17, 18, 81–84
identity: accommodation to different cultures and, 180–81; based on conformity, 160; changes resulting from choices, 14; cross-cultural families and, 87; development of, 134, 145; evaluation of actions and, 85; moral evaluation and, 175; sense of freedom to act and, 84
ideology, concept/function of, 38–41. See also gender ideologies
inclusion, 13, 77, 159
independence: decision making and, 77; developed by Lucy, 121; implementation of new ideology and, 46; of Marianne Katoppo, 118–19, 120; obstacles to, 85–86; strength for lifestyle choices and, 77
indigenous cultures: *adat* customs of, 16n. 2, 20n. 9, 30, 44–45; bride price and, 44; concept of reason in, 54; education of youth and, 76–77n. 1; Islamic influence on, 8; male authority patterns in, 60
indigenous religion: Dutch colonizers and, 67; integration with Christian theology, 116; legal status of, 25; stories of creation in, 68n. 12; world religions' influence on, 8, 19–21
Indonesia: arrival customs, 71–72n. 15; concept of reason in, 53–54; construction of social worlds in, 177; dominant gender ideology of, 9, 13n. 7, 27–31, 42–43, 53; etiquette in, 16, 64, 117, 135, 164; independence and new ideologies in, 39; methods of conflict resolution in, 69n. 14; population of, 21n. 12; as study field, 8; women's status in government, 34–36. *See also* Constitution of Indonesia; government; indigenous cultures; indigenous religions
Indonesian Consortium of Theological Schools, 7
In Memory of Her (Schussler-Fiorenza), 144
international conferences, 101
"Interpretation and the Sciences of Man" (Taylor), 148
intolerance, 32–33, 40
Irian Jaya: Catholic predominance in, 25; Christian experience in, 16; colonization of, 19; economy of, 24n. 21, 25; Islamization of culture in, 25–26; political influence of, 24; position of women in, 18; women's role in development in, 37
Islam: call to prayer, 23n. 19; concept of reason of, 54; gender equality and, 43–44; influence on culture of Indonesia, 8, 20, 21, 22–23; practice of in Java, 17, 19; preferential treatment of, 25–26; proliferation of universities, 9; submissive role of women in, 78–79; view of hospitality, 107; view of women's role, 30–31; women creating beauty for, 111. *See also* religion

Index

Jakarta Theological Seminary, 7, 55, 56
Jane (pseud.), 17, 58
Java: conflicting ideologies in, 13; cultural diversity of, 17; displays of power in, 134–35; gender ideology of, 42, 43–44, 156; Islamic predominance in, 25; kinship systems of, 76–77n. 1; position of women in, 18, 65; powerful political/social group in, 24–25; power games in, 49–50; protocol for women in, 64, 180–81, 182; religious influences in, 19, 22; relocation programs in, 26; roles of women in, 30n. 36; views of nontraditional dress in, 33; women creating beauty in, 111
justice principle of gender equality, 161, 165

Kartini, Raden Ajeng, 43n. 18
Ibu Kartini (pseud.), 97–100, 101, 102–3, 105, 108
Katoppo, Marianne: creation of beauty by, 120; Gilligan's model and, 163–64; hospitality of, 117–20; marital status of, 89; on matriarchal societies, 46–47; resistance strategies of, 86; theology of, 116–17, 119–20
kebatinan, 21n. 11, 25
kinship structures, 8, 10n. 5. *See also adat*
knowledge: author's search for, 139, 141; developing a theory of, 142–46; discourse on across cultures, 152; Indonesia power to define, 130; interpretive understanding of, 145–46, 174–75; mediation of, 132

kodrat, 44, 68, 78–79, 162
Kohlberg, Lawrence: cognitive model of, 163–64; emphasis of, 170; gender bias of model, 168; moral development theory of, 12, 85, 135, 153–54; noncontextual aspect of model, 159, 160n. 10; religion-identified resistance and, 160–61; study of Filipino boys, 152
Kompas, 10n. 6, 149
Krier, Jennifer, 60, 96
Kuhn, Thomas, 143

leadership: acceptable modeling of, 97–103; challenges to, 10–11, 27; Christian views of women in, 59–61; conflicting gender ideologies and, 12–13; deterrents to, 108–10, 112, 115–16, 121–22, 125; double burden and, 47; everyday practices and, 7, 105, 125; as modeled by *Ibu* Kartini/*Ibu* Lena, 98–102; religious calling to, 77–80; state agenda vs. personal agendas, 49–50; strategies for overcoming resistance, 13–14
Ibu Lena (pseud.), 97–101, 105
lifestyle choices: change in communities from, 14; foregoing marriage, 77, 83, 88–89; of Ida, 80–81, 84; introduction of strangers and, 33–34; of Marianne Katoppo, 122; of Lena/Kartini, 99, 102; of Marlene, 82–83, 84; moral agency and, 13; of Ratna, 76–77
literature, representation of women in, 45n. 20, 48
Lucy (pseud.), 121–25, 165–67

MacIntyre, Alasdair, 142
Magdalena (pseud.), 67–71
Making the Connections (Harrison), 144
Manado people: effects of Christianity on, 17; gender equality of, 9–10n. 5, 178; position of women in, 18; protocol for women, 64, 98; women in church leadership in, 101
Mannheim, Karl, 174n. 5
marginalization of women, 91–95, 96, 101, 162
Marlene (pseud.), 82–84
marriage: changes wrought by, 156–57; changing blueprints for, 65–67; Christian leadership and, 89–90; delaying/foregoing of, 77, 83, 88–89, 99, 122; polygamy, 23; roles of women in, 162
Martha, Sister (abbess of Gedono), 82
Ibu Masooma (pseud.), 107, 108
matrifocal societies: effects of Christianity on, 19; gender equality in, 9n. 4, 156; power of women in, 29, 44; roles of women in, 18, 30n. 36
matrilinear societies, 61–62n. 9
McCoy, Charles C., 142, 143, 145n. 14
McCutcheon, Russell T., 131
Mead, George Herbert, 142–43
meaning: construction of, 130, 134; interpretation of, 7, 152; religion/culture and, 20n. 5; use of theory to investigate, 132
media, women's issues and, 10, 86n. 5
megalithic culture, 20n. 6
men: assertion of dominance in women's meetings, 72–73; attitude toward women in graduate school, 58; dedication to Islam, 23; dominance in mosques, 31; individualism of, 30n. 34; Indonesian views of, 42–43; position in *adat*, 16n. 2, 45; presence in home, 51; reasoning abilities of, 54; response to dialogue on gender equality, 185; social training of, 54–55; as speakers in convention of women theologians, 101, 114, 115; stereotype of, 73n. 17; struggles with gender ideologies, 59–64
methodology, 12, 146–48
middle-range theory, 148–53
Minahasa people, 44, 67
Minangkabau people: conflicting ideologies of, 13; gender equality of, 9–10n. 5; prestige structures of, 62n. 9; roles of women of, 30n. 36; sphere of women's power, 44
Moluccas, 18–19
moral agency: author's interest in, 146; decision making and, 6–7, 13; development models and, 159; development of, 76; everyday practices and, 105–6, 125; exercised by Dewi, 160–62; gender ideologies and, 103; as highest stage of cognitive moral development, 154; hospitality and, 108; Indonesian concept of, 84–86; of Marianne Katoppo, 118–19; lifestyle choices and, 150; religion-identified resistance and, 34n. 6; skill acquisition model and, 165; social pressures and, 80–84; study of, 5
moral development models. *See* development theories
morality, 16n. 1, 85, 160
Morrison, Toni, 174
motivation, 39–40

Ms. Magazine, 139, 140n. 2
Mudflower Collective, 176
Murniati, Nunuk Prasetyo, 44, 47
Muslims. *See* Islam

Nani, 22n. 16
narrative method, 5–6, 7–8, 12, 135
Nasikun, 44–45, 47
National Convention of Women Theologians of Indonesia, 96, 98, 101, 113–14, 115–16
nationalization, 27
Nias, 20n. 6
Nicomachean Ethic (Aristotle), 144n. 12
Niebuhr, H. Richard, 143, 178
nihilism, 177n. 7
Ibu Nona (pseud.), 182–84
Nora (pseud.), 17, 18

other/otherness: as a chosen path, 124, 141, 150, 151; foregoing marriage and, 89; Ida as, 81; Marianne Katoppo as, 86–87, 116, 119, 124; Lucy as, 124; meeting of, 145–46, 185–86; power of not understanding and, 187; researcher as, 134, 138–39, 141; results of, 86–87, 156; women's fears of, 159
Our Struggle to Serve, 140

Pak Otto (pseud.), 59–61
Pancasila, 24, 147
Parks, Sharon, 100n. 25
partnership in Christianity, 96
partnership in development: creation of double burden by, 28; National Convention of Women Theologians of Indonesia on, 114; power struggle over, 49; prestige structures and, 62; reality vs. legality, 34–38, 149, 156; wording of, 158n. 7
paternalism, 95
patriarchy: in Batak Church, 90n. 14; dominance of in Indonesia, 9, 13n. 7, 18; effects of Christianity on, 19; roles of women and, 30
Paul, Apostle, 78
peer pressure, 162
pluralism, 18–20, 22, 31, 42
Polanyi, Michael, 175
politics. *See* government
polygamy, 23
Porterfield, Amanda, 3, 104–5
postmodern era: cross-cultural communication in, 12; ethnographic research in, 11; use of theory in, 131–32; views of truth in, 176
Post-Modern Ethics (Bauman), 147
postmodernism, 147–48
power: expression of in Java, 134–35; familial structures of under *adat*, 160n. 2; of gender globally, 4; home as center of, 46–47; Indonesian concept of, 130; Javanese expression of, 49–50; in Javanese families, 29, 44; legitimation of existing systems of, 114; of men, 43; of not understanding, 183–84, 187; organizational structures of, 141; resistance to change in structures of, 184
practices: as agents of social change, 84–86; changes in from women's leadership, 49–50; changes needed, 51; creation of beauty as, 110–12;

decision making and, 85, 155;
development of, 49–50; gender
ideology and, 39–40; honoring
relationships as, 112–16;
hospitality as, 107–10; impact of,
104–5, 124–25; of Marianne
Katoppo, 117–21, 124, 125; as
link to leadership, 7, 14; otherness
and, 156; purpose of, 11, 104;
reflections on, 116–17; study of, 5;
transformation by, 105–6;
usefulness of studying, 12, 136
prayer, Muslim calls to, 23n. 19
prestige structures, 61–63, 94,
163–64, 187n. 12
Protestantism: authoritative theology
of, 79; Catholicism and, 83; in
Java, 19; models of feminine
leadership in, 97; predominance in
Ambon/Sumatra, 25; women in
leadership in, 77. *See also*
Christianity; religion

Qur'an, 43–44, 54, 107n. 3

Rabinow, Paul, 177n. 7
Ratna (pseud.), 76, 84
reality, 14, 20n. 5
reason, Indonesian concept of, 53–54
relational model of moral
development, 154–55, 163–64
relationships: changes resulting from
prioritizing, 14; decision making
and, 85; as deterrent to leadership,
115–16, 121–22, 125; domination
of in women's lives, 156–57;
Gilligan's model and, 163–64;
honoring of, 7, 11, 14, 105–7;
impact on decision making,
161–62; Indonesian view of, 10;
Marianne Katoppo's care for, 117,
118–19, 120–21, 125; loyalty in,
134; Lucy and, 121–25;
maintaining harmony in, 10;
religion and, 104; social change
and, 134; for support of women,
74–75, 112–14, 136; traditions
ordering, 59–61; university women
and, 65–67. *See also* family relations
religion: changes in theology, 14;
definition of, 77; demands of
women in, 77; diversity of in
Indonesia, 8, 17; feminist
reexamination of, 173–74;
government intervention in,
26–27, 92; historical location of,
130; in Indonesia, 8;
meaning/reality and, 20n. 5;
mixing of rituals of, 20–21; as
oppression/opportunity, 6;
partnership in development and,
37, 41n. 15; reinterpretation of
gender roles, 51; role of in world
construction, 129–30; support of
patriarchy, 31; tension between
groups, 21–22, 25, 26–27;
transformation by gender
consciousness, 3–4. *See also*
indigenous religion; *specific religion*
religion-identified resistance strategies:
challenges to, 53, 119; concept of
religious calling as, 77–80;
contempt for women and, 179;
development of, 173; Dewi's use
of, 160–62; ethnographic research
on, 6–8, 11; in light of moral
development theories, 153–71;
North American vs. Indonesian,
135–36, 180–82; results of, 156;
sense of agency and, 34n. 6; social

religion-identified resistance strategies (*cont.*)
  change from, 13–15; study of, 5; thesis of Magdalena as, 67–70
  religious calling: acceptance of, 91–95; examples of women following, 80–84, 160–61; gender ideologies and, 83–84, 102–03, 156;
  resistance to institutional structures and, 6–7, 13, 77–80, 162
  relocation programs, 21, 25–26
  research, 11–12, 74
  Research Center for Women, 74
  researcher: Frances Adeney as, 141, 147–48; approach of, 133–35, 184–85, 189; complexities for in fundamentalist groups, 136; embeddedness of, 130–31, 132, 148; feminists as, 172–73; test case of, 149–51
resilience, 163–64
resistance strategies: avoiding marginalization, 91–95; becoming other, 86–87; exposing double standard, 89–91; foregoing marriage, 77, 83, 88–89, 99, 122; graduate students' use of, 11, 76–80; resisting stereotypes, 95–97. *See also* religion-identified resistance strategies
resistance theologies: definition of, 34n. 6; development of, 156; of Marianne Katoppo, 118–19; reflections on, 116–17, 125
resistance theology, 34n. 6
Responsible Self, The (Niebuhr), 143
Ria (pseud.), 42
Riceour, Paul, 39
Ibu Rita (pseud.), 28, 29
rituals, 104–5, 110–11, 114
Robb, Carol, 178–79

Royce, Josiah, 134
Ruggiero, Vincent, 164n. 12

Ibu Sabariah (pseud.), 58, 109–10
Sangir Terlud conference, 98
Sartika, Dewi, 46n. 22
Satya Wacana Christian University: goals of program at, 147; graduate program of, 10–11, 56–64; struggles with gender issues at, 56–67; teaching experience at, 16; test case of gender ideologies, 67–71; weekend retreat and, 4–5, 112–14
Sayers, Dorothy, 141
Scanzoni, Letha, 139–40
Schussler-Fiorenza, Elizabeth, 96–97n. 22, 144
science, 174n. 5, 175
Sears, Laurie, 38
Sekolah Istri (Sartika), 46n. 22
service, 63–64
Shaw, Rosalind, 132
skill acquisition model of moral development, 155, 164–69, 193–94
Smith, Archie, 143
social change, 12–15, 134–35, 149, 150, 151–52
social networks, 30, 84. *See also* support networks
society: changes from women's leadership, 7; changes motivated by new ideologies, 39–41; conflicts of change within, 158; construction of practices in, 33n. 3; contextual-relationship theory of change in, 133–35; controls exerted by, 162; delineated roles in, 35; integration of ideologies into, 40–41; opportunities for changes in, 51;

positions held by women in,
46–47; religion-identified
resistance and, 14–15
socioeconomic status, 84
solidarity, 3–4, 112–13, 115, 150,
178–80
South East Asia School of Theology, 7,
56
spirituality, 7
status hierarchies. *See* prestige
structures
Stoler, Ann Laura, 54
Structure of Scientific Revolutions, The
(Kuhn), 143
Struggle to Be the Sun Again (Chung),
116
Suharto regime: ban on *becas,* 117n. 8;
censorship of, 10n. 6; demise of, 9,
94; dissatisfaction with, 24;
emphasis on family obligations,
149–50n. 21; relocation of
Javanese, 21n. 13; women's
emancipation and, 13n. 7
Sukarno, 24
Sukarnoputri, 94
Sulawesi: Dutch Reformed Church of,
19; economy of, 25; effect of
Protestantism in, 17; gender
ideology of, 156; kinship systems
of, 76–77n. 1; matriarchal societies
of, 44, 65; protocol for women in,
64
Sullivan, Norma, 29, 38, 96
Sumatra: controversy over church
leadership in, 92; gender ideology
of, 42, 156; matrifocal societies in,
18, 44; patriarchy of church in,
169–70; political influence of,
24; protocol for women in, 64,
85; religious influences in, 19,
25
Sunindyo, Saraswati, 65

support networks: conflict of
ideologies and, 49; functions of,
11; for graduate students, 71–75;
impact on gender ideology, 156; in
North America/Indonesia, 136;
solidarity of, 112–13, 115; value
of, 178–80

Tan, Mely G., 41–42, 47n. 25
Tangkudung, Magdelena, 177n. 8
Tannen, Deborah, 59n. 7
Tarule, Jill Mattuck, 3, 79
Taylor, Charles, 85, 145n. 15, 148,
175
ten-point program, 45
theology: development of, 156,
163–64, 173; of gender equality,
14; honoring relationships and,
113–14; as major at universities,
54; reflected in hospitality, 108;
reflection on practices and, 14. *See
also* Christian theology; feminist
theologians; feminist theology;
resistance theologies
theories: approach of, 133–35;
appropriation of, 151–52; assessing
everyday practices by, 125;
cognitive model, 153–54;
development of, 133–35;
engagement of, 135–38;
framework for use of, 148–52; of
knowledge, 142; usefulness of in
different contexts, 136; use of in
postmodern age, 131–32, 137. *See
also* feminist theories; Western
theories; development theories
three-phase theory of society, 33n. 3
Tilaar, Martha, 47
tolerance, 20, 33–34, 57
Torajan people, 9–10n. 5, 64, 76–77n.
1, 178

traditions: as basis of ethics, 160; clashes between, 145–46; for dress, 33, 100n. 26, 110–11, 156; making changes in, 144; Western influences and, 32–34

"Unity in Diversity," 24–25
university life: challenges for women, 53–56; evaluations of women and, 53; men's struggles with females, 59–64; power of, 130; prestige structures and, 61–63; protocol for women in, 64; religion-identified resistance and, 76; at Satya Wacana Christian University, 56–58; service in, 63–64; thesis defense, 67–71; transition from old to new ideologies, 70–71; women as instructors, 93; women's struggles with gender ideologies and, 64–67; women's support groups for, 71–75

values: accommodation to different cultures and, 180–81; conscious evaluation of, 132; of gender equality across cultures, 177–78; impact on decision making, 161–62; means of understanding, 186–87; social change and, 134–35

Wahid, Abdurrahman, 37, 41n. 15
Walker, Alice, 174
Ward, Barbara, 10n. 5
Wayang Kulit, 19n. 4

Weber, Max, 148
Western cultural studies, 9–10
Western influences, 5, 32, 133, 156
Western theories: cross-cultural communication and, 12; influence on culture of Indonesia, 54; non-Western contexts and, 12, 135, 149. *See also* development theories; feminist theories
women: basis of ethical decisions of, 154, 168; disposition of incomes of, 47–48; Indonesian views of, 42–44; lifestyle changes of, 158; as professors in Indonesia, 182–85; social expectations for, 156–57, 162; struggles with gender ideologies, 64–67; university training of, 55–58; view of capacities of, 53
Women's Research Center, 6n. 1
women's rights: guarantee of, 8, 36; historical accounts in *adat,* 46; lack of respect for, 43–44; women's role in establishing, 34n. 7
women's role: in *adat,* 44–45; Christian view of, 78; double burden of, 41–42; Islamic influence on, 22–23; in Java, 43–44; as leaders, 47; North American vs. Indonesian struggles with, 135–36; practices showing continuity with, 106; prevailing ideology, 27–31; social controls over, 149; social expectations, 156–57, 162

Yolanda (pseud.), 16–17, 18, 58